★CLASSIC★ ROCK

Future PLC Quay House, The Ambury, Bath BA1 1UA

David Bowie bookazine
Editor **Dave Everley**
Subbing: **Alex Burrows**
Art Editor **Big John**

Editorial
Editor **Siân Llewellyn**
Art Editor **Darrell Mayhew**
Features Editor **Polly Glass**
Production Editor **Paul Henderson**
Reviews Editor **Ian Fortnam**
News/Lives Editor **Dave Ling**
Online Editor **Fraser Lewry**
Content Director (Music) **Scott Rowley**
Head Of Design (Music) **Brad Merrett**

Advertising
Media packs are available on request
Commercial Director **Clare Dove**
clare.dove@futurenet.com
Advertising Sales Director (**Music Portfolio**) Lara Jaggon
lara.jaggon@futurenet.com
Account Director **Ayomide Magbagbeola**
ayomide.magbagbeola@futurenet.com
Account Director **Steven Pyatt**
steven.pyatt@futurenet.com
Graduate Sales Exec **Saskia Pemberton**
saskia.pemberton@futurenet.com

International licensing and syndication *Classic Rock* is available
for licensing and syndication. To find out more contact us at
licensing@futurenet.com or view our available content at
www.futurecontenthub.com.

Head of Print Licensing **Rachel Shaw**

Digital
Editor In Chief, Louder **Briony Edwards**
Executive Editor, Louder **Merlin Aldersdale**
Staff Writer, Louder **Lizzie Capewell**

Subscriptions
New orders: **www.magazinesdirect.com / 0330 333 1113 /**
email help@magazinesdirect.com
Renewals: **www.mymagazine.co.uk / customer service: 0330
333 4333 /**
email queries: help@mymagazine.co.uk
Acquisitions Director **Sharon Todd**

Circulation
Head of Newstrade **Tim Mathers**

Production
Head of Production **Mark Constance**
Production Project Manager **Clare Scott**
Senior Ad Production Manager **Joanne Crosby**
Digital Editions Controller **Jason Hudson**
Production Manager **Keely Miller**

Management
Managing Director, Music **Stuart Williams**
Bookazine Editorial Director **Jon White**

Printed in the UK

Distributed by Marketforce, 5 Churchill Place,
Canary Wharf, London, E14 5HU
www.marketforce.co.uk
Tel: 0203 787 9001

FUTURE Connectors.
Creators.
Experience
Makers.

Future plc is a public company
quoted on
the London Stock
Exchange (symbol: FUTR)
www.futureplc.com

Chief executive **Zillah Byng-Thorne**
Non-executive chairman **Richard Huntingford**
Chief financial officer **Penny Ladkin-Brand**

Tel +44 (0)1225 442 244

Widely Recycled

ipso. For press freedom with responsibility

H as there ever been a greater or more influential run of albums than the ones
David Bowie released between 1970 and 1980? From mystical hard rock and
extra-terrestrial glam to 'plastic soul' and icy Mittel European art rock, Bowie
breathed new life into rock'n'roll, frequently pushing it into territories it had
never previously conceived of entering.

As astounding as that 10 year period was, Bowie's entire career is no less remarkable, from
his days as a wannabe superstar in Swinging London right up to the release of *Blackstar*, easily
the greatest parting gift any musician has given the world. Yet he was so much more than
a musician – he was an actor on film and on album, an internet early-adopter, an art lover,
a cultural lightning rod.

This special 132-page magazine, drawn from the archives of *Classic Rock* magazine, charts
Bowie's unique journey. In it, we dive deep into the making of his key albums, from *Hunky Dory*
and *The Rise And Fall Of Ziggy Stardust And The Spiders From Mars*, through The Berlin Trilogy and
Let's Dance, right up to his remarkable comeback with *The Next Day* and the final, valedictory
Blackstar, all with input from key participants, including The Thin White Duke himself.

So turn the volume up on *Ziggy Stardust* or *Low*, or maybe one of his great overlooked albums
(personally, I'm going for *Earthling*), and enjoy…

Dave Everley – Editor

Contents

Features

IIIIIIIIIIIIIIIIIIIIIIIIIIIIIIIIIIIIIIIIIIIIIIIIIIIIIIIIIIIIIIIIIIIIIIIIIIIIIIIIIIIIIIIIIIIIIIIIIIIIIIIIIIIIIIIIIIIIIII

WATCH THAT MAN

Rock'n'roller, mod, mime artist, hippie – the young David Bowie tried everything in the search for fame before a sci-fi epic inspired his breakthrough hit. But even that would be a false start.

Words: **Julian Marszalek**

The London that David Bowie was born into on January 8, 1947 still bore the scars of World War II. This was a landscape pockmarked by bombsites, the detritus of destruction and inhabited by a shell-shocked population living with rationing, austerity and making do.

Then again, nothing was conventional about him right from the start. Born David Robert Jones in Brixton, south London to Haywood 'John' Jones – a PR executive for the children's charity Barnardo's – and cinema usherette Margaret 'Peggy' Burns, the future Starman was eight months old before his parents married. Both had children from previous relationships and his father had had showbiz ambitions of his own when he tried to launch his previous wife, Hilda, as a singer. His efforts came to naught.

By all accounts, Bowie's early years were far from straightforward. In 1996, he told the BBC's Alan Yentob: "It wasn't a particularly happy childhood. My parents were cold emotionally and there weren't many hugs. I always craved affection because of that."

Despite a 10-year age difference, Bowie was close to his older half-brother, Terry Burns, who would prove to be a huge influence on his life as well as trying to protect him from the schizophrenia on

A shoot with a model for *Boyfriend* magazine in London, summer 1963.

his mother's side of the family.

"I'm not so sure how much of it is madness," Bowie would ruminate to Yentob. "There's an awful lot of emotional and spiritual mutilation that goes on in my family."

The half-brothers would split for a couple of years when, in 1956, Terry was called up as part of his National Service. A year later, the Jones family left Brixton for the more staid environs of Bromley, an outer borough of Greater London where he met his lifelong friends Geoff MacCormack – who would later work with Bowie as his backing singer – and George Underwood who'd later make an inadvertent yet significant impact on Bowie's life. The trio bonded over a love of Americana and rock'n'roll.

"The country was very grey," McCormack told Carrie Kania at the Bowie 75 convention in 2022. "The only chink of light came from America via its fashion and its music. David's father had access to music from America. We'd listen to Elvis and Fats Domino. Little Richard was rebellion, like a thunderbolt. Everyone wanted to be Elvis, but David wanted to be Little Richard."

Joining Bromley Technical High School in 1958, further influences hit the young Bowie. After being de-mobbed, his half-brother Terry returned and introduced him to the beat poets and Jack Kerouac's *On The Road*. Terry would take David into the demi-monde of Soho where he acquainted him with jazz and R'n'B as well as pointing out the sleazier aspects of the central London neighbourhood. With his father giving him a saxophone, Bowie took a greater interest in art via an experimental school programme spearheaded by Owen Frampton, Peter's dad. A burgeoning interest in fashion would find the young Bowie playing around with his image.

"I spent all those formative teenage years adopting guises and learning to be somebody," Bowie told the BBC's Jeremy Paxman in 1999.

The biggest and arguably most significant change to the teenage Bowie occurred in 1962. Falling out with his pal George Underwood over a girl called Carol whom Bowie had tried to steal, the former took matters into his own hands.

"I was so aggrieved that I just walked up to him, turned him around and went 'whack!' without even thinking," recalled Underwood to ITV's *London Tonight* in 2012. Unfortunately, his punch to Bowie's left eye would have serious consequences. Needing three operations to save his sight, Bowie was left with a permanently dilated pupil that gave the appearance of having differently coloured eyes.

In his poem *Annus Mirabilis*, Philip Larkin identified 1963 as the real start of the 1960s as they are understood today. This was when *"sexual intercourse began... Between the end of the Chatterley ban /And the Beatles' first LP."* By this point, Bowie had already been playing in showband the Kon-Rads. Though the band split before Bowie left school in 1963, he'd informed his parents of his desire to become a pop star. He would spend the next six years floundering on the edge of success.

Part of the problem with Bowie's inability to break through in the 60s was exactly what would propel him to the huge success the following decade – himself. So enamored was he of the idea of fame and absorbing influences like a sponge, that he would flit from one fad to the next without giving it the single-minded focus needed to see a project through.

"I've always been a very curious and enthusiastic person," Bowie admitted. "I had a very short attention span and would move from one thing to another quite rapidly." ▷

IIIIIIIIIIIIIIIIIIIIIIIIIIIIIIIIIIIIIIIIIIIIIIIIIIIII
"I spent all those formative teenage years adopting guises and learning to be somebody."
David Bowie

At home in London, 1966.

Such was the case with his next band, the R'n'B-flavoured Davie Jones And The King Bees, which he formed with George Underwood. Released in 1964, their sole release, *Liza Jane*, sank without a trace. Compared to contemporaries the Pretty Things' *Rosalyn* – released the same month and later covered by Bowie on *Pin Ups* – the former came across as dilettantes rather than serious blues devotees with an added penchant for amplified hooliganism.

But it got Bowie noticed. Signing with impresario Leslie Conn and swiftly joining the Manish Boys, the pair hatched the kind of publicity stunt that Bowie would excel at during the 70s. Through his father's PR connections, the *London Evening News* ran a story about a group of young men who'd suffered abuse because of their long hair. Naturally, these youths were the Manish Boys and this exercise in media manipulation soon gained traction when they appeared on BBC show *Tonight*. Claiming to be the leader of the Society For The Prevention Of Cruelty To Long-Haired Men, Bowie – his own hair resting on his eyebrows and collar – bemoaned the lot of the hirsute man to presenter Cliff Michelmore.

"We're all fairly tolerant but for the last two years we've had comments like 'Darling' and 'Can I carry your hand bag?' thrown at us and I think it just has to stop now," said Bowie as his band

mates sniggered behind him. Though a significant publicity coup for Bowie and the Manish Boys, there remained a flaw in their strategy: their debut single wouldn't be released for another four months, by which point they'd been forgotten. Another release, another flop.

Come 1965 and Bowie had re-styled himself as a mod and was fronting his fourth band – Davy Jones And The Lower Third. Significantly, he changed his name to David Bowie to avoid confusion with future Monkee Davy Jones – fast emerging as a star in his own right. Their single, *Can't Help Thinking About Me*, flopped in early 1966, but it did mark a change in Bowie's songwriting as it reveled in a narcissistic, self-aware glee.

Despite a lack of record sales, Bowie was a face on the London scene of 1966. Backed by yet another band – this time the Buzz – he was a regular performer at the Marquee but he still lacked that indefinable X-factor that could take him to the next level.

It was at one of these shows that Bowie was introduced to his next manager,

Ken Pitt. For the next three-and-a-half years, the pair worked hard to free him from the gravitational pull of obscurity. Pitt had worked as the UK publicist for Judy Garland, Frank Sinatra and Jerry Lee Lewis. Advising Bowie to develop a cabaret act, the singer opted for the singer-songwriter route, inspired in part by the acetate of the Velvet Underground's debut album that had been given to him by his new manager.

Another major influence on Bowie was the homegrown all-round entertainer Anthony Newley. Bowie's faux vocal Americanisms were replaced by an accent much closer to home.

"He had this fixation with Anthony Newley," said producer Gus Dudgeon in a 1992 TV interview. "Every time Bowie opened his mouth, Anthony Newley would pop out."

Signing to Deram Records, Bowie released another pair of flop singles in the shape of *Rubber Band* and *The Laughing Gnome*. His eponymous debut album, a combination of Baroque pop and music hall influences, was released in the shadow of the Beatles' landmark *Sgt. Pepper's Lonely Hearts Club Band*.

"It didn't stand a chance," producer Mike Vernon told director Francis Whately in 2019, but it did contain many of the themes that would appear in his later work: the gender blurring of *She's Got Medals* and flawed messiah in *We Are Hungry Men* would later re-appear in *Queen Bitch* and *Ziggy Stardust* respectively.

"It was very difficult to get him noticed at the time," admitted Pitt in a 1985 BBC radio interview. He encouraged Bowie to turn to acting. His first role was that of a painting brought to life in the short film, *The Image*, but again, Bowie's efforts were thwarted. Flitting once again, he studied mime under dancer and choreographer Lindsay Kemp before hitting another wall.

Falling in love with dancer Harmione Farthingale who he'd met through Kemp, the pair teamed up with former Buzz guitarist John Hutchinson to form Feathers but their blend of folk, poetry and mime was always going have a quite limited appeal.

"He wasn't taken that seriously on the London underground scene because he was

"Every time Bowie opened his mouth, Anthony Newley would pop out."
David Bowie

into mime and he wasn't a total hippy. There was something about him that didn't quite fit," singer-songwriter and Bowie obsessive Robyn Hitchcock told this writer in 2013.

Hitchcock was perfectly correct in his assessment. It's a view that Bowie himself subscribed to. Speaking to *Melody Maker* in 1966, he opined: "As far as I'm concerned the whole idea of western life – that's the life we live now – is wrong."

"I was very stoned when I went to see *2001: A Space Odyssey*, and it was a revelation."

David Bowie

His sense of isolation and fear must have increased when, returning home from a concert by Cream with his half-brother, he witnessed Terry suffering a severe schizophrenic incident. They would gradually drift apart with Terry living in a variety of mental institutions while Bowie threw himself into his work.

He would later say in a 1993 BBC radio interview: "One puts oneself through such psychological damage in trying to avoid the threat of insanity."

Though all might have seemed lost, two key events occurred that would pave the way to Bowie's success in the 1970s. It was after performing with Feathers at the Roundhouse in London in September 1968 that Bowie met his future wife and champion Angie Barnett. Attending the show with her was Calvin Lee who, while sharing her enthusiasm, would soon play an integral part in getting Bowie signed to Mercury Records in 1970.

And then, finally in 1969 after years of skirting around the periphery of success, came Bowie's breakthrough with the single *Space Oddity*. In common with many of his generation, the singer had been deeply affected by Stanley Kubrick's seminal 1968 sci-fi classic, *2001: A Space Odyssey*, not least thanks to his altered state of consciousness.

"I was very stoned when I went to see it, several times, and it was really a revelation to me," Bowie admitted in a 2003 interview with writer Bill DeMain. "It got the song flowing."

Released in July 1969 to coincide with the first ever NASA moon landings and peaking at No. 5 in the UK singles chart in October of that year, *Space Oddity* would combine all the crucial elements that would beat at the heart of his triumphant 70s oeuvre: a sense of unease (*"Your circuit's dead/There's something wrong"*), material dissatisfaction (*"The papers want to know whose shirts you wear"*) and alienation from the mainstream (*"Sitting in my tin can far above the world"*).

It should have propelled David Bowie into the big time. Instead, his next few singles failed to trouble the charts. Cruelly viewed as a one-hit wonder, he would, like Major Tom, drift listlessly further away from his destination. Would he ever make it? ❷

GETTY x2

David Bowie

Space Oddity

Intergalactic lullaby, break-up tune, moonshot tie-in, the five-minute, wildly inventive story song began Bowie's fertile decade of ground-breaking pop.

Words:
Bill DeMain
Portrait:
Michael Ochs Archives/Getty Images

In the darkness of London's Casino Cinerama, a 21-year-old David Bowie stared at the space embryo floating across the theatre's huge, 70mm screen. It was summer 1968, and this was the third time the singer-songwriter had been to see *2001: A Space Odyssey*, released in April that year.

"It was the sense of isolation I related to," Bowie tells *Classic Rock*. "I found the whole thing amazing. I was out of my gourd, very stoned when I went to see it – several times – and it was really a revelation to me. It got the song flowing."

While Stanley Kubrick's film provided the setting and title for Bowie's first Top 10 hit, *Space Oddity*, there were other inspirations shaping the song's sound and vision. That summer, Bowie was hooked on Simon & Garfunkel's *Bookends* album – especially *Old Friends*, whose breezy chords he borrowed for the '*tin can*' section of his song. More significant was the downward spiral of Bowie's relationship with his actress girlfriend Hermione Farthingale. "It was Hermione who got me writing for and on a specific person," Bowie says. The break-up would yield a handful of songs, but the lonely void that Bowie felt in her absence found its perfect metaphor in the marooned space capsule of Major Tom.

While Bowie has never commented on the origin of his astronaut's name, there is one intriguing theory. As a kid growing up in Bromley, he saw posters advertising the well-known music hall performer Tom Major (Prime Minister John's dad), and the name lodged in his brain.

Whatever the source, Major Tom became the first in a long line of mythical characters to float through Bowie's musical universe (and one who would return in 1980's hit *Ashes To Ashes*).

With the song's neatly designed, rocket-like structure in place – it had seven distinct sections, as opposed to the three or four of most hits – Bowie recorded a demo in late 1968 for the short promotional film *Love You Till Tuesday*. That version, thin and reedy, with Bowie mimicking the spaceship sounds himself, failed to make commercial waves. But it got him signed to Mercury Records. With that mission

accomplished, the first order of business was to record a proper, full-on version.

Bowie assumed that he'd be working with his friend and producer Tony Visconti. But Visconti hated the song, calling it "a cheap shot – a gimmick to cash in on the moonshot." Into the breach leapt Visconti's young engineer Gus Dudgeon.

"In those days a gimmick was a big deal and people who had gimmicks were taken more seriously than those who hadn't," Dudgeon has said. "Bowie's was that he'd written a song about being in space at a time when the first US moonshot was about to take place. I listened to the demo and thought it was incredible. I couldn't believe that Tony didn't want to do it."

Recorded on June 20, 1969 at Trident studio in London, the track was plotted out with the precision of a space launch. From the well-timed entrances of Herbie Flowers's bass and Rick Wakeman's Mellotron, to the controlled chaos of the lift-off and the spooky distress calls dotting the outro, the clever arrangement propelled the song into an atmosphere far beyond the demo. The song's majesty is even more remarkable when you consider the session costs were under £500. Dudgeon mixed the track in stereo, which was almost unheard of for radio singles at the time.

It was rush-released on July 11, nine days ahead of the Apollo 11 Moon landing. Copies were air-mailed to US disc jockeys. But despite the efforts to piggyback on NASA's moment of glory, it got little play in the States. The reception in England was much warmer, however.

"It was picked up by British television and used as the background music for the landing itself in Britain," Bowie says, then adds with a chuckle: "Though I'm sure they really weren't listening to the lyric *at all*; it wasn't a pleasant thing to juxtapose against a moon landing. Of course, I was overjoyed that they did. Obviously, some BBC official said: 'Right, then. That space song, Major Tom…' blah blah blah, 'That'll be great.'

Nobody had the heart to tell the producer: 'Um… but he gets stranded in space, sir.'

Space Oddity remains Bowie biggest-selling single in the UK and his signature song. It won an Ivor Novello Award in 1969. And although there were a few commercial bumps in the years following, it was kind of a scouting mission for the worldwide fame that would come in 1972 with the extraterrestrial Ziggy Stardust.

A theatrical set piece of his live set, Bowie used to sing *Space Oddity* while being lowered by a hydraulic lift into a giant hand. The song has been covered by more than 20 artists, including Def Leppard, Tangerine Dream and Cat Power, and featured in the videogame *Rock Band 3*. In 1979 Bowie recorded a stark version of it for BBC TV's *The Kenny Everett Show* and performed it inside a padded cell.

Intergalactic lullaby, break-up tune,

> ## "I don't think it was like anything anybody had done before, and that's why the record is still a classic."

NASA tie-in, *Space Oddity* is all this and more. A five-minute, wildly inventive story song which began Bowie's fertile decade of ground-breaking pop. "I don't think it was like anything anybody had done before, and that's why the record is still a classic," Gus Dudgeon said.

Even Tony Visconti admitted: "I wish I'd dropped my peacenik hippie ideals and recorded this classic track."

"When I originally wrote about Major Tom," Bowie says, "I thought I knew all about the great American dream and where it started and where it should stop. Here was the great blast of American technological know-how shoving this guy up into space, but once he gets there he's not quite sure why he's there. And that's where I left him."

And that's where he remains, an icon of rock music, and a glittering star in the firmament of Bowie's career. ❼

STYL' LEADER
"David Bowie plays Stylophone on *Space Oddity*!" trumpeted the magazine ad, which pictured the curly-headed singer poised thoughtfully above the device – a miniature toy keyboard played with a pen-like stylus.
   Invented by Brian Jarvis in 1967 and promoted on TV by Aussie entertainer Rolf Harris, the "pocket electric organ" sold millions in the early 70s. Kids loved it, as did budding electronic musicians (Kraftwerk, Pulp and Daft Punk were eventual users). But "the greatest craze since the yo-yo" began with Bowie and those interstellar noises on *Space Oddity*.

THE FACTS
RELEASE DATE
July 1969
HIGHEST CHART POSITION
UK No.1 (1975 re-release), US No.15 (1973 re-release)
PERSONNEL
David Bowie
Vocals, acoustic guitar, Stylophone
Rick Wakeman
Mellotron
Mick Wayne
Guitar
Herbie Flowers
Bass
Terry Cox
Drums
Paul Buckmaster
String arranger
WRITTEN BY
David Bowie
PRODUCER
Gus Dudgeon
LABEL
Mercury

David Bowie: glad the BBC didn't actually listen to the lyrics to *Space Oddity*.

THE MAN WHO SAW THE FUTURE

In 1970, **David Bowie** the one-hit wonder was on the brink of becoming David Bowie the decade-defining artist. *The Man Who Sold The World* was the album that helped him recalibrate his sound and vision.

Words: **Bill DeMain**

By March 1970, Major Tom was becoming something of an albatross to his 23-year old earthly counterpart David Bowie. The single of *Space Oddity*, which reached No.5 in the UK and sold nearly 150,000 copies, had pushed up fees for Bowie's live shows and made him flush for the first time in his six-year career. But the song's connection to the Apollo Moon landing had coloured it with a novelty status that he was finding it hard to get past. His latest single, *The Prettiest Star*, written for his new bride Angie and featuring Marc Bolan on lead guitar, moved only 800 copies, never denting the charts.

Bowie had other troubles on his mind too. He was grieving his father, who died a few months earlier at age 56. His management contract with Ken Pitt had soured to the point where he wanted out. There was also the delicate matter of his schizophrenic half-brother Terry, who'd been living with his parents. After Bowie's dad passed, his mom, unable to cope with Terry, committed him to Cane Hill Asylum. Bowie visited him regularly but felt increasingly guilty over not being able to do more to help.

Looking back in a 1971 *Phonograph* interview, Bowie summed up his state of mind: "I really felt so depressed, so aimless, and this torrential feeling

> ## "I really felt so depressed, so aimless, and this torrential feeling of 'What's it all for anyway?'"
>
> **David Bowie**

of 'What's it all for anyway?' A lot of it went through that period."

So it made sense to stay cocooned with Angie in their flat at Haddon Hall, a shambling old Victorian house in Beckenham. Sharing the rent was Bowie's producer pal Tony Visconti, and his girlfriend. The record that became *The Man Who Sold The World* started with late night conversations about the idea of moving away from singles toward albums.

"We wanted to make an art rock album," Visconti said in Dylan Jones's book, *David Bowie: A Life.* "On the *Space Oddity* album, we had no idea what we were doing. It was all over the map. So we tried something different, something harder. We just threw caution to the wind. It had to be seen by our peers as a work of art rather than just a pop album, along the lines of a Frank Zappa album, as David and I were into the idea of a concept album. The single went out of favour for a while because the likes of Led Zeppelin and Yes were making albums that were outselling singles for the first time We wanted to be seen as a great album group."

With Visconti on bass, Bowie's new band began to come together that spring with the arrival of two musicians from Hull – guitarist Mick Ronson and drummer Woody Woodmansey. Ronson had met Visconti on a session for Mike Chapman's *Fully Qualified Survivor*, a now-forgotten record that, thanks to Ronson's touch, has pre-echoes of *Hunky Dory*. Ronson attended a Bowie show and returned with him to Haddon Hall for a late night jam.

In *Beside Bowie,* the 2017 documentary about ◆▸

With Tony Visconti at Trident Studios, May 1970.

Bowie as a musician who was being an artist 24/7. "Although he really hadn't got it figured out at that time, I looked on him as an artist in preparation. He had all these ideas but he hadn't really sorted out a direction. And he didn't really know rock'n'roll music at that time. Which is where the band came in."

The other major player who entered Bowie's life that spring was Tony Defries. In April, Bowie had his fateful first meeting with the bushy-haired, cigar-smoking 26-year-old litigation clerk and would-be show business agent. His role model was Colonel Tom Parker, and he was convinced he'd found his Elvis. He seemed to intuit all Bowie's career angst, and made big promises. We'll get you out of your management contract with Ken Pitt. We'll get you onto a better label. We'll make you "bigger than everybody." All you have to do is be creative and write songs. I'll take care of the rest.

Three years later, Bowie told BBC Radio 1, "He said, 'I'm going to make you a star!' 'Oh yeah?' And he did… so they say. I've read about it. That's when Tony Defries entered my life – and me wallet!"

Many legal battles loomed ahead, and it would be 1982 before Bowie would fully extract himself from the management contract he called "the worst decision of his life."

Meanwhile, back at Haddon Hall in spring 1970, the new group started rehearsing in the wine cellar. Visconti said in *The Golden Years*: "We cleaned it up and put up eight crates on the wall as soundproofing – to this day I don't think those crates ever worked. We got a lot of complaints from the neighbours, as we spent weeks down there. We made this album our job, and by the time we got into the studio we were very well-rehearsed. It was just a matter of putting all the tracks down and recording it."

But upon entering the studio, Bowie was procrastinating on finishing melodies and lyrics for the instrumentals that the band were assembling. Speaking in *The Golden Years*, Visconti recalled: "Mick, Woody and myself would be making up backing tracks having got a brief from David – it was E chord for 16 bars, then an A chord for four bars – and we were just banging out these backing tracks, and David would come into the studio and say whether he liked it or not."

Royal Academy-trained pianist Ralph Mace was

Ronson, Bowie recalled, "I started playing some of my songs on my 12-string and he plugged in his Gibson. Even though he was playing at a very low volume, the energy and grit cut through the room and he immediately established himself as a very well-defined player."

"Mick was like Jeff Beck, Eric Clapton and Jimi Hendrix all rolled up in one person," Visconti told *Performing Songwriter*. "He had it all, and his technique was phenomenal, as were his sensibilities. He knew the right notes to play, the right way to play a song. Give him a song for 10 minutes and he was there."

That idea was tested two days later, when Ronson, with zero rehearsal, did his first gig with

Bowie on the *BBC In Concert* series. "It was incredibly exciting," Visconti said in *David Bowie: The Golden Years*. "Because we knew that Mick was going to work out – he had something we needed."

With his enthusiastic demeanor and deep musical vocabulary, Ronno was a perfect foil to Bowie. After he moved into Haddon Hall, the two became inseparable, sitting for hours across from each other, working out chord progressions and designing the riffs that would inspire the songs on *The Man Who Sold The World*.

Ronson also became quickly frustrated with Bowie's current drummer John Chamberlain, and suggested a replacement. Mick "Woody" Woodmansey recalled his first impression of

On the chaise longue: at Haddon Hall in 1970.

drafted in to play a Moog synthesizer. "It was creation in the studio," Mace said in Peter and Leni Gillman's *Alias David Bowie*. "They began with a basic idea from one instrument or one vocal line. They would start adding and would change according to their whims. David bounced ideas off people. There was a lot of creative interplay."

But for all the collaboration, only Bowie's name would appear on the songwriting credits. "It's hard to say how much you do when you write a song with someone else," Visconti said. "And even though we weren't credited as writers, Mick and I were getting the chord changes together. *The Width Of A Circle* was the only track that was written, and that was only the first part of the song. The second part was written in the studio, and Mick and I definitely wrote all that, and David just threw all his words and melody on top."

It's not clear why Bowie didn't assert control more. It could be that he wasn't yet confident enough to assert himself, thinking it best to let the more experienced musicians run the show. Engineer Ken Scott, who would move into the producer chair for Bowie's next three breakthrough albums, said in a YouTube interview: "Tony and Mick did take over. How much it was

David not wanting to have anything to do with it, and how much was Tony taking over, I don't know. But I think it was more Tony's ideas on the album than David's."

Or it could've simply been that he was formulating the working method that would give his coming decade of albums such spontaneity and

IIIIIIIIIIIIIIIIIIIIIIIIIIIIIIIIIIIIIIIIII
"As far as the label was concerned, this was the last they had to do with David."

Tony Visconti

character. On *TMWSTW*, the songs are almost more interesting for what they hint at than what they are. *The Width Of A Circle*, with its eight-minute ramble through tempo and mood shifts, is a precursor to *Station To Station*. *She Shook Me Cold* foreshadows Ziggy's glam sexuality. *Saviour Machine* is a queasy dystopian preview of *Diamond Dogs*. *All The Madmen* and *The Supermen* move deep into the lyrical themes of alienation and loneliness that Bowie explore throughout his career.

But for much of the album, the songs seem to

wander away from the singer, turning into extended jams. Then suddenly, on the last two songs, everything snaps into focus.

It was the final day of mixing, and Bowie still hadn't come up with words for the second-to-last track on the album. With Visconti waiting impatiently at the mixing console, the singer hunkered down in the studio lobby and scratched out what became the title track and best song on the album.

Bowie later referred to the song as "trance-like," saying, "My state of mind when I was writing it was as near to a mystical state as a 19-year-old can get into. It was at a time when I was sort of studying Buddhism."

Visconti referred to this as "writing on microphone." He said in *David Bowie: A Life*: "David would start singing spontaneously. It was really wonderful. When he was hot, he was hot. But for me the whole thing was not so good. I had two big conflicts – getting this done technically, which I was struggling with, and also managing to get a good performance out of David. I had a record company screaming for final mixes, not even sure that they wanted this album. As far as they were concerned, this was the last they had to do with David Bowie and I wasn't delivering the goods." ➤➤

"I enjoyed being able to hybridize these different kinds of music. As if to say, 'Wow, this is no longer rock n' roll'"

David Bowie

Quick cig break during sessions at Trident Studios.

The album was released on November 4, 1970 in the US and April 10, of the following year, in the UK. *Rolling Stone* called it "intriguing and chilling." Phonograph Record praised it for "trying to define some new province of modern music."

In support, Bowie did a brief tour of US college radio stations, showing up in his Mr. Fish dress, confounding and charming disc jockeys. But since Olav Wyper – his champion at the label – had departed Mercury did little to promote the record. By early 1971, Tony Defries was already busy engineering Bowie's move to RCA Victor.

The pushy manager's increasingly hands-on presence in Bowie's life ended up forcing Visconti out of the picture and on towards his fruitful partnership with Marc Bolan and T.Rex. "David was assigning his power to other people," Visconti said in *The Golden Years*. "When he meets someone, and he falls in love – forget it. The person's the one

until he's severely hurt. I said to David, 'If you go with Tony Defries, I'm not going to go with you.'"

The album enjoyed a brief resurgence in 1974 after Lulu took a cover of the title track to No.3 on the UK charts. Produced by Bowie and Mick Ronson, and featuring the Spiders From Mars as a backing band, it veered even further towards the Berlin cabaret feel that was hinted at in the original.

"I didn't think *The Man Who Sold The World* was the best song for my voice, but it was such a strong song in itself," Lulu told Marc Spitz in *Bowie: A Biography*. "I had no idea what it was about. In the studio, Bowie kept telling me to smoke more cigarettes, to give my voice a certain quality."

In 2020, Tony Visconti returned to the original tapes of *The Man Who Sold The World* to create a 50th anniversary stereo remix. To distinguish it from the usual remasters, it was given its intended title, *Metrobolist*, and used the sleeve illustration

from the alternative US 1970 release. But even with the fresh take, the album still occupies a strange place in Bowie's discography. Rarely listed as a favourite or Top 5 entry, it's a preview of the conceptual, harmonically adventurous artist who will find much fuller flower on the two albums just around the bend, and an entrance way to the unparalleled string of masterpieces to follow over the decade – from *Aladdin Sane* to *Scary Monsters*.

David Bowie once described his artistic vision to me as it bloomed in the early 1970s. "What my true style was is that I loved the idea of putting Little Richard with Jacques Brel, and the Velvet Underground backing them. What would that sound like? It really seemed what I was good at doing and what I enjoyed was being able to hybridize these different kinds of music. As if to say, 'Wow, this is no longer rock'n'roll. This is an art form. This is something really exciting!'" 🔊

THE BIRTH OF GLAM

The audience at 1970's Atomic Sunrise Festival was largely indifferent to **David Bowie**'s new band, Hype, with their Lurex outfits and make-up. But one man wasn't: Marc Bolan.

Words: **Rob Hughes**

We're having a moment here. It's March 25, 1971 and this Thursday's episode of *Top Of The Pops*, the BBC's flagship chart show, has reached its finale. So far we've had Andy Williams, Gilbert O'Sullivan, Fleetwood Mac, even the Plastic Ono Band. Now it's time for this week's No1. Mungo Jerry's *Baby Jump* has been swatted from its perch by *Hot Love*, an insidious little boogie from T.Rex that will stay put for the next month and a half.

It's a great song all right. And with his satin and curls, a Gibson Les Paul slung across his chest, Marc Bolan cuts a dramatic figure. The most striking thing, however, is the splash of glitter on each cheek. The work of T.Rex publicist Chelita Secunda, who's already applied a thin caking of mascara to Bolan's eyes, it fires the imagination of hordes of young viewers. Bolan claims he prettied himself up on the spur of the moment, just for laughs. But his next gig finds him greeted by hundreds of adoring teenage fans, all decked out in various degrees of glitteration. There was no escaping it: Bolan had introduced glam rock to the masses.

But it wasn't quite as spontaneous as that. A year earlier, Bolan had been in the audience at a London Roundhouse show by Hype, fronted by David Bowie. This was a gig that flew directly into the wind of the times. One that brought colour, playfulness and a hint of self-mythology into what was an overwhelmingly monochrome era.

Then known as the curly-haired creator of *Space Oddity*, a sci-fi tune that had landed him a surprise hit in 1969, Bowie was looking for a new direction. Everything around him seemed drab and overly serious. Denim was the unofficial uniform of the music fraternity, be it worn by earnest singer-songwriters with acoustic guitars or tribes of unsmiling prog bands. Where was the flash? Where was the fun?

"At that point in time, rock seemed to have wandered into some kind of denim hell," Bowie recalled in 2003's *Moonage Daydream*, photographer Mick Rock's visual account of the rise of Ziggy Stardust. "Street life was long hair, beards, leftover beads from the 60s and, God forbid, flares were still evident. In fact, all was rather dull attitudinising with none of the burning ideals of the 60s."

Bowie and his soon-to-be wife Angie Barnett were sparked into action by photographer Ray Stevenson. A comic-book nut and regular visitor to the couple's base at Haddon Hall in Beckenham, South London, Stevenson recalled an evening spent talking about "supermen and superstars". Next time he called, Bowie and Barnett were busy with a sewing machine. The idea of flamboyant stage gear had taken hold.

In February 1970, Bowie had brought in guitarist Mick Ronson, largely on the recommendation of drummer John Cambridge, for a new band that also included his producer Tony Visconti on bass. A phone call to Bowie's manager Ken Pitt sparked a discussion over what to call themselves, with a chance remark – "The whole thing is just one big hype" – providing a name that seemed to suit.

> **"You can see Bolan looking up at Bowie, going, 'I'm gonna have a bit of that.'"**
>
> **Hype drummer John Cambridge**

ALAMY

Original gangster: Hype guitarist Mick Ronson.

Tony Visconti on bass as 'Hypeman' in Hype at The Roundhouse, 11 March 1970.

PHOTOSHOT x3

"Bowie used to think that everything was hype," recalls Cambridge today. "It was all shit, in other words. So he said we should just go with it."

What happened next is still open to conjecture. Pick up any Bowie biography and it'll tell you that the band's live debut, supporting Fat Mattress at the Roundhouse, Chalk Farm, on February 22, marked the first occasion that they wore costumes. Visconti even says so in his autobiography, *Bowie, Bolan And The Brooklyn Boy*. Yet Cambridge, who kept a diary, insists they didn't dress up until they returned to the Roundhouse a fortnight or so later.

With Barnett and Visconti's girlfriend Liz Hartley as seamstresses, each member had been assigned the role of a spoof superhero. Bowie had a blue cape, Lurex tights and thigh boots in his guise as Rainbowman. Visconti, in green cape and white leotard, a giant 'H' emblazoned on his chest, was the Superman-styled Hypeman. Ronson borrowed Bowie's suit from a recent awards show – the singer had been voted *Disc And Music Echo*'s 'Brightest Hope For 1970' – and became Gangsterman. While Cambridge, in frilly shirt and 10-gallon stetson, was Cowboyman.

It was a transition that wasn't merely sartorial. Positing himself as a psychedelic folkie, Bowie's previous work had been mostly acoustic. Now he was fronting an electrified rock'n'roll band. They didn't go down well at all. Fans of the headline act made no secret of the fact they didn't go in for post-hippie songs like *Memory Of A Free Festival* or Velvet Underground's *I'm Waiting For The Man*.

Bowie's new band weren't actually billed as Hype at the Roundhouse. It wasn't until they played Basildon Arts Lab, six days later, that he finally decided on using the name, if not the clothes. Though for their next major engagement, back at Chalk Farm on March 11, they most definitely did break out the faux-superhero gear.

Appearing as part of the venue's Atomic Sunrise Festival – Seven Nights Of Celebration, organised by the Living Theatre collective – Hype took their place alongside Quintessence, Graham Bond, Hawkwind, Third Ear Band, Kevin Ayers and Arthur Brown.

|||||||||||||||||||||||||||||||||||||||||

"I was a big Bowie fan. He and the band were wearing costumes, and I hadn't seen that before."

Genesis keyboard player Tony Banks

"Danae Brook, who was associated with the Living Theatre, wanted to do this mad week at the Roundhouse," recalls DJ and scenester Jeff Dexter. "So she and I organised it. I booked all the bands and Allan King Associates decided to film it all. They had two or three cameramen at the festival."

Hawkwind's Nik Turner was there for the duration. "I knew the people who ran the venue," he says, "so they'd let me come and go. It was all pretty casual and LSD was the drug of choice. People were either giving it away or spiking each other with it. The acts were really cool and everything was very mystical and magical. I remember David Bowie playing with his guys, all dressed as superheroes."

Bowie headlined on the Wednesday night. Opening the show that evening were Genesis, then a relatively unknown band, testing out songs from their soon-to-be-recorded second album, *Trespass*. "We were trawling around the country," recalls ex-guitarist Anthony Phillips, "and the festival did have the feel of being something pretty big. I don't

think there was a large audience, though. I would've thought that Bowie might've pulled in a bigger crowd, because he'd had a hit with *Space Oddity*. But he was nowhere near the Bowie that we all know. We weren't thinking superstar, we were thinking quirky guy who'd had that hit."

Phillips' memory of the night remains fuzzy, but Genesis keyboard player Tony Banks has a sharper recollection. "I remember Bowie quite well," he offers, "because I was a big fan already. I'd bought an early single of his, *Can't Help Thinking About Me* [1966, with The Lower Third]. So I'd followed him since then and *Space Oddity* had brought him into the public eye. He and the band were all wearing costumes, and I hadn't really seen that kind of thing before. It was pretty interesting."

Not every Hype member was keen on the get-up, though. Dressing up was one thing, but cosmetics was another. "Both me and Mick [Ronson] went: 'There's no way I'm doing that!'" laughs Cambridge. "Cowboys don't wear make-up. But compared to Visconti, in his cape and tights, me and Mick got away lightly in the end."

They certainly looked the part. Bowie's outfit consisted of a silver jacket with metallic belt, silver tights, billowy satin cape and thigh-high leather boots. Visconti was similarly spacey in his

REGULAR SUPERSTAR

How David Bowie met Mick Ronson – and an unlikely partnership was born.

"Mick Ronson just floored us," Tony Visconti recalled of his first encounter with Bowie's most celebrated guitarist. "When David and I met him we knew he'd fit in looks-wise, but we had no idea what was coming until he picked up his Les Paul."

The story of how Ronson ended up with Bowie couldn't be more prosaic. Convinced that Ronson would be an ideal fit for the band that morphed into Hype, John Cambridge recommended him from their days in Hull band, The Rats. The drummer returned home, where he found Ronson working as a municipal gardener with Hull City Council, marking out lines on a school rugby pitch. Bringing him to London, Cambridge introduced Ronson to Bowie after a show at the Marquee on February 3, 1970. Two days later he joined the band for a BBC radio session with John Peel. "I didn't know

anything, none of the material," he said in 1984. "I just sat and watched David's fingers. I really didn't know what I was doing, but I suppose it came across OK."

Ronson was to become Bowie's key foil. Not only was he a formidable player, but his classical training and arrangement skills proved invaluable when it came to the run of albums between 1970-'73: *The Man Who Sold The World*, *Hunky Dory*, *The Rise And Fall Of Ziggy Stardust And The Spiders From Mars*, *Aladdin Sane* and *Pin-Ups*.

Essentially a shy man with a dry wit, Ronson made a strange first impression on Visconti. "We thought he was just a cool, silent type," said Visconti. "Later we found out that our apartment in Beckenham was very 'big time' for him. I remember us going to the pub and he became tipsy after half a pint of shandy!"

"We thought we were kind of smart, but nobody even looked at the stage. So it was all to no avail. But that was a wonderful show in as much as I knew that theatre was for me after that."

It certainly wasn't a new idea. Little Richard had camped it up in sequined vest and mascara, Elvis and Billy Fury had their gold suits, The Stones and The Kinks had flounced around London like foppish Edwardian dandies. But what was fascinating about Bowie was that he was beginning to take it further. Dressing up at the Roundhouse was the first manifestation of the rock star asa projection; adopt a fictional persona and play it out on stage. Design your own future, then will it into being. '*So inviting, so enticing to play the part,*' he would later sing on *Star*. '*I could play the wild mutation as a rock'n'roll star.*' Ziggy was still a couple of years away, but the seed was sown.

Hype wasn't designed to last. Two nights later, after a show at Sunderland's Locarno Ballroom, they ditched the costumes. Bowie carried on with the name until the end of March, when John Cambridge played his final gig at the Star Hotel in Croydon. A week later, he was replaced by another ex-member of The Rats: Woody Woodmansey. Cambridge had at least played a part in the birth of Ziggy Stardust, which in turn would signal the arrival of Bowie the superstar. "I always say that I wasn't in the Spiders," he says, "but I helped weave the web."

The reconstituted version of Hype backed Bowie on sessions for *The Man Who Sold The World* in April and May 1970. Though by the time it was in the can, he'd acquired hard-nosed businessman Tony Defries as manager. One of his first conditions was to drop the band. "Defries only saw David as the star," says Visconti. Ronson and Woodmansey, for the time being, also headed home to Hull.

The footage from the Roundhouse lay on a shelf for two decades after Allan King Associates went bust. In 1990, it was bought by producer Adrian Everett, though the original soundtrack had long been lost. An edited version, *Atomic Sunrise Festival 1970*, was finally screened in the Roundhouse's Studio Theatre on March 11, 2013.

It remains a defining moment in the trajectory of Bowie and, by extension, 70s rock. Just around the corner were T. Rex, Roxy Music, Sweet and a host of glittery glam icons.

"I just stopped after that performance," Bowie told *NME* years later, "because I knew it was right. I knew it was what I wanted to do and I knew it was what people would want eventually." ●

Hypeman ensemble, while Ronson's borrowed Gangsterman suit was given added zing by his appropriation of a loud tie with giant dots.

John Cambridge recalls how his own outfit came together: "I remember meeting Visconti at his offices on Oxford Street one day. We were crossing the road together and saw this cowboy hat in a store. He just went in and bought it. I've still got it actually, it's been up in the loft."

The setlist that night included Bowie originals *Memory Of A Free Festival* and *The Supermen*. The latter, with its allusions to Nietzsche and HP Lovecraft, was soon to find a home on *The Man Who Sold The World*, his third album, issued later in the year. Among the covers played were *I'm Waiting For The Man* and John Lennon's *Instant Karma*.

"We'd always do a couple of covers," explains Cambridge. "We'd play Canned Heat *Let's Work Together*, which was in the charts in 1970.I remember Bowie saying to me, 'I really like that lyric, "*Together we'll stand/Divided we'll fall*". I wish I'd written a song like that.' I said, 'You know it's in another song as well? Brotherhood Of Man have got a single out called *United We Stand*.' He went, 'They haven't! Oh shit!'"

All parties remember the crowd as convivial, if largely indifferent. Cambridge likens it to audience footage of the Woodstock festival, albeit ona micro scale, full of people in headbands, waving their arms about, "stoned out of their heads".

But there was at least one attendee who was paying full attention: Marc Bolan. Bowie and Visconti had no idea that he was even there. It was only much later, when going through Ray

Stevenson's shots of the gig at the back end of the 70s, that the discovery was made. "There is a photo somewhere and Marc Bolan is at the very front of the stage," confirms Cambridge. "The photo is taken from the back of us, looking out at the audience, and Marc's there. This was when he was still doing Tyrannosaurus Rex. Woolworths used to sell these plastic shields, like copies of armour, and he had it strapped to the front of him, just to be different. You can see him looking up at Bowie with all this make-up on and his Lurex tights. And his eyes are saying: 'Ahh, I'm gonna have a bit of that!' So he took it on. When it comes to this big debate about whether it was Marc Bolan or Bowie who started glam rock, it was definitely Bowie."

Visconti has credited both Bowie and Bolan for having "simultaneously kind of invented" the glitter movement. Though in his autobiography he states that that Roundhouse gig "will always be the very first night of glam rock". The most hyperbolic assessment, however, belongs to Mick Rock: "If David Bowie was the Jesus Christ of glam. Then Marc Bolan was John the Baptist!"

Bowie, himself, has mixed feelings about that first night of glam. "It was really just the most depressing night of our lives," he recalled later.

Wild west hero: Hype drummer John Cambridge.

"It was really just the most depressing night of our lives. Nobody even looked at the stage."

David Bowie

The Freakiest Show

Words: Bill DeMain

J ANUARY, 1971. THERE was trouble in outer space. Major Tom's signal was growing fainter by the day. And Ziggy Stardust was still an undefined blip on the interstellar radar.

Meanwhile, back at ground control, David Bowie was staring at the grey sky outside his Beckenham flat and worrying about his career.

His last single, *The Prettiest Star*, had been a flop, failing to build on the momentum of *Space Oddity*. His third album, *The Man Who Sold The World*, was languishing in the vaults of Mercury Records without a firm release date. His guitarist, Mick Ronson, had moved from London back to Hull to work as a gardener. Meanwhile, Bowie had fired his manager of five years, Ken Pitt. Although Pitt's replacement, the cigar-chomping Tony Defries, had offered the age-old promise of "I'll make you a star", nothing celestial had yet materialised. In fact Defries's most significant gambit at that point had been a financial squeeze-play that ousted Tony Visconti, robbing Bowie of both a producer and close friend. Alienated and in serious limbo, Bowie was reduced to gigging at pubs around south London for a few pounds a night.

In an unguarded low moment, he admitted to journalist Steve Peacock that he felt "washed-up – a disillusioned old rocker".

At 24, with seven years in the business, three albums under his belt and one too many thwarted dreams, Bowie brooded on the sidelines as his friendly rivals Marc Bolan and Elton John ascended the first rungs of the ladder to stardom. When would he get his turn?

But even in his winter of discontent, Bowie refused to quit. "I might have had moments of, 'God, I don't think anything is ever going to happen for me,'" he later said, "but I would bounce up pretty fast. I still liked the process. I liked writing and recording. It was a lot of fun for a kid."

After years of aping R&B and coffeehouse folk styles, the blond-tressed kid was finally discovering his own sound. Or, as he'd put it so poetically in a song he'd written that December, he was learning to 'Turn and face the strange'.

"In the early 70s it really started to all come together for me as to what it was that I liked doing," Bowie told *Classic Rock* in 2011, "and it was a collision of musical styles. I found that I couldn't easily adopt brand loyalty, or genre loyalty. I wasn't an R&B artist, I wasn't a folk artist, and I didn't see the point in trying to be that purist about it.

"My true style was that I loved the idea of putting Little Richard with Jacques Brel, and the Velvet Underground backing them. 'What would that sound like?' Nobody was doing that, at least not in the same way."

This revelation would help create *Hunky Dory*, the kaleidoscopic pop collection that announced Bowie's arrival and began a streak of landmark albums through the 1970s – from *Ziggy Stardust* to *Aladdin Sane* to *Heroes*.

Bowie's artistic vision was doubtless brought into sharper focus by a dose of domestic reality – he was about to become a father for the first time. Ex-wife Angie Bowie said: "I think that changed how he was writing songs. He really started to think about how he was going to have a kid. That was interesting to him. He got along very well with his father, so from that relationship he had an optimistic prognosis on what it was going to ⟶

In 1971 David Bowie had everything to prove. Inspired by New York, (?) gay bars and philosophy, backed by his greatest band and produced by the engineer for The Beatles, he made his first classic.

Hunky Dory

be like. It wasn't a scary thing for him. *Changes* and *Eight Line Poem* were about that. And, of course, *Kooks*."

David and Angie, the self-described "kooky" couple, lived in an £8-a-week, ground-floor flat in a Victorian-era mansion called Haddon Hall. Furnished with Carnaby Street bric-a-brac, art-deco lamps, Oriental rugs from Kensington Market, and heavy black drapes blocking out the already dim natural light, it was the Bowies' version of a decadent pop-star pad. Or, as one visitor had it, "It looked like Dracula's living room."

In those early months of 1971, Count Bowie could often be found hunched over Haddon Hall's centrepiece, an ancient grand piano. Swapping his usual instrument, a Harptone 12-string acoustic guitar, for the less-familiar keyboard had a galvanising effect on his songwriting.

"He loved that piano," Angie remembered. "David is a fantastic musician, because his approach is not studied, it's by ear. He has an ability to pluck a song from those first moments when he plays with an instrument. Writing on the piano opened up his possibilities, because of its association with so many kinds of music – classical, cabaret, every style."

Bowie was also discovering interesting possibilities at his new favourite nightclub, a gay disco in Kensington called the Sombrero. Enchanted by the sexual freedom and outré hair and make-up on display, he found inspiration for both his songs and his own appearance. "*Oh! You Pretty Things* came directly out of David observing that scene, as did his [Ziggy] look," Angie said.

Excited about his growing cache of songs and ideas for a new direction, he rang Mick Ronson,

saying: "There's nothing doing up in Hull, is there? Why don't you come back here? You can stay with me and Angie." With the promise of recording sessions and a place to crash, Ronson, with drummer Woody Woodmansey and bassist Trevor Bolder in tow, moved into Haddon Hall.

Woodmansey, who had played on Bowie's *The Man Who Sold The World* was immediately struck by Bowie's new material. "I think he focused more as a writer and managed to keep his unique approach, especially lyrically, while streamlining everything," he says. "The songs were more structured. Honestly, I didn't think he had these songs in him."

Bolder, who'd been playing with Ronson and Woodmansey for about eight months in the band Ronno, was also surprised. "I had an impression of Bowie as a bit of a folkie. I didn't realise how good he was until we started doing *Hunky Dory*."

In the makeshift studio at Haddon Hall or in a practice room above the nearby Thomas A. Becket pub, Bowie and the future Spiders From Mars began working up arrangements for songs such as *Changes* and *Oh! You Pretty Things* (which had already been covered and taken to No.12 in the UK singles

chart by Peter Noone), as well as *Ziggy Stardust* tunes like *Hang On To Yourself, Suffragette City* and *Moonage Daydream*.

At the end of January, Bowie departed for a promotional tour of America, his first-ever visit. He was greeted at customs by a snarling dog, and an official who detained him for over an hour. Maybe it was the full-length purple suede coat and white chiffon scarf Bowie was sporting. Or his suitcase, which was packed with six dresses by designer Mr. Fish. The customs official finally sent the long-haired singer on his way with a mumbled parting shot of "fag".

But Bowie was too excited to let that get him down. At last he was in the land of his heroes Jack Kerouac and Andy Warhol. Over the next two weeks, he crossed the country, chatting up radio DJs and journalists about *The Man Who Sold The World* (the UK sleeve, featuring Bowie lounging in one of his dresses, was replaced in the US with a pop-art drawing of a cowboy). At night Bowie indulged, swallowing as many pills and bedding as many women as he could. But what fascinated him most about America were two artists and kindred spirits-to-be: Lou Reed and Iggy Pop. Bowie scrawled down an idea for "an ultimate pop idol" who would combine Reed's urban songwriting with Iggy's cartoon stage persona. But before Ziggy Stardust was born, Reed and Iggy would etch their way into the grooves of *Hunky Dory*.

"The whole *Hunky Dory* album reflected my new-found enthusiasm for this new continent that had been opened up to me," Bowie said in 1997. "It all came together because I'd been to the States. That was the first time that a real outside situation affected me so one hundred per cent. It changed my way of writing and changed the way that I looked at things."

Before he flew back to London, Bowie made his artistic resolve clear to *Rolling Stone* magazine: "I refuse to be thought of as mediocre. If I am mediocre, I'll get out of the business."

Upon his return, rehearsals resumed – by now Ronson, Woodmansey and Bolder had rented their own flat in nearby Penge – and plans were made to record an album, which Tony Defries would then use to secure a new label deal. But first a producer had to be found.

As engineer on Beatles classics from *Sgt. Pepper* to *Abbey Road*, as well as on Bowie's previous two records, Ken Scott seemed a logical choice (Bowie would later call Scott "my George Martin").

"I was getting fed up with engineering," Scott told *EQ* magazine, "and I happened to say to David: 'I want to start moving into the production side.' He said: 'Well, I've just got a new manager and I'm about to start a new album. I was going to do it myself but I don't know if I can. How about working with me?' And that was *Hunky Dory*, which then led to the other three albums."

Sessions began at Trident Studios in London's Soho in early June 1971. In the world outside, US president Nixon ended a 21-year-old trade embargo on China; Russia launched the Soyuz 11 craft for the first-ever rendezvous with a space station; Frank Sinatra announced his retirement; and topping the pop chart in Britain was Tony Orlando & Dawn's *Knock Three Times*.

Inside Trident, however, none of that registered. Working from 2pm to midnight, Monday to Saturday, with quick breaks for tea, sandwiches and the occasional bottle of wine, the band were swept up in a colourful world of bipperty-bopperty hats, Garbo's eyes and homo superiors (the album's recurring theme of children ch-ch-changing into enlightened beings was influenced by Bowie's love of the occult writings of Aleister Crowley, and sci-fi novels by Arthur C Clarke).

Bolder recalled the excitement: "*Hunky Dory* was the first recording session I ever did in my life, and just to be in a studio was amazing. Our approach was very off-the-top-of-our-heads. We'd go in, David would play us a song – often one we hadn't heard – we'd run through it once and then take it. No time to think about what you're going to play, you'd have to do it there and then. In some respects it's nerve-racking, but it gives a certain feel. If you play a song too many times in the studio it can become stale, and I think David wanted to capture the energy of it being on the edge."

Woodmansey agreed: "There was incredible pressure in getting a track recorded right. Many times, we'd go in with a track to record, and at the last minute David would change his mind and we'd

David and Angie married in March 1970 and son Duncan Zowie Haywood Jones was born in May 1971.

do one we hadn't rehearsed! We would be panicking, as he didn't like doing more than three takes to get it. Nearly every track I recorded with David was first, second or third take, usually second. He knew when a take was right."

This was a change from the sessions for the previous album, where Bowie was reportedly distracted and undisciplined. Tony Visconti later complained that during the recording of *The Man Who Sold The World* David had spent more time in the lobby cuddling with Angie than worrying about finishing the tracks. But the Bowie on *Hunky Dory* was a man with a mission

Ken Scott: "With David, unlike the Beatles sessions, it was very much him knowing what he wanted right from the get-go. I think he knew all along what was going to happen, but he didn't always tell you. You had to be ready. And with David almost all of the lead vocals are one take."

A late addition to the team was keyboard virtuoso Rick Wakeman, who had played Mellotron on *Space Oddity* and was now drafted in to dress up Bowie's piano parts. "He told me to make as many notes as I wanted," Wakeman ➤➤

"It was like 'Wow – this is no longer rock 'n' roll, this is an art form!'"
— David Bowie

once said. "The songs were unbelievable – *Changes, Life On Mars?*, one after another. He said he wanted to come at the album from a different angle, that he wanted them to be based around the piano. So he told me to play them as I would a piano piece, and that he'd then adapt everything else around that."

If Wakeman was a featured performer, so too was the 100-year old Beckstein piano he played. Scott: "It was the same piano used on *Hey Jude*, the early Elton John albums, Nilsson, Genesis and Supertramp, among many others. That was one of Trident's claims to fame – the piano sound. It was an amazing instrument."

Nowhere was that piano better featured than on the kitchen-sink ballad *Life On Mars?* The song has often been compared to Sinatra's *My Way* (the album liner notes even say: "Inspired by Frankie"), and for good reason. In 1968 Bowie was asked by a publisher to submit English lyrics to a popular French chanson, *Comme D'Habitude*. His version, titled *Even A Fool Learns To Love*, was rejected in favour of another by former teen idol Paul Anka.

Bowie: "There was a sense of revenge in that, because I was so angry that Paul Anka had done *My Way*. I thought I'd do my own version. There are clutches of melody in that [*Life On Mars?*] that were definite parodies."

A week before the sessions began, on May 30, Duncan Zowie Haywood Jones was born, cracking his mother's pelvis in the delivery. Bowie greeted his boy with *Kooks*, a charming ditty meant as both a paternal tribute and a warning. In the 1971 press release for *Hunky Dory*, he explained: "The baby looked like me and it looked like Angie and the song came out like, 'If you're gonna stay with us you're gonna grow up bananas.'"

Actually, Zowie (now known as Duncan Jones and an acclaimed film director) turned out fine, despite a mostly absentee father and being raised by a revolving cast of nannies and grandparents. Bowie confessed: "I might have written a song for my son, but I certainly wasn't there that much for him. I was ambitious, I wanted to be a real kind of presence. And I had Joe very early. And with that state of affairs, had I known, it would've all happened a bit later. Fortunately everything with us is tremendous. But I would give my eye teeth to have that time back again, to have shared it with him as a child."

Drawing on the "collision of musical styles" idea, *Hunky Dory* ricochets playfully through its 11 songs. From the lounge-meets-boogaloo gear shifts of *Changes* and the glam-ragtime stride of *Oh! You Pretty Things*, through the Tony Newley-does-the-blues of *Eight Line Poem* to psyche-Dylan swirl of *The Bewlay Brothers*, it's a thrilling hybrid.

"It was like, 'Wow, this is no longer rock'n'roll. This is an art form. This is something really exciting!'" said Bowie. "I think we were all very aware of George Steiner and the idea of pluralism, and this thing called post-modernism which had just cropped up in the early 70s.

"We kind of thought, cool, that's where we want to be at. Fuck rock'n'roll! It's not about rock'n'roll any more, it's about how do you distance yourself from the thing that you're within? We got off on that. I think certain things had been done that were not dissimilar, but I don't think with the sensibility that I had."

That sensibility was abetted by the album's secret weapon: guitarist and creative foil Mick Ronson. "What I'm good at is putting riffs to things, and

Piano practice at home in Haddon Hall, 1971.

GETTY

> ## "Hunky Dory shows that David had the kind of range and versatility as a writer to handle anything."
> — Angie Bowie

hook-lines, making things up so songs sound more memorable," the guitarist (who died in 1993) once said. And the proof abounds: his spare, searing licks on *Eight Line Poem*; the explosive acoustic on *Andy Warhol*; the nasally distorted power blast on *Queen Bitch*. All electrifying moments.

"I would put him up there with the best I've ever worked with," said Ken Scott. "I think Ronno was better than any of The Beatles as a guitarist. His playing was much more from a feel point or melodic point of view."

Woodmansey: "Mick didn't really know how good he was. He would do a solo, first take, never played it before, and it would blow us away. David would always get Ken to push the record button without Mick knowing. He would do another six solos, but it was always the first or second one that we kept."

Ronson's gifts extended beyond his guitar playing. In the months prior to the sessions, he had been studying music theory and arranging with a teacher back in Hull. That bit of knowledge, combined with his innate musicality, made for the stunning string arrangements on songs like *Life On Mars?* and *Quicksand*.

"Ronno was great the way he'd go down to just one or two violins, then have the others come slowly but surely," said Scott. "He didn't quite know what he was supposed to do, so he was much freer. Much like The Beatles. He would do things other arrangers would never do."

Angie Bowie said of the communication between her ex-husband and Ronson: "They were two Yorkshiremen chatting away. Very full of respect for each other. They were young and very sweet, well-mannered, trying to be as professional as they could. I know that sounds boring, but it's the truth. There were no drugs. They were just doing this wonderful album and everyone was thrilled at having a chance to participate instead of having to work horrible jobs."

Side Two of the album featured a trio of "hero songs" inspired by Bowie's visit to America. *Queen Bitch* was an exhilarating nod to the Velvet Underground (Lou Reed later said he "dug it"). Bowie says he had been fixated on the Velvets since the first time he heard their single *Waiting For The Man*. "It was like, 'This the future of music! This is the new Beatles!' I was in awe. For me it was a whole new ball game. It was serious and dangerous and I loved it."

For this coded tale of seduction, Bowie taps into Reed's style of urban poetry, even tossing in New York-isms like 'you betcha'. As the only electric guitar-dominated track on *Hunky Dory*, it also previews the shapes of things to come on *Ziggy*.

Of *Song For Bob Dylan*, Bowie said in 1976: "That laid out what I wanted to do in rock. It was at that period that I said: 'Okay, Dylan, if you don't want to do it, I will.' I saw that leadership void. Even though the song isn't one of the most important on the album, it represented for me what the album was all about. If there wasn't someone who was going to use rock'n'roll, then I'd do it."

As for the song *Andy Warhol*, Bowie wrote what he thought was a tribute. That is until he returned to New York in September 1971 and played it for Warhol. "He hated it," Bowie recalled with a chuckle. "Loathed it. He went [imitates Warhol's blasé manner] 'Oh, uh-huh…' then just walked away. I was kind of left there. Somebody came over and said: 'Gee, Andy hated it.' I said: 'Sorry, it was meant to be a compliment.' 'Yeah, but you said things about him looking weird. Don't you know that Andy has a thing about how he looks? He's got a skin disease and he really thinks that people see that.' It didn't go down very well.

"I got to know him after that. It was my shoes that got him. They were these little yellow things with a strap across them, like girls' shoes. He absolutely adored them. Then I found out that he used to do a lot of shoe designing when he was younger. He had a bit of a shoe fetishism. That kind of broke the ice."

The album's cryptic closer, *The Bewlay Brothers*, with its images of '*mind warp pavilions*' and '*grim faces on cathedral floors*', has been one of the most analysed of all Bowie's songs, with interpretations finding everything from a gay manifesto to an account of Bowie's relationship with his schizophrenic half-brother, Terry.

Angie: "It's always a good idea to get a two-fer: write a song and get your therapy. I always teased him about that one, because it was a big, autobiographical confessional song. All folk singers have to write a few of those."

Ken Scott offered a different take: "That was almost a last-minute song. Just down the street from Trident, there was a tobacconist which apparently gave him the inspiration for the name. He'll probably deny this to death. As I remember, he came in and said: 'We've got to do this song for the American market.' I said: 'Okay, how do you mean?' He said: 'Well, the lyrics make absolutely no sense, but the Americans always like to read into things, so let them read into it what they will.'"

In 2000 Bowie said of the song: "It's another vaguely anecdotal piece about my feelings about myself and my brother. I was never quite sure what real position Terry had in my life, whether Terry was a real person or whether I was actually referring to another part of me."

From start to finish, the album took two weeks to record and two to mix. Defries shopped the acetate to labels in New York, and got Bowie signed, with a $37,500 advance, to RCA, who were keen to hip up their roster beyond country music and Elvis.

Released on December 17, 1971, *Hunky Dory* was hailed by *Melody Maker* as "the most inventive piece of songwriting to have appeared on record in a considerable time". NME said it was "Bowie at his brilliant best", while the *New Yorker* dubbed Bowie "the most intelligent person to have chosen rock music as his medium". With a sleeve image suggesting a George Hurell portrait of Veronica Lake, Bowie seemed ready for his close-up.

Despite glowing reviews, first-quarter worldwide sales barely reached 5,000. Not that Bowie noticed. The man who'd sung '*I'm much too fast to take that test*' was already back in the studio with his Velvets-meets-Iggy-in-outer-space masterplan, recording the album that within six months would transform him into a Martian messiah and worldwide glam rock superstar: *Ziggy Stardust*.

Because of *Ziggy Stardust*'s rise and all-encompassing effect on Bowie, *Hunky Dory* has remained in its shadow as the quiet, talented brother. But those close to *Hunky Dory*, while acknowledging its vital role in opening the space hatch and clearing the way for *Ziggy*, secretly prefer it as the stronger work.

Angie Bowie divorced from David in 1980. She now works as a journalist specialising in gender issues. "David had interesting songs and important subjects to talk about," she says, "and *Hunky Dory* shows that he had the kind of range and versatility as a writer to handle anything."

Woody Woodmansey, who worked with Bowie up to 1973's *Aladdin Sane*, said: "*Hunky Dory* was the album where David's ability as a songwriter came through. It showed us all what it took to create quality products, how you had to tick all the boxes, from good song ideas, arrangements, rhythmically, sound-wise, emotionally and the rest. It was the start of David's career, really."

Bassist Trevor Bolder stayed with Bowie until 1973's *Pin-Ups*. He was with Uriah Heep from 1983 until his death in 2013. "It's my favourite Bowie album, hands down," he said. "I put it on constantly, and I will play it forever. A lot of musicians in the business that I've met were young kids when that album came out and it's one of their favourites too. It's got great songs, his singing is brilliant, and the lyrical content is superb. I don't think you could've wished for a better album."

Reflecting on its place in his five-decade-spanning catalog, Bowie saw the album as the springboard to all his chameleonic changes.

"*Hunky Dory* gave me a fabulous groundswell. First, with the sense of 'Wow, you can do anything!' You can borrow the luggage of the past, you can amalgamate it with things that you've conceived could be in the future and you can set it in the now. Then, the record provided me, for the first time in my life, with an actual audience – I mean, people actually coming up to me and saying: 'Good album, good songs.' That hadn't happened to me before. It was like, 'Ah, I'm getting it, I'm finding my feet. I'm starting to communicate what I want to do. Now… what is it I want to do?'" ●

THE STORIES BEHIND THE SONGS

David Bowie

Changes

How a young Bowie's artistic manifesto was captured
in three and a half perfect minutes.

Words: **Bill DeMain**

In the spring of 1971, when David Bowie wrote the now classic line 'Turn and face the strange', he created a mission statement for the next decade of his career.

At the age of 24, seven years into that career, three albums and 'a million dead end streets' behind him, Bowie had been brooding on the sidelines as friendly rivals Marc Bolan and Elton John started to find stardom. Determined not to be left behind, he pooled his creative strengths and began writing songs that were "more immediate".

"In the early seventies it really started to all come together for me as to what it was that I liked doing," Bowie told me in 2003. "After I came back from my first trip to America, I had a new perception of songwriting, and it was about a collision of musical styles. I found that I couldn't easily adopt brand loyalty, or genre loyalty; I wasn't an R&B artist, I wasn't a folk artist, and I didn't see the point any more in trying to be that purist about it. What my true style was is that I loved the idea of putting Little Richard with Jacques Brel and the Velvet Underground backing them. What would that sound like? Nobody was doing that. At least not in the same way."

Changes began, he once said, as "a parody of a nightclub song". But it quickly became one of his new hybrids, fusing cocktail jazz, boogie woogie and beat poetry to a Beatlesque chorus. Significantly, as Bowie worked on the song – and all the material for the *Hunky Dory* album – he would often swap his usual instrument, a Harptone 12-string acoustic guitar, for the ancient grand piano at Haddon Hall where he lived.

"He loved that piano," Angie Bowie told me. "David was a fantastic musician, because his approach was not studied, it was by ear. He had an ability to pluck a song from those first moments when he played with an instrument. Writing on the piano

opened up his possibilities, because of its association with so many kinds of music – classical, cabaret, every style."

Listening to Bowie's home demo of *Changes*, the song is all there, although his playing is a bit plodding. That's why he brought in session ace Rick Wakeman to play piano and embellish and add more of a nuanced touch to the recording.

"David knew what he wanted to do," Wakeman tells *Classic Rock*. "He knew how the music needed to be and he would pick musicians that he felt could achieve what it was he was after. I went to his house, and he had his guitar and he played all of the songs, and every single one was a winner. I took some manuscript paper and I was writing stuff down, and I stopped and said: 'Do you know what you've got here? This is the finest collection of songs, and I tell you what, I don't have any money but if I did I would put it all on saying that this particular record – which he already told me was going to be called *Hunky Dory* – will still be around and important long after you and I are gone.' And he laughed. I said: 'I'm serious.' He gave me total freedom to play what I liked, really. The vamping bit in *Changes* was his idea because that's how he wrote the song, so that's how it stayed. Sometimes when there's something simplistic, if it works then keep it."

Sessions for *Hunky Dory* at London's Trident Studios ran through June and July 1971. Bowie, his musicians and producer Ken Scott worked from two p.m. to midnight, Monday to Saturday, with quick breaks for tea, sandwiches and the occasional bottle of wine. There was a sense of excitement on the sessions, fuelled by Bowie's new material.

"Honestly, I didn't think he had these songs in him," recalled drummer Woody Woodmansey. "They were more structured. He'd obviously focused more as a writer, yet he'd managed to keep his unique

Changes helped Bowie's rapidly rising star get higher.

approach, especially lyrically, while streamlining everything."

"*Hunky Dory* was the first recording session I ever did in my life, and just to be in a studio was amazing," the late bassist Trevor Bolder said. "Our approach was very off-the-top-or-our-heads. We'd go in, David would play us a song – often one we hadn't heard – we'd run through it once and then take it. No time to think about what you're going to play, you'd have to do it there and then. In some respects it's nerve-racking, but it gives a certain feel. If you play a song too many times in the

PERFECT PIANO

It's been called "the best rock'n'roll piano ever." The Bechstein grand at Trident Studio was on The Beatles' *Hey Jude*, Queen's *Killer Queen* and Elton John's *Levon*, to name just three songs. And Rick Wakeman played it on *Changes*.

"It had a cut-through sound," Rick recalls, "beautifully balanced from top to bottom. From about 1970 through 1973 it was an absolutely perfect instrument. It went to auction when Trident closed. It had a guide price of £100,000 and it didn't sell. Nobody truly knows what happened to it after that, because nobody had the serial number."

> **"David was a fantastic musician. He had an ability to pluck a song from those first moments when he played with an instrument."**

GETTY

THE FACTS
RELEASE DATE
December 1971
HIGHEST CHART POSITION
UK: did not chart,
US: No.66
PESONNEL
David Bowie
Vocals, saxophone
Rick Wakeman
Piano
Mick Ronson
Guitar, string arrangement, backing vocals
Trevor Bolder
Bass
Mick Woodmansey
Drums
WRITTEN BY
David Bowie
PRODUCED BY
Ken Scott
ENGINEER
Ken Scott
LABEL
RCA

studio it can become stale, and I think David wanted to capture the energy of it being on the edge."

"There was incredible pressure in getting a track recorded right," Woodmansey agreed. "David didn't like doing more than three takes to get it. Nearly every track I recorded with David was first, second or third take, usually second. He knew when a take was right."

Changes was released as a single in January 1972, but failed to chart in the UK, and in the US it made it only to No.66. But it became a staple of FM radio, and in Bowie's live sets, evolving through different arrangements as his stylistic calling card. As the lyric says, he was always '*much too fast to take the test*' of being pigeonholed.

The song, which has become an anthem of youthful freedom, has been covered by several artists, perhaps most creatively by Seu Jorge in Wes Anderson's film *The Life Aquatic*. It was also a preamble to John Hughes's teen movie *The Breakfast Club*.

Did Bowie know back in 1971 that he was making a career-defining single? Putting it in context of the album that it kicked off, he told me: "*Hunky Dory* gave me a fabulous groundswell. First with the sense of: 'Wow, you can do anything.' You can borrow the luggage of the past, you can amalgamate it with things that you've conceived could be in the future, and you can set it in the now. Then the record provided me, for the first time in my life, with an actual audience – I mean people actually coming up to me and saying: 'Good album, good songs.' That hadn't happened to me before. It was like: 'Ah, I'm getting it. I'm finding my feet. I'm starting to communicate what I want to do. Now… what is it I want to do?'" ⊘

LOV⚡NG THE AL⚡EN

By 1972, glam rock was kicking in but Bowie was still waiting for his big break. And then he hit on the character that would redefine him forever. This is an oral history of *The Rise And Fall Of Ziggy Stardust And The Spiders From Mars*.

Words: **Julian Marszalek**

Half a century on from his creation, Ziggy Stardust arguably remains the most beloved character from David Bowie's illustrious seven-decade career. Combining glamour and a then-outrageous sexuality, this bisexual alien rock star fell to earth as the 60s dream had turned sour in the wake of Altamont, and the economic boom of the previous decade had finally burst.

The music scene was becoming as grim as the outside world. Clive Dunn's mawkish single, *Grandad* topped the charts at the start of 1971 while Benny Hill's *Ernie (The Fastest Milkman In The West)* brought it to a close. By 1972, the likes of Donny Osmond and David Cassidy hit the top spot as compilation albums dominated their respective charts.

Yet from this morass of tedium came a glimmer of hope. First T. Rex brought the glitter to the pop kids while Slade stomped their stack heels hard. And then, as if from nowhere, former one-hit wonder David Bowie introduced Ziggy Stardust to sweep aside all competition to leave a legacy that's still felt to this very day.

Having failed to successfully crack America in January 1971, David Bowie returned to the UK. Encouraged by his wife, Angie, and manager, Tony Defries, Bowie developed the idea of the "ultimate pop idol" by combining his underground heroes Lou Reed and Iggy Pop with cult British rock'n'roller Vince Taylor…

David Bowie: I wanted to define the archetype messiah rock star; that's all I wanted to do. And I used the trappings of kabuki theatre, mime technique, fringe New York music – my reference was The Velvet Underground. It was a British view of American street energy.

Woody Woodmansey (drummer): Angie was a very flash-talking, buzzing American girl. She got him on what he wanted to do before anybody else. So when David had a few doubts in the beginning or when he said, 'I'm thinking of doing

"I wanted to define the archetype messiah rock star; that's all I wanted to do."
David Bowie

this', she said, 'Do it, David!' If she hadn't have been there, it might not have gone the way it did. She was very influential.

Suzi Ronson (hairstylist, later Mick Ronson's wife): Angela really was a driving force behind David. She was very influential with the costumes. She made him brave. She would have her hair cut first if she thought that he wouldn't like it.

Dana Gillespie (singer and confidante to Bowie): She was always encouraging him and always on his side. She would always be dressing

him and helped with his image. She was always a positive force.

During a January 1972 interview with Melody Maker's Michael Watts, David Bowie unveiled his new Ziggy image and made an outrageous claim that reverberated across the nation…

David Bowie: I'm gay and always have been, even when I was David Jones.

Mick Ronson (guitarist): When David came out, I felt a bit funny about it. My family took a bit of flak for it. I gave my mother and father a car and somebody threw paint over it.

Trevor Bolder (bassist): There were plenty of girls. I think he was spinning them along, but it sold papers and therefore records, so we didn't give a toss.

While Marc Bolan spearheaded the glam charge with T.Rex by smearing glitter under his eyes, swapping his hippy gear for satin clothing and altering his music for a teen audience and Slade's Dave Hill became more sartorially outré, David Bowie set about creating something completely and utterly unique.

David Bowie: Ziggy Stardust was this surreal cartoon character brought to life. He was half out of sci-fi rock and half out of the Japanese theatre. The clothes were, at that time, simply outrageous. Nobody had seen anything like them before.

Hang on to yourself: Hammersmith Odeon on 3 July 1973 when Ziggy Stardust was retired.

Mick Ronson: Just after *Hunky Dory* and before *Ziggy*, there was a lull in the scene; it needed jarring and excitement. Bowie's dressing us up and the make-up was needed. It wasn't what I usually did but it was exciting. On stage I became someone else.

Trevor Bolder: We were his droogs. David edged us into (wearing the) clothes. Originally he wanted us to wear bowler hats and boiler suits like in the movie *A Clockwork Orange* but we refused to do that so he commissioned our stage clothes.

Woody Woodmansey: We were in Liberty in the material department and David and Angie were passing rolls of material down. I thought, 'Oh, nice – we're getting new curtains, but they're a bit bright'. Then a few days later, he got a friend of his in who's a really incredible fashion designer and we started having the clothes made from the material. The hair came about a month later.

David Bowie: Writing a song for me never rang true. I found it quite easy to write for the artists I would create because I did find it much easier having created a Ziggy to then write for him. Even though it was me doing it.

David Bowie's fourth album Hunky Dory was barely finished when he and the band swiftly reconvened at Trident Studios in London to begin work on their following album, which would eventually be released in June 1972.

Ken Scott (producer): One of David's talents was picking a team to give him exactly what he wanted at any given time. And that team knew what it was supposed to be. We didn't have to tell each other all the time; we just instinctively knew this is what's going to happen here, this is what's going to happen there.

||||||||||||||||||||||||||||||||||||||||||||||||||||||||

"When he did *Starman* on *Top Of The Pops* – that blew me and everybody away."

Def Leppard's Joe Elliott

David Bowie: Mick Ronson was very much a salt-of-the-earth type; the blunt northerner with a defiantly masculine personality, so what you got was the old-fashioned yin and yang thing. As a rock duo, I thought we were as good as Mick and Keith.

Ken Scott: *Ziggy Stardust* didn't start as a concept album. *It Ain't Easy* was left over from the recording of *Hunky Dory*.

Angie Bowie (wife and mover and shaker): David is a fantastic musician, because his approach is not studied, it's by ear. He has an ability to pluck a song from those first moments he plays with an instrument.

Ken Scott: His greatest talent was performing in a studio. Ninety-five per cent of the

songs he recorded were done one take, first take from beginning to end.

Woody Woodmansey: Mick didn't really know how good he was. He would do a solo first take, never played it before and it would blow us away.

Ken Scott: The mainstay of the whole story – the 'man coming from up there somewhere' – is *Starman*. That was the last thing recorded for *Ziggy* Stardust and… it was never meant to be on the album. The album was sent into RCA and they said, 'The album's great but we don't hear a single. Can you go and record a single?' Of course David could! He goes away and comes back with *Starman* and then suddenly the whole album is a concept album.

With the album in the bag, David Bowie took to the road in his new guise as Ziggy Stardust. Starting in tiny clubs, the band's popularity began to rise throughout 1972, which culminated in two sell-out shows at the Rainbow Theatre in London.

Kris Needs (journalist and author): He told me: "Next time I come back (to Aylesbury Friars), I'm going to be something different. I'm going to be a big rock star." And sure enough, the following January in 1972 he returned as Ziggy Stardust. It was the first time in the world he'd played as Ziggy Stardust and he came out to the Beethoven music from *A Clockwork Orange* in his silver jumpsuit with the Spiders and nothing was going to be the same again.

David Bowie: During the very early days of Ziggy Stardust, we often used to play these fairly grotty clubs. Backstage one night I was desperate to use the bathroom. I was dressed in my full battle finery of Tokyo-spaceboy and a pair of shoes high enough that it induced nosebleeds. I went up to the promoter – actually I tottered over to the promoter – and I asked, 'Could you please tell me where the lavatory is?'

And he said, 'Yeah, look down that corridor? On the far end of that wall? You see that sink? There you go.'

I said, 'My good man, I'm not taking a piss in the sink.' He said, 'Listen son, if it's good enough for Shirley Bassey, it's good enough for you.'

Nick Kent (journalist): I went to the first official Spiders From Mars gig in London at Imperial College. After four bars of *Hang On To Yourself*, the PA just stopped. Bowie was standing there, and for a split second, you could see the panic in his eyes, thinking, What the fuck am I going to do? And what he did was put his hands on his hips in this really camp way, and proceeded to give a rundown of what he was wearing. He just did this camp routine, and then after about a minute, the sound came back on. In that minute, Ziggy Stardust's destiny was manifest.

Mick Rock (photographer): The fellatio picture is one of the most striking images from the Ziggy period. If you look at the picture, he's chomping on Mick's guitar. He was hugging Mick's buttocks in a cute way, but he only did that because of the way Mick was swinging his guitar around.

Kris Needs: Bowie returned to Friars for a third performance on 15 July.

Trevor Bolder: Friars in Aylesbury on 15 July was the big one. That was sold out. Everybody wanted to see the band. So that was when we realised it was taking off.

Lindsay Kemp (dancer and mentor): That Rainbow show was a big shock. When I saw how he captured an audience of thousands and knew exactly what to do. It was absolutely electric – I was numb from beginning to end.

The Rise And Fall Of Ziggy Stardust was released in June 1972. A loose concept album, it's held together by the idea of an alien, bi-sexual rock star who visits the Earth during its last five years before being killed by his fans. Straddling the gap between the serious rock album market and the singles-orientated pop charts, it rocks hard on Ziggy Stardust, Suffragette City and Hang On To Yourself and revels in the pop sensibility of Starman and Soul Love.

Crucial to Bowie's meteoric rise was his appearance on Top Of The Pops on 6 July 1972 to perform Starman. For many fans, this was the moment they irrevocably fell under Bowie's spell.

Nick Rhodes (Duran Duran): I think people have forgotten the significance *Top Of The Pops* had throughout the 70s. It really focused the entire nation on music, on what was going on.

Trevor Bolder: We went to the pub together; nobody knew who we were. *Top Of The Pops* changed all that.

Joe Elliot (Def Leppard): *Starman* on *Top Of The Pops* – that blew me and everybody away. ➢

Posing for a portrait as Ziggy Stardust in New York, 1973.

Another 1973 TV appearance with the Spiders: the landmark 1972 TOTP performance of *Starman* shot the band into the stratosphere.

GETTY X3

Trevor Bolder: We did it live, straight through, and then went to the BBC bar. People kept coming up to us and asking if we were in *Doctor Who*.

Robert Smith (The Cure): I immediately put on some of my sister's make-up. I loved how odd it made me look, and the fact that it upset people.

Mary Conelan (writing to the David Bowie fan club): David Bowie on *Top Of The Pops* – it took hours for the grin on my face to wear off! Auntie Beeb has gone Bowie-mad! The establishment has now recognised you as a STAR, David. Long may it last!

Trevor Bolder: It all happened after that night. We went out on the road and did a British tour, and where we'd [previously been] playing to maybe 50-60 people a night in small venues, we were selling them out.

As Bowie's star rose, Tony Defries' MainMan management company took on new clients including Lou Reed, Mott The Hoople and Iggy & The Stooges. Their respective albums – Transformer and All The Young Dudes – were produced by David Bowie while the latter's Raw Power was remixed by him.

Kris Needs: Bowie plugged into Mott the same way that he'd plugged into Iggy and Lou Reed. He

was inspired, but also vaguely frightened, by these highly influential people, so he ended up working with them. They were giving him something. Lou Reed gave him a New York attitude with his lyrics, Iggy gave him the wildest rock star-type mentality and Mott gave him a sense of danger.

Iggy Pop (Iggy And The Stooges): We did a session in a little room called Western Recorders in Hollywood. It was David Bowie, James Williamson and myself, to mix it. And I think it was done in two days, or a day-and-a-half. The

||||||||||||||||||||||||||||||||||||||||||||||||||||||||||||||||||

"One of David's talents was picking a team to give him exactly what he wanted at any given time."

Ken Scott

mix on that sounds, to me, a lot like the records David was making at the time. He took off the bottom and at the top and there was a lot of clarity. And you really, really heard the vocal and the lead guitar.

Ian Hunter (Mott The Hoople): He played *All The Young Dudes* on an acoustic guitar. I knew straight away it was a hit. We grabbed hold of it.

James Williamson (Iggy And The Stooges): I could never stand Bowie personally. I was one of the people saying I didn't like the mix (of *Raw Power*), but in retrospect it was actually a good job.

Lou Reed (solo artist): *Transformer* is easily my best-produced album. Together as a team, (Bowie and Ronson) are terrific.

Angie Bowie: David was very smart. He'd been evaluating the market for his work, calculating his moves, and monitoring his competition. And the only really serious competition in his market niche, he'd concluded, consisted of Lou Reed and – maybe – Iggy Pop. So what did David do? He co-opted them.

As the tour and promotion continued to roll on, the character of Ziggy began to consume David Bowie.

David Bowie: It became apparent to me that I had an incredible shyness; it was much easier for me to keep on with the Ziggy thing, off the stage as well as on.

Ian Hunter: He came in with an entourage and he'd gone a bit weird. His clothes were more flamboyant and he was starting to live his image to the hilt.

Live in Los Angeles, 1973.

Ain't easy: Bolder, Ronson and Bowie on the Ziggy Stardust tour, 1973.

David Bowie: I wasn't getting rid of Ziggy at all. In fact, I was joining forces with him. This doppelganger of myself was becoming one and the same person. And then you start on this trail of chaotic and psychological destruction. You become what's called a 'drug casualty' at the end of it all.

Trevor Bolder: We lived and breathed the Spiders. As the tour went on, we actually became the characters, to go along with the Ziggy thing. So we tried to live up to people's expectations of us when we came offstage.

David Bowie: I was having a ball at first, and then around the end of the Ziggy period, I found drugs in a major way. If that hadn't happened, I wonder how different life would've been… But I can't dwell on that. In all seriousness, that's why it all went wrong, then, when I was virtually on top of the world. I can't say it wasn't fun; the whole of that time was terrific.

With the British dates ending in triumph, manager Tony Defries booked a 28-date US tour. Employing the risky and expensive strategy of positioning David Bowie as a superstar, the tour fared well on the USA's east and west coasts, but less so across the mid-west. And while the addition of pianist Mike Garson widened the scope of the music, it unwittingly planted the seeds of the demise of Ziggy Stardust And The Spiders From Mars.

Leee Black Childers (MainMan US rep): He had two bodyguards and he dressed then up in karate costumes and they flanked him wherever he went. Everyone assumed then that he was just as big as Mick Jagger or Elton John. And of course he wasn't. We were having to create this myth.

Woody Woodmansey: I was sat on an airplane with (Mike Garson) and I was reading a magazine and there was a Lamborghini in it. I went, 'Oh, that's nice.' And he went, 'Why don't you buy one?' I went, 'Yeah, I wish' And he said, 'You must be able to afford one' and I went, 'Actually, no'. I went, 'What do you think I get?' and he went, 'Well, I know what I get' and he told me and it was like, three times what I got.

Trevor Bolder: We went to Bowie and said, 'Unless things change and you give us the money, we're going home.'

Angie Bowie: David was furious, just furious. 'They can't hold me up like that,' he told me. 'I don't care who they are, I simply won't have that kind of disloyalty.' From then on, his passive-aggressive machinery engaged gears and the lads' days were numbered.

A combination of MainMan's parlous financial affairs, the rhythm section's perceived mutiny and Bowie's increasing

▌▌▌▌▌▌▌▌▌▌▌▌▌▌▌▌▌▌▌▌▌▌▌▌▌▌▌▌▌▌▌▌

"We went to Bowie and said, 'Unless things change and you give us the money, we're going home.'"

Trevor Bolder

boredom with the music he'd created saw him finally "retire" Ziggy Stardust at London's Hammersmith Odeon on 3 July, 1973.

David Bowie: Of all the shows on this tour, this particular show will remain with us the longest, because not only is this the last show on the tour, but it's the last show that we'll ever do.

Scott Richardson (confidante to David Bowie and Mick Ronson):
To break up a band like that is astonishing. I have to

credit Bowie with having a lot of courage: to say, 'I'm not coming back'.

Trevor Bolder: He's fuckin' sacked us!

As all the children boogie, a trail of those who David Bowie influenced and whose lives he touched are like sign posts on popular music's highway…

Siouxsie Sioux (Siouxsie And The Banshees): Bowie was the catalyst who'd brought a lot of us – the so-called Bromley Contingent – together. And out of that really small group of people, a lot happened.

Ian Astbury (The Cult): He served as one of the most formative teachers in my life.

Robert Smith: I look back at some the things we've done and I can see echoes of some of Bowie's stuff in it. I got my dream come true when he invited me to sing with him at his birthday in New York.

David Bowie: I'm very happy with Ziggy. He was a very successful character and I think that I played him well. ●

Additional Sources: Starman – David Bowie: The Definitive Biography by Paul Trynka; David Bowie: A Life by Dylan Jones, Melody Maker, Iggy Pop: Open Up and Bleed by Paul Trynka; Raw Power: An interview with Iggy Pop, Trey Zenker, Tidal; Mojo; Melody Maker.

Just under a year after *Ziggy Stardust*, Bowie released *Aladdin Sane*. His last album with the Spiders From Mars, it was a record written on the road, inspired by the USA and steeped in sex, drugs and ruthless ambition.

Words: **Max Bell**

|||||||||||||||||||||||||||||||||||||||||||||||||||||||||||||||||||||||||||||||||||||||||||||||||

n September 10 1972, David Bowie and wife Angie – "Britain's most famous bisexual couple" – boarded the Queen Elizabeth 2 at Southampton Docks bound for New York City. Where were the Spiders? Mick Ronson, Trevor Bolder and Woody Woodmansey joined them a week later in NYC where a chartered Greyhound bus would take them on tour. First stop: Cleveland, Ohio. As the bus pulled away from Grand Army Plaza, a woman on the sidewalk pulled down her skirt and defecated into a paper bag. Welcome to America.

It wasn't Bowie's first stateside visit. Three months earlier, Dave'n'Ange had tottered down Pennsylvania Plaza in their freak flamed-hair finery to see Elvis Presley at Madison Square Garden. They sat next to fellow VIPs John Lennon, Led Zeppelin, Simon and Garfunkel and Bob Dylan.

"Elvis was a major hero of mine," Bowie said later. "And I was probably stupid enough to believe that having the same birthday as him actually meant something. I came over for a long weekend. I was in the middle of a Ziggy Stardust tour and I flew over on a Friday to see Elvis on the Saturday night. I remember coming straight from the airport and walking into Madison Square Garden very late. I was wearing all my clobber from the Ziggy period and had great seats near the front, about 10 rows in. The whole place just turned to look at me and I felt like a right idiot. I had brilliant red hair, some huge padded space suit and those red boots with big black soles – the full kit. I wished I'd gone for something quiet, because I must have registered with him. Elvis was well into his set. I had to walk down through these really quite conservative Americans… and I thought it was the worst, most humiliating feeling ever. I flew back again on Sunday for the Monday night gig at Bristol.

For about two weeks I was Presley [laughs]. It was a fantastic experience."

And before that, in January 1971, Bowie had jetted to New York and witnessed the American touchstones that underpinned his love for the bizarre and the decadent: the Velvet Underground at Max's Kansas City, and a rowdy club date by the Stooges. He would soon introduce both Lou Reed and Iggy Pop to his British audience, working on their groundbreaking albums *Transformer* and *Raw Power*. On that debut visit, the wild-eyed boy from south London was all over his new-found promised land. "I think I've been in prison for the past 24 years. Coming to America has opened [a] door."

If that initial trip kick-started the burst of creativity that became *The Rise And Fall Of Ziggy Stardust And The Spiders From Mars* album, the 1972 adventure proved even more fruitful. Bowie wrote the songs for his next venture, *Aladdin Sane*, on the bus, in limousines, trains and hotel rooms. Though not as conceptually overt as Ziggy, *Aladdin Sane* was his most ambitious lyrical work to date: a cooler, more loveless affair than its summery, blustery predecessor. Describing worlds falling apart, the end of Western civilisation, Bowie fixed Aladdin Sane at the epicentre. He was the stranger in a strange, dystopian land populated by sexually predatory celebrities, terrorists and snipers, coke dealers, ferocious groupies, Andy Warhol starlets, smacked-out rock-star casualties – and he was loving every cocaine-tooting minute. The Top Rank Suite, Stoke-on-Trent, the last British date before his departure, this was not.

With latest hit *John, I'm Only Dancing*, that song for swinging lovers with bisexual tastes, creaming the UK charts, Bowie and the boys were on their A game. After their debut gig, wowing the Music Hall, Cleveland, Bowie and Ronson concocted a follow-up, *The Jean Genie*, nicking The Yardbirds' version of Muddy Waters's *I'm A Man* and turning it into an erotic coke-and-fuck fest in keeping with the jubilant mood of the tour. Roadie Will Palin recalled the song's birth as an on-the-road chant, jammed up by Ronno and Bowie's pal George Underwood, Ronno's riff accompanied by shouts of "Bus, bus, bus, bus, bus, bus, we're bussin."

Trevor Bolder revealed: "We regarded it as a rip-off of *I'm A Man*, which I'd played in bands when I was young. We played it on the bus. [When we recorded it] it was knocked out in an hour on the second or third take."

Bowie had the lyrical idea within hours of stepping off the QE2. He and Angie went to the Mercer Arts Center to see the New York Dolls – or The Dolls Of NY as they currently called themselves – in the midst of a 17-week residency in the venue's Oscar Wilde Room. According to Dolls guitarist Sylvain Sylvain, the Bowies enjoyed a five-day orgy at the Plaza Hotel with Billy 'Doll' Murcia and 21-year-old Marilyn Monroe lookalike Cyrinda Foxe. The foursome were at it hammer and tongs while room service champagne bottles and cocaine phials littered the floor. "David Bowie was now infatuated with Cyrinda and Angie had a new lover – Billy Doll!" said Sylvain.

Basing his Jean Genie tale on a fictional variation of new pal Iggy Pop, who'd also snuck into the tryst at the Plaza suite, Bowie wrote the song to amuse Cyrinda in between bouts of 'Snow White' ingestion. Aladdin Sane was in the building. The pharmaceuticals were good. Watch that man.

But New York's a go-go where everything tastes nice, and a prestigious ➥

ZIGGY IN
AMEI

RICA

With make-up artist Pierre La Roche, 1973.

weren't all that did. The next day, Bowie sat in his suite and regurgitated the night. *Watch That Man* was born.

The tour in full swing, manager Tony Defries reminded Bowie he wasn't in America to have fun. RCA were pressing for the next album. Known as Deep Freeze behind his back, Defries saw himself as an English gent with a cut-glass accent. He was a ruthless motherfucker.

"I never liked Defries," Trevor Bolder told *Classic Rock* in 2012. "Never. Ever. I didn't trust him. Obviously Bowie did, though later on he discovered he shouldn't have. He always wore a fur coat and had a huge cigar. He was a consultant lawyer who'd worked with Allen Klein."

In early October, the band returned to New York and booked RCA Studios on Avenue of the Americas to cut *The Jean Genie* with Bowie and Ronson producing, rather than Ken Scott, the regular console master. Scott wasn't unduly bothered. "It's designed to be a big hit. It's cute, but it's not one of my favourites."

It was debuted live in Chicago the next day. Bowie described the song as a "lightweight riff thing written for Cyrinda's enjoyment, an otherwise wordless pumper; ultimately it turned into a smorgasbord of imagined America… based on an Iggy-type persona. The title, of course, was a clumsy pun upon Jean Genet."

That pseudo-intellectual reference added nothing to the song which soon became – like Ms Foxe – Bowie's new favourite thing.

On November 21, the song was possibly remixed at RCA Studio B in Nashville in mono. Scott maintained that carbon dating this era is notoriously problematic, but that mix was earmarked as the single. Three days later it was, later rising to No.2 in the UK, beaten off the top spot by Little Jimmy Osmond's vile *Long Haired Lover From Liverpool*, then The Sweet's glam-stomp siren *Blockbuster*, which bore a remarkable similarity to *The Jean Genie*. *Blockbuster*'s co-writer Nicky Chinn met Bowie soon afterwards. "He looked at me completely deadpan and said, 'Cunt!'" remembered Chinn. "Then it was all hugs and kisses."

Suzi Fussey (later Suzi Ronson) was Bowie's hairdresser, make-up artist and personal wardrobe assistant during the entire period as Ziggy/Aladdin Sane. 'DB' also changed her life. "I was working in a salon in Beckenham," she said. "I was going to marry the banker round the corner but I wanted to go on the road. Boy, did I go on the road! Before Bowie and the Spiders, I'd never met anyone black, or gay, let alone someone with a Yorkshire accent like the boys from

concert at Carnegie Hall was attended by Andy Warhol, Lou Reed, the Dolls, Todd Rundgren and Anthony 'Psycho' Perkins. Andy Warhol sat poker faced when the *Hunky Dory* song bearing his name was introduced. By contrast, Lou Reed died and went to heaven as the Spiders crawled over his 60s epics *White Light/White Heat* and *Waiting For The Man*. At the aftershow, arch bitch Wayne County – who could eat you with a fork and spoon – shimmied on the dance floor in his stilettos with Warhol's gal Cherry Vanilla. Angie and Cyrinda waltzed and groped and tongued each other. The men from RCA ogled and wished they hadn't brought their wives. The champagne bubbles got up your nose, and they

Linda Lewis: helping Bowie to *Watch That Man*.

LINDA LEWIS
The backing singer

Linda Lewis's career as an R'n'B singer/songwriter was in full swing in 1973 (she had a No.15 hit in July with *Rock-A-Doodle-Doo*, co-written with then-husband Jim Cregan) but she still found time to do session work.

"I sang on *Panic In Detroit*, *Watch That Man* and *Lady Grinning Soul* with Juanita 'Honey' Franklin. Bowie knew I was a new songstress on the block but I'd met him before. He came to the commune I lived at in Hampstead Way with Marc Bolan and we talked about astrology and he remembered chatting to me at the first Glastonbury Festival when I was off my trolley. I didn't know of his glamour and fame but I did say, 'Why have you got all that make-up on?' He laughed and said, 'I've just come back from a photo session.' I tried on his lip-gloss. Ken Scott, who'd engineered my *Say No More* album, hired me. The message was just: 'Trident 3pm. David Bowie.'

"He was quite shy. When he looked at me he glanced at me from the corner of his eye as if I was nutty. He seemed a little bit fragile. We sang to the track. Mick Ronson had a quick chat about what we could do and David said, 'Sing what you want. Make whatever noises you like.' I wasn't attracted to him particularly; he was just like a chatty Londoner, a nice pixie boy who reminded me of Anthony Newley. At the time, I was doing a session for money. I sang. I left. I was invited to his Ziggy thingy farewell concert and I went to the party. I remember that because Mick Jagger tried to pull me at the buffet. He certainly tapped my bum."

At Earls Court Arena in 1973 during the Ziggy Stardust tour.

Hull. The first time I saw two guys kissing, I was shocked! On tour David would try and find the most hardcore leather and jockstrap clubs in town and force the Spiders to accompany him. Mick, Trevor and Woody sat with their backs to wall, trembling, hands over eyes, mumbling, 'Oh fuckin' 'ell!' Bowie took everyone to those places but he was never as gay as he said he was. He did like to wind people up.

"There were a lot of girls on tour. One of my jobs was to pull the girls at the concerts for the band, load them on the bus and bring them back to the hotel. The technique was the boys would say, 'See her? Try and get her.' And I'd stand on stage and throw a towel at the chosen ones and we'd see who'd grab it. They knew what it meant. Sometimes I'd get it wrong and we'd end up with a big beefy one but they still didn't complain. Much.

"It was a tough job," Suzi laughed. "Very complicated because of age. There were 16-year-olds desperate to get into the dressing room but you had to be careful with local laws. It was very touch and go. I was the procurer to all the boys and if you're in Kansas, take care or all hell breaks loose."

When things got too hectic, Suzi was the band's link to the outside world: "I'd be off buying lamé tights and feather boas and I looked after the clothes. Two shows a night, all that sweat, the material was disintegrating."

As the tour rolled across America, Bowie was hard at work writing at the back of the bus with Ronson close by, both men clutching guitars in case the muse struck. Fussey remembered: "Angie wasn't around much on the first tour. Dave was working and she was so loud. She could talk you to death. The rest of us were like a big gang running around America, and it hadn't gotten too intense. That changed later."

The band played strait-laced Salt Lake City, of passing interest to Ronno since he'd been brought up as a Mormon, but decadence returned with a bang when the 46-strong entourage hit Los Angeles and stayed in the Beverley Hills Hotel, running up a $100,000 tab. In LA Bowie started writing *Cracked Actor* after taking a stroll down Hollywood Boulevard. Borrowing a cue from the Velvet Underground's *Loaded* epic *New Age*, written about Shelley Winters ('*Can I have your autograph/He said to the fat blonde actress*'), Bowie's song depicted a 50-year-old has-been homosexual entering into an S&M tryst with a 'trick' he's picked up on Sunset and Vine. The most debauched lyric he'd written, *Cracked Actor* is often interpreted as an old lecher taking advantage of a young lad: it's actually the other way around.

In California, the band played Santa Monica Civic – captured as a quality bootleg thanks to FM radio (and officially released in 2008). Bowie hooked up with Iggy Pop and started writing another song in his honour, *Panic In Detroit*, while the Ig regaled him with lurid gossip concerning the Stooges, anarcho rockers MC5 and partner in crime John Sinclair of the White Panthers, who now became the National People's Gang. Bowie tucked in an allusion to an old friend he'd bumped into in Detroit who left him a cryptic note: 'Let me collect dust.' Bowie recalled, "I know why I associated with that character. It was somebody I used to go to school with who ended up as a very big drugs dealer down in South America and who flew to see one of the shows and reintroduced himself. And I said, "I don't believe it. Is that what you are now?"'

High as kites, Bowie and Iggy remixed the latter's *Raw Power* at Western Sound Recorders in one day. Bowie remembers: "Out of 24 tracks there were just three tracks used. I said, 'Jim, there's nothing to mix…'"

Signing autographs for fans in the final days of the Ziggy Stardust era, London, 1973.

In San Francisco, the promo for *The Jean Genie* was shot with trusted English photographer Mick Rock – it starred Bowie and Cyrinda Foxe cavorting at the Mars Hotel, a 4th Street flophouse associated with The Grateful Dead. Grace Slick's ex-husband Jerry Slick was the cameraman.

The band caught a train to Seattle and then Phoenix. During that journey, Bowie wrote *Drive-In Saturday*, a futuristic post-apocalyptic sci-fi twist on American 50s rock'n'roll that namechecks Carl Jung, NY Doll Sylvain Sylvain (Bowie misspelled his name and used it as a brand name for a pre-Viagra pick-me-up: '*He's crashing out with Sylvian/The Bureau Supply for ageing men*'), the model Twiggy ('*Twig the Wonder Kid*'), Mick Jagger and was remarkably prescient in predicting a time when video pornography would be mainstream.

At a gig in Cleveland, Bowie sat on a stool and played *Drive-In* acoustic, explaining: 'It's about a future where people have forgotten how to make love, so they go back to video films that they've kept from this century. This is after a catastrophe of some kind, and some people are living on the streets and some people are living in domes, and they borrow from one another and try to learn how to pick up the pieces."

Ken Scott was summoned to America in December. "When the tour ended, the band returned to New York and we cut Bowie's version of *All The Young Dudes*, *Drive-In Saturday* and *The Prettiest Star*," he said.

The latter tune was a remake of the 1970 single, written for and about Angie, featuring Marc Bolan's guitar, which sold 800 copies. "We attempted a couple of others that were never completed but didn't get too far. God knows ▸▸

"BEFORE BOWIE I'D NEVER MET ANYONE GAY, BLACK OR FROM YORKSHIRE."
SUZI FUSSY (NÉE RONSON)

The Spiders in London, 1972: Ronson, Bolder, Bowie and Woodmansey.

GETTY IMAGES X3

TREVOR BOLDER
The bass player

||||||||||||||||||||||||||||||||||||||||||||||||||||||||||||

When *Classic Rock* spoke to original Spiders From Mars bassist Trevor Bolder in 2012, he was taking time out from his role as bass man for Uriah Heep – a job he had, on and off, since 1976 – as he battled the pancreatic cancer that would sadly claim his life the following year.

On drugs: "David was dead against them. There were a lot of people spiking your drinks in America. We went to a party at Wolfman Jack's in California and we took all our own alcohol. Bowie had three or four bodyguards pouring the drinks. We weren't allowed to touch anything just in case we got spiked. We were a drinking band and there were no drugs at all. I was amazed later when I heard about Bowie in Berlin and the drug side of things. We certainly avoided it. David used to drink wine. I never even saw him drunk. He was totally in control of himself because he had to be to get to where he wanted to be.

His whole thing was he had a standard to maintain."

On Bowie's fear of flying: "The reason why David eventually stopped flying – and why he thought he was going to die on a plane – stems from a time when me, Woody, him and Angie went on a holiday to Cyprus and on the flight back, the plane was hit by lightning and David was having a heart attack! After that he said, 'I'm not flying again, that's it.' Back then we were great mates who could go away together and have a great time and just enjoy it all."

On the end of the Spiders: "When David fired Woody, I was actually at his wedding. That's the day it happened. He called him up that day and sacked him. Or he got someone to do it. I was with Woody. The following Monday I went to see Bowie to discuss *Pinups* and I had a go at him. I told him that wasn't a nice way to do it – on the man's wedding day. He turned round and said, 'Well, if you don't like it you can go and we can replace you as well.' That's exactly what he said. Mick grabbed a hold of me and said, 'Look just keep your mouth shut. Do the album.'

"Did he fire me? Not really. To this day I don't know why he did. I didn't get any kind of golden handshake, or a thank you. He didn't call me up and say, 'I don't want to use you any more' – it was just taken for granted. I never knew I was fired. That was just it. I earned nothing from Bowie. To this day I don't. If he'd paid us what we were promised, I'd have quite a lot of money. It's dreadful. I make no money out of *Ziggy* or *Aladdin* or anything other than PPL. None of the albums will get me a penny.

"David would say, 'One day we'll all be really, really rich,' so we thought, 'Great.' But we had no contract. Defries refused to give us one. It didn't matter what David said, Defries would override everything."

why he did *All The Young Dudes* – it wasn't likely to make the album but that was typical of Bowie. He had his reasons. He'd done *It Ain't Easy* for *Hunky Dory* but then changed his mind and saved it for *Ziggy*. It was all part of his mystique, which could be very secretive. There were two versions of *John, I'm Only Dancing*, for example. One he did with me at Trident and then, apparently, in the evening he took the band to Olympic Studios and mimicked the entire session. Don't ask me why."

Scott noticed: "Bowie's confidence level had exploded. All our ears and ideas had changed, and we were looking for different things. The drum sound was much more live than it had been before. With David's arrangements, he threw a lot more in than he did in *Ziggy*. Then there was the addition of Mike Garson. There'd been acoustic piano before, which Ronno or Bowie had done, but they're not the greatest keyboard players in the world, so Mike made a big difference. On *Ziggy* it was all very sparse – there had been two bits of synth – that was it. On *Aladdin Sane* there were a lot more keyboards, Mellotrons, a Moog synthesiser, as well as acoustic piano."

At the time, Scott said: Some *Aladdin Sane* tracks were recorded in New York but mostly in Trident. As for RCA's New York Studios, he just suddenly got the urge to record. He had some idea of getting an American sound."

Forty years later, he adds: "He liked to keep everyone on the edge. When we recorded *Drive-In*, Ronno knew the song but Trevor and Woody certainly didn't have a clue. He preferred to treat the rhythm section that way and he didn't like being in the studio for too long. He got very bored very easily. Everyone was fearful of his saying, "'Look, we've had three runs at it and we haven't nailed it so we'll have to move on.'"

Having been what Bowie once called "my George Martin", Scott (who started working with The Beatles in 1964 as a 16-year-old 'button pusher' on side two of *A Hard Day's Night*) was in a good position to assess the singer's mood. "There was a lot of pressure because record companies back then demanded an album every six months and so *Aladdin Sane* had to be recorded and mixed in about three weeks. He was always totally professional at work. When I first worked with him I never thought he'd become a superstar and so leading up to *Hunky Dory*, my first ever production, I felt quite comfortable because I thought I could make any number of mistakes and no one would ever hear them. Then, while sorting out which songs we should record for the album, I realized, 'Fuck – he really is talented after all.'"

On the back of the success of *Ziggy*, three of Bowie's previous albums were also shooting up the British charts. In 12 months he sold over a million LPs and even more singles. America was, Scott said, an unknown quantity. "It was going to be a hard sell. There were no guarantees with *Aladdin Sane*. It could easily flop. A lot of people hated him pushing the bisexual androgyny thing. They were scared of that image in America."

Dave and Angie Bowie eventually returned to London on December 10 on the Royal Hellenic Mail Ship Ellinis, where he wrote the title track *Aladdin Sane (1913 – 1938 – 197?)*. Album copies would bear the name (R.H.M.S. "Ellinis") beneath the title. Inspired by his on-deck reading of Evelyn Waugh's *Vile Bodies* novel, where people Bowie's age indulged in reckless hedonism while civilisations collapsed on the brink of war ('*Battle cries and champagne*'), the singer looked at himself. "People like Lou Reed and I are probably predicting the end of an era," he mused. "Any society that allows people like me to become rampant is pretty well lost. If we're the spearhead of anything, we're not necessarily the spearhead of anything good."

On return, Bowie offered Mott The Hoople first crack at *Drive-In Saturday* but the band were bamboozled by what he called "all these weird time changes". Unconvinced, Overend Watts suggested Bowie keep it for himself. Since he reckoned he'd rescued Mott with *All The Young Dudes*, Bowie was miffed. He'd later claim he shaved his eyebrows off as a result. That seems unlikely since Suzi Fussey recalled, "Angie had already done that so he was copying her. He shaved them in Phoenix and we'd painted the gold circle on his forehead. I remember he rushed off stage screaming, 'Oh my eyes! My eyes!' because having no brows meant all the glitter and sweaty make-up cascaded down and blinded him."

There may have been another reason why Mott The Hoople turned down the song. Where Bowie had sat cross-legged in Mott's management office and somewhat nervously played them *Dudes*, this time, Ian Hunter says, "He came with an entourage and he'd gone a bit weird. His clothes were more flamboyant and he was starting to live his image to the hilt."

Before Christmas, Bowie and t'Spiders played two nights at the Rainbow Theatre and unveiled pianist Mike Garson. God, it was different. Garson's arrival had enormous repercussions for the sound of *Aladdin Sane* and the eventual break-up of the band. Brooklyn-born Garson came to Ronson's attention first when the guitarist heard him play on Annette Peacock's 1972 RCA album *I'm The One*, an experimental masterpiece featuring the cream of the new-wave New York avant-garde. Bowie's interest piqued, he and Ronno decided the Spiders needed gingering up. Garson was called to audition in New York. "I played Mick eight bars of *Changes* and he said, 'You've got the gig.' I was hired for eight weeks but stayed three years. That was thanks to Ronson because he told me, 'It's all very well being a paid session man but to last with David you need to make yourself indispensable.'"

Garson heeded the advice. "Bowie and I got on great because he loved my fractured, conservatory jazz piano and he liked the fact I was searching for creativity. It wasn't easy

Off the rails: Bowie takes the train in July 1973.

from the outset because the rhythm section were so tight-knit. They were decked out in wild clothes, gold and silver, blond hair – all looked kinda gay to me. But I was a starving jazzer and since I don't like playing in a comfort zone, I laughed it off and got on with my work."

Significantly, Bowie was also immersed in Van der Graaf Generator's ultra progressive Trident produced albums – *H to He, Who Am The Only One* and *Pawn Hearts* – both stuffed with saxes and synths.

"IN THE U.S. THEY HATED THE BISEXUAL THING. THEY WERE SCARED OF IT."
PRODUCER KEN SCOTT

The Rainbow homecoming shows were mayhem. Bowiemania was now a reality. Mick Rock, snapping from the pit, witnessed "two girls I called the agony and the ecstasy: one was in ruins and the other was having an orgasm". It was an eye-opener for Garson. "Suddenly I'm playing with these guys and it's like Beatlemania! And their scene was definitely sex and drugs and rock'n'roll. It was a freak show. I didn't care. Jazzers on heroin or rockers on coke – nothing to do with me. I stayed on my game. I didn't want to end up in rehab. I know there was antipathy towards me from Trevor and Woody because I changed Bowie's paradigm. I found him open-minded and generous, others may not have. Y'know, some people would rather be right than happy."

In the New Year of 1973, the band returned to Trident's basement to finish *Aladdin Sane*. Scott says: "Everything was fine with Garson in the band. His playing on the title track is magnificent and he pushed the others on. Bowie brought him into the fold and told him to play his Cecil Taylor avant-garde stuff and he let rip on the Trident's famous handmade Bechstein – the same instrument heard on *Hey Jude* and *Life On Mars?*, which Rick Wakeman still insists is one of his greatest works."

As the sessions took shape, Bowie was convinced he'd discovered his Grail. "Suddenly my songs didn't seem so out of place. All the situations that we were going through were duly noted down and all the remarks I had heard, real ➡

Bowie with Ringo, Lulu and Edgar Broughton at the Cafe Royal party where he snubbed the Spiders.

Garson was also integral to *Time*, a Brechtian discourse on death, part-written in New Orleans, with nods to the Master of Ceremonies character played by Joel Grey in recently released Bob Fosse movie *Cabaret*. Bowie's lyric depicted a Grim Reaper who *'flexes like a whore/Falls wanking to the floor.'*

Increasingly partial to cocaine, Bowie was starting to study his own mortality. He'd turned 26 in the studio and found himself staring at a list of rock casualties, the latest of whom was Billy 'Doll' Murcia, immortalised here: *'Time – in Quaaludes and red wine/ Demanding Billy Dolls and other friends of mine.'*

Dave and Angie's NY Doll friend died from a heroin and barbiturate OD in London the previous November, a few days after the Dolls supported The Faces at Wembley Empire Pool. Murcia passed out at a party where attempts by other junkies to revive him with black coffee only led to his asphyxiation. He was 21.

Time was another musical triumph. Guitarist Ronson quoted a section from Beethoven's Ninth – the band's pre-show music – while Bowie's mate Geoff MacCormack mimicked him perfectly on the choral fades. Mike Garson: "*Time* is my second favourite performance. It's got a kinda New Orleans jazz stride – a little left-field, with an angle. Bowie pulled me out as a producer. On my favourite song, *Aladdin Sane*, I played him my most obsessed blues and he said, 'Nah. Don't want that.' I played him my finest Latin. 'Nah, I already know you can do that. Play one of those weirdo things.' I trusted his intuition because any of my other attempts would have done most people."

On January 17, Bowie appeared on TV's *Russell Harty Plus* and debuted his crash course for the ravers, *Drive-In Saturday*. It would be the album's next single. Chatting to Harty, Bowie appeared to be somewhat under the influence although Scott insistsed, "In the studio he was always cool. People don't believe me but on the albums I worked on, I never saw any sign of drugs at all. Everyone was straight – maybe a couple of beers for Ronno. Oh, and nicotine. Lots of nicotine." Bolder said, "I never saw Bowie take drugs." Most likely, the singer was discreet. What was cool with pals like Iggy wasn't done in front of more impressionable folk. Not long afterwards, Bowie admitted, "I like fast drugs. I don't like drugs that slow me down."

Last in the can were the remodelled *The Prettiest Star*, the stereo remixed *The Jean Genie* and a cover of the Rolling Stones' *Let's Spend The Night Together*. Bowie's take on his heroes '67 proto-hippy free love single – a precursor to the *Pin Ups* project – loitered with menace. Again, Garson and the Spiders stepped up to the mark with fractured solos and vicious rhythms that punched out the singer's carnal interpretation. This wasn't a love song, this was a fuck song. Most likely Bowie wanted to throw down a marker to Jagger's boys: "I've got your women, I'm taking your audience – next I want your Greatest Rock'n'Roll Band In The World crown."

Bowie's Midas touch remained intact elsewhere. Lou Reed's *Transformer* album, produced by David and Ronno, had just gone Top 10. Its single, *Walk On The Wild Side*, was also flying in America when the second leg of the US tour began with a brace of shows at New York's Radio City Music Hall on February 14. This gig could be tagged the St Valentine's Day Massacre. Learning on the flight over that Mike Garson was being paid $1,000 a week while they were on £30, Bolder and Woodmansey confronted Defries. "We said, 'What's going on here?'" recounted the bass player. "We demanded a rise, or we were going home on the next plane."

Ronson intervened and the tour went ahead but Bowie blew his top. According to Angie Bowie: "David was furious, just furious. 'They can't hold me up like that,' he told me. 'I don't care who they are, I simply won't have that kind of disloyalty.' From then on, his passive-aggressive machinery engaged gears and the lads' days were numbered."

Americanisms that caught my ear. Just the look of certain places like Detroit really caught my imagination because it was such a rough city and it almost looked like the kind of place that I was writing about. I thought, 'Christ, these places really exist and people live in them! I wonder if Stanley Kubrick has seen this town? It makes his kind of world in *Clockwork Orange* look kind of pansy!'"

Utilising the studio's 16-track console, Scott added his magic: "For *Cracked Actor* I put Bowie's harmonica through Ronno's Marshall amp because it sounded tiny before. Now it was very nasty and very lovely," the producer recalled.

Scott also insisted on keeping a deeply buried vocal mix on *Watch That Man*, despite RCA's disappointment with the results – probably because Bowie sounds like he's in a different room to the others. Maybe that was the point. "I probably went overboard but it seemed right at the time. That was the only problem we ever had with a Bowie mix."

Watch That Man was a perfect opener. It told the story of a wild party thrown by Shakey (a sarcastic reference to an RCA executive) and all-night debauches with the Dolls in New York, high on cocaine and lust. The girl backing vocals, expertly provided by Linda Lewis and Juanita 'Honey' Franklin, added to the druggy claustrophobia.

The perfect closer to this American sojourn was *Lady Grinning Soul*, theme song for an imaginary James Bond movie, supposedly written in honour of Bowie's latest girl at arm, Claudia Lennear – also the subject of the Stones' *Brown Sugar*. Bowie was more obsessed with this composition than anything else and oversaw the mixing, making sure Scott phased his vocals properly.

For Garson, "*Lady Grinning Soul* brought out the romantic playing in me that comes from composers like Franz Liszt and Chopin. I mixed this with elements of Liberace and Roger Williams, styles of music that were always put down because they were so mainstream. I played in a very undissonant way here, whereas *Aladdin Sane* is about as dissonant as you can get."

"I LIKE FAST DRUGS. I DON'T LIKE DRUGS THAT SLOW ME DOWN."
DAVID BOWIE

Bolder and Woodmansey sulked while Defries blanked them. "All we wanted was a fair deal," says the bass player. "CBS offered the Spiders a huge deal and Defries crushed it. He took Ronson aside and said, 'You go solo and we'll get rid of these two.' Ronson was played along. He got the 'I'm going to make you a star, just like I did David Bowie' treatment."

The old camaraderie jeopardised, Bowie's entourage stayed at The Plaza in New York. "Not us," says Bolder. "Me, Woody and Ronno were staying in a cheap hotel and going down the Village to get drunk. David became more separate and distant. We weren't arty enough for him and the Andy Warhol and Mick Jagger crowd any more."

Defries flogged them on, insisting his star travelled first class and stayed in the best hotels – all paid for from RCA's advances. Debts mounting, Defries's solution was to book a third US tour. Facing bankruptcy, that was promptly cancelled.

Trevor Bolder said: "We had to crack America because Defries had borrowed so much money, but it meant the *Aladdin Sane* tour wasn't pleasant. Fair enough, David couldn't be Ziggy forever but he had this expensive lifestyle while me and Woody could barely exist. The royalties weren't arriving; they never arrived. We got nothing in the end and either David didn't know what was going on or he ignored it. In the end, Defries did the same thing to him. People will rob you in this business."

Moving on to Japan, in Tokyo Trevor and Woody were told by Defries that RCA had agreed to up their wages to £500 a week. He added: "I don't think you're worth a penny of it. In fact, I'd rather give it to the road crew because they're worth more than you." Woodmansey got up and told Defries, "In that case you can stuff this tour, and everything else." Again, Ronno's intervention saved the day.

The second US tour over, Bowie took stock: "I was surrounded by people who indulged my ego, who treated me as Ziggy Stardust." After a side trip to Moscow and Paris, Bowie arrived home at Charing Cross Station where thousands of fans lay in wait. His life had completely changed.

Continuing to live in the old Haddon Hall community with the Spiders was impossible – girls were breaking in through the basement – so he moved out of Beckenham in May and rented Diana Rigg's flat in Maida Vale. Of course, he went back on the road, but his mental state was beginning to mirror the title of his new record. Driving from concert to hotel in a chauffeured Daimler, he'd started drinking heavily and consuming cocaine by the phial. Those around him muttered about a nervous breakdown, or worse. The opening night at Earls Court was disastrous. Fights broke out and Bowie's plea of "don't be so silly" sounded feeble.

It wasn't all gloom. In Glasgow's Green's Playhouse, he was delighted to discover a section of the audience ripping out the seats. "Can you imagine the physical effort that takes? It sounds like the 50s to me. And we had four couples fucking in the back row. That was fabulous – first time I've heard of that happening."

In June, Defries summoned a meeting and showed Bowie the books, a mass of red. RCA's underwriters were owed thousands. The manager suggested David should announce his retirement. It would be great publicity and the old adage 'leave them wanting more' would only up his profile. Bowie wasn't sure but on July 3 at the Hammersmith Odeon, he bit the bullet and made his onstage announcement. "Everybody… this has been one of the greatest tours of our lives… Of all the shows on this tour, this particular show will remain with us the longest… [mass cheering]…because not only is it the last show of the tour, but it's the last show we'll ever do. Thank you."

Those who heard the speech were devastated but as a career move, it was a brilliant coup. Defries was right. David to him was "a real star … Not a Rod Stewart style, if you like, or a Cat Stevens, but… a Marlon Brando or a James Dean-type star. I see him more in that category of large-scale untouchable. It's like he doesn't quite belong here."

And Bowie was certain he'd taken the Ziggy/Aladdin persona to the limit. Trouble was, he hadn't told Woody and Trevor, though Ronson was in on the secret. Woody's initial reaction was "because of his character, there were always things of that nature thrown around. We weren't sure that it wasn't just a publicity stunt."

The truth dawned not at the aftershow party at the Inn On The Park but at an exclusive gathering on July 4 at Café Royal, where Bowie held court with Mick and Bianca Jagger, Lou Reed, Rod Stewart, Jeff Beck, Keith Moon, Cat Stevens, Lulu, Barbra Streisand, Sonny Bono, Tony Curtis, Ryan O'Neal, Elliot Gould, DA Pennebaker and Paul and Linda McCartney. Peter Cook and Dudley Moore provided ribald cabaret. Dr John played the piano.

It was quite a night, unless you were a drummer or bassist. Bolder said: "Bowie and his mates were sitting at a table having a jolly good time, and me and Woody were ignored like we weren't even in the band." Even Angie Bowie was surprised by her husband's callous attitude. "Trevor said, 'We're out of a job, Angie. He's give us the fookin' sack!' What is freaky – chilling – is the fact that he kept them on… and only once they'd given him their best and were enjoying their most triumphal moment, did he let them have it – full bore… in the most public, humiliating manner possible."

Angie thought this was "ruthlessness – non-confrontational cowardice, and cruelty".

Years later, Bowie justified his decision. "I didn't quite know what I was getting myself into, because I knew it was the end of the Spiders. I knew that I had done as much as I could within the context of that band. And I was so weary of touring that I actually did wonder whether I really wanted to tour again. So I just said, 'We will never tour again,' and I really meant it. And about 48 hours later, I'm sitting there thinking, 'What have I said? I don't really think I meant that, because I'm feeling better already,' but it was too late. I really pissed off Woody and Trevor because they were so angry, I think because I hadn't really told them that I was splitting the band up. But that's what Ziggy did, so I had to do it too."

In Ken Scott's view, "Bowie doesn't see himself as using and dumping people. He 'parts company' when it suits him. He also didn't realise how in control of his entire life Tony Defries really was. There are stories about Mr Defries's treatment of him that I can't possibly repeat."

There was a calculated logic to Bowie's madness. "*Aladdin Sane*, that's me having a go at trying to redefine Ziggy, and making him what people wanted. The *Ziggy Stardust* album told the whole story. There was nothing more to say. And I knew when I was making *Aladdin Sane* that the bottom had just fallen out of the whole idea. That was a tough period and I felt for the first time and the only time like I was working for somebody else. Yeah, *Aladdin Sane* was kind of a sellout."

A lad insane. Not quite yet. If anyone thought Bowie had taken himself to breaking point, they were wrong. Soon he'd unleash the dogs. Things were about to get really messy. ❼

"WE HAD FOUR COUPLES FUCKING IN THE BACK ROW. THAT WAS FABULOUS."
DAVID BOWIE

Twiggy and Bowie on the cover of
Pin Ups. The photo was originally
shot for *Vogue* magazine

ZIGGY'S SUMMER HOLIDAY

After killing Ziggy and breaking up the band, **David Bowie** holed up in a French castle to record an album of fan-pleasing, critic-baiting 60s covers. This is the inside story of *Pin Ups'* creation.

Words: **Bill DeMain**

In July 1973, a week after announcing Ziggy Stardust's retirement, David Bowie flew to France to record an album of 60s-era cover versions. Although the resulting *Pin Ups* remains the dark horse of his 1970s catalogue, it captures Bowie at his most relaxed, and his right-hand man Mick Ronson at the height of his powers. Even Starmen need to come down to earth now and then.

Consider David Bowie's gravity-defying release schedule of the early 1970s: *Hunky Dory*, December 1971. *Ziggy Stardust*, June 1972. *Aladdin Sane*, April 1973. Even by the standards of the era, that's prolific. Then consider that all three are classics, two of them regulars on Greatest Albums round-ups. Then throw in constant touring, press and the day-to-day of trying to live up to lofty accolades such as "brilliant songwriter", "darkling prophet" and "TS Eliot with a beat". Bowie may not have been ready to *'kick it in the head when he was twenty-five'* (he was 26), but he sure needed a breather to recharge his creative batteries.

His idea of a break was a walk down Memory Lane – in this case Wardour Street in London's Soho – to a time when he was a mod teen at the Marquee club, soaking up sounds by his favourite bands, such as The Pretty Things, Pink Floyd, Them, The Yardbirds and The Who. Bowie planned to repay the debt of inspiration with an album of cover versions. And really, he'd already been indulging his fanboy tendencies with homage songs to Warhol, Dylan and the Velvets. There was also *Let's Spend The Night Together* on *Aladdin Sane*. Even the Ziggy Stardust character was a kind of mash-up tribute to Iggy Pop and Vince Taylor.

The vacation began on a dramatic note. On July 3, 1973, Bowie closed out an 18-month world tour at Hammersmith Odeon. There had been triumphs along the way (two sold-out nights at Santa Monica Civic Auditorium, later turned into a live album) and disappointments (more than a few venues in America's heartland were half-empty, audiences lukewarm to a flame-haired androgynous alien). If the *Rock 'N' Roll Suicide* finale at Hammersmith didn't make it clear enough, Bowie famously announced: "This is not only the last show of the tour, it's the last show we'll ever do."

Explaining himself to the *NME* that summer, Bowie said of Ziggy: "The star was created; he worked, and that's all I wanted him to do. Anything he did now would just be repetition, carrying it on to the death. Now he's up there, there would be very little point in doing anything else with him."

If fans were shocked, imagine how the Spiders From Mars felt. Bowie's manager Tony Defries informed guitarist Mick Ronson and pianist Mike Garson that they would be joining Bowie and producer Ken Scott the following week for recording sessions in France. Drummer Woody Woodmansey was fired – on the day of his wedding, in fact – and replaced by Aynsley Dunbar.

"I was officiating at Woody's wedding and had to tell him he was let go," Bowie's long-time pianist Mike Garson tells *Classic Rock*. "I felt terrible. He was my friend. They were all my friends. But it wasn't a personal thing with David – it was his musical restlessness. He had to stretch his wings, just like when Diana Ross left The Supremes. These people have to go on and do other things. Of course, we all take it personally. Every album of David's I didn't play on, I wish I played on. I took personally. But it was just him saying: 'This is the direction I'm going in now, what I'm hearing next.'"

"It was a dreadful way to let the band go," Suzi Ronson tells *Classic Rock*. "David was so cold to have done it like that. It took Woody a long time to come around, and I understand that completely. The Spiders were a fantastic band. They didn't deserve that."

Reportedly, an invitation was extended to Cream's Jack Bruce to replace Trevor Bolder on bass, but Bruce declined and so Bolder stayed on. But it would be the final album for both him and Mick Ronson. On July 9, Bowie took the boat and train from London to Paris, then a limo to the Château d'Hérouville, an 18th-century castle outside the city that had been converted into a 16-track recording studio. "A studio where you could sleep, be fed, record on your own schedule and never leave the premises?" says Garson. "That was an unprecedented, amazing thing at the time. I loved it. It was a magical place."

In the outside world in July 1973, US President Richard Nixon's Watergate scandal was deepening by the day, the Soviet Mars 5 space probe launched, and three separate commercial jets crashed in the space of a month. Almost symbolically, legendary actress Veronica Lake,

> "Those string parts that Mick Ronson wrote were magical. He was a terrific natural string writer."
>
> **Mike Garson**

Bowie with Lulu, a regular visitor to the Château.

whose coiffed look Bowie had borrowed for *Hunky Dory*, died the same week the *Pin Ups* sessions started.

Meanwhile, in the idyllic world of the Château, it was all nostalgia and sunshine, cigarettes and coffee. And rock'n'roll. Each morning, Bowie and Ronson spun a couple of 45s from Bowie's collection for the band to listen to. They'd learn the songs, gather in the George Sand Studio, located in the Château's converted stables, and bash them out to tape. "Most of the basic tracks were captured on the second or third take," Garson says, "and often David would get his vocal on the first take."

During the three weeks at the Château, visitors including Nico, Mick Rock, Ava Cherry, Suzi Fussey (the Spiders' hair stylist, later Ronson's wife) and Lulu (who recorded covers of *Watch That Man*

and *The Man Who Sold The World* while she was there) lent the proceedings a convivial vibe.

"Meals were eaten family-style in the large kitchen," Suzi Ronson recalls. "There was a pool outside the Château that wildlife had taken over, so no one was going in. The studio was great. The control room had a window seat that looked out over the courtyard. The rooms were French country style – not huge, but comfortable. The whole place was made of stone, so it was cold. Mick and I didn't care. It was where we first got together, so it was a little like our honeymoon."

The Château's chef entertained everyone with his nightly impressions of Charlie Chaplin, and there was a green Cadillac with a driver on hand for anyone game for nightly jaunts to the Malibu Club or Crazy Horse in Paris. Ken Scott and his assistant

> ### "People say it was just a stopgap album, but it was a genius idea."
> **Mike Garson**

Andy always stayed behind and played pinball, occasionally returning to the control room for further tinkering on the tapes of the final Hammersmith gig, planned as a live album (tentatively titled *Bowie-ing Out*). Bowie mostly kept to himself, reading the newspaper and working on songs for his ambitious next project, a musical based on George Orwell's novel *1984*. Ronson was usually at the dining room piano, with a felt-tip pen and manuscript paper, working on his next arrangement.

And on *Pin Ups*, it's Ronson who shines the brightest. His arrangements are inventive and startlingly modern in places, especially on the two centrepieces: *See Emily Play* (Pink Floyd's second single) and *Sorrow* (a hit for The Merseys in '66). The first is a whirlwind of dramatic scene shifts, from bass and one-finger piano to power chords and vari-speeded vocal harmonies, to interludes of dissonant noise and a modern string quartet. It plays like a forecast to the cut-and-paste music of Beck and Radiohead 25 years later.

Sorrow threads its spare elegance around a single cello line, back beat and layer-cake vocal harmonies. Again, there's a prescience about it. In the moment where Bowie's singing: '*With your long blonde hair, I didn't sleep last night,*' one can almost hear the DNA for *Raspberry Beret*-era Prince.

"I knew when we did these arrangements that no one would get them," Garson says with a chuckle. "And I still didn't care. David and Mick didn't care. I think it's undeniable that David affected Prince, Beck, Kate Bush, all these artists. You can hear his influence everywhere today. And those string parts that Mick wrote were magical. He was a terrific natural string writer. The fact that he wasn't trained served him well, because he thought outside the usual boxes that arrangers think in. His guitar playing was tremendous, of course, so lyrical and strong.

"He was the perfect foil for David. Those of us who knew him weren't surprised by the depth of his talents, but I think the public didn't know, and still don't. Just a once-in-a-generation talent."

"Writing and arranging music came very easily to him," says Suzi Ronson. "David trusted him and didn't interfere with the process. I loved that about David. He was open to other people's ideas, and when Mick came along, what a gift for David. He was so lucky to have found such a talented musician. Lucky for Mick, too. He found someone whose music inspired him. David's music was calling out for Mick, and Mick did not disappoint."

That summer, Ronno was also being groomed by Bowie's manager Tony Defries for a solo career, which may have caused some ripples between him and Bowie. But if so, it's certainly not apparent on the album. *Pin Ups* is often dismissed for being frivolous and light, but that's a big part of its charm, especially sandwiched between the seriousness of *Aladdin Sane* and *Diamond Dogs*.

Ronson made it easy for Bowie to clown around behind the mic in a way that he never had before, and never would again in quite the same playful way. *Rosalyn, Here Comes The Night, Friday On My Mind,* they all capture the singer at his most loose-limbed and freewheeling. Significantly though,

THE COVER: ZIG & TWIG THE WONDERKID

The iconic *Pin Ups* photo was originally intended for a different cover – that of British *Vogue*. The magazine flew photographer Justin De Villeneuve to France to shoot his girlfriend Twiggy with David Bowie (to the model's excitement, Bowie had name-checked her in *Drive-In Saturday*). How could a pic of two of the world's most compelling faces possibly go wrong?

"When Twigs and Bowie were together and lit up," de Villeneuve said, "I looked through the viewfinder and realised that David was pure white, whereas Twiggy was tanned from a holiday in Bermuda. There was a moment of panic because I knew it would look bizarre, but the make-up artist ,Pierre LaRoche, suggested drawing masks on them, and this worked out even better. I remember distinctly that I'd got it with the first shot. Too good to be true. When I showed Bowie the test Polaroids, he asked if he could use it for the *Pin Ups* sleeve. I said: 'I don't think so, since this is for *Vogue*... How many albums do you think you will sell?' 'A million,' he replied. 'This is your next album cover!' I said.

"When I got back to London and told *Vogue*, they never spoke to me again. Several months later, Twigs and I were driving along Sunset Boulevard and we passed a 60-foot billboard of the picture. I knew I had made the right decision."

ALAMY x2

Specs appeal: Bowie the 70s pin-up.

Bowie and Mike Garson rehearsing at Sigma Sound Studios in Philadelphia, 1975.

the album ends with The Kinks' cranky *Where Have All The Good Times Gone*. Like Davies, Bowie had a pessimistic bent that never squared with the 60s' sunny optimism. The run-out message of *Pin Ups* seems to be: "This has been fun, but time to move on now." Much too fast to take that test indeed.

It turned out that 1973 was the year of the covers album. In June, Harry Nilsson had released *A Little Touch Of Schmilsson In The Night*, a collection of Tin Pan Alley standards recorded with Sinatra's arranger Gordon Jenkins. Laura Nyro put out *Gotta Be A Miracle*, remaking Brill Building-era pop. John Lennon had begun the dark odyssey of *Rock 'N' Roll* with Phil Spector. But treading much closer to Bowie's stylistic turf was Bryan Ferry, who was halfway through recording his own covers of English pop for *These Foolish Things*.

There are differing reports of how Ferry's anger over the competing project played out. Some say he asked his label, Island Records, to file an injunction to prevent RCA from rush-releasing *Pin Ups*. Others say he bombarded Bowie with telegrams and calls at the Château d'Hérouville. Bowie certainly hadn't forgotten Ferry's comment to the press about how, in concert, David liked to "push all his band back, like props in their little boxes". Either way, both sides agreed to let it be.

Released on October 19, *Pin Ups* entered the UK chart at No.1, with Bowie's three previous albums lingering nearby at 13, 19 and 16 respectively (he was the best-selling album artist of the year). Led by its first single, *Sorrow*, it shipped 147,000 copies, then continued to sell 30,000 a week through Christmas. "It's the kind of music your parents will never let you play loud enough!" teased the tagline on RCA's ad campaign, and fans loved it.

Critics were less enthused. *Rolling Stone* said: "Even in 1965, any of a thousand bands could have done better." *NME* said: "David Bowie should know well enough not to succumb to everyone else's idea of how-to-make-your-next-album." John Peel said: "I'll be glad when Bryan Ferry and David Bowie get this oldies business out of their normally diverting systems."

Because it's covers, *Pin Ups* will never have the artistic heft of Bowie's other 70s albums, but it remains an energetic and highly charming throwaway, a kind of glossy Pop Art reassembly of 60s singles. Spending five months on the chart, it gave Bowie the respite he needed to plot his

next move. The *1984* musical was scrapped after Orwell's widow denied Bowie the rights, and its apocalyptic visions were folded into what was essentially Ziggy's epilogue, *Diamond Dogs*. It was the last straight-up rock album that Bowie would make. Just ahead lay Philly soul, chilly Krautrock and the Berlin trilogy.

Bowie tipped his hand that summer by telling the *NME*: "The rock business has become so established, and so much like a society, that I have revolted against it. That's what wasn't liked; that I won't take it seriously, and I'll break its rules, and I won't listen to it, and I won't take much notice of it. It doesn't worry me."

Although he was too restless to see it through, *Pin Ups* was planned as a two-part release, with the second leaning on covers of American music, such as the Lovin' Spoonful's *Summer In The City*, the Beach Boys' *God Only Knows* and the

> ## "I knew no one would get the arrangements. We didn't care."
> ### Mike Garson

Velvet Underground's *White Light/White Heat*. The version of Bruce Springsteen's *Growing Up* that surfaced later as a bonus track hints at what might have been. Mike Garson, who has been leading a worldwide tour of alumni musicians called the Bowie Celebration, says: "Over the years, David talked about doing a *Pin Ups 2*, even as late as 2002, but it didn't happen. There were a lot of projects that we never got to – a Broadway show, *Outside 2* and *3*, a big-band album where we'd rearrange the least-known song on each of his albums.

"But I think the original *Pin Ups* has been overlooked for too long. That's why I put *Sorrow* in the set for this tour. People say it was just a stopgap album, but it was a genius idea, another change of direction in his seventies story. I want every Bowie fan, new and old, to listen – or relisten – to it. It's just more proof that his creativity never stopped." ●

HIS BARK MATERIALS

Diamond Dogs was the point at which an unsettled **David Bowie** was shedding his glam-rock skin and shaping up to become the 'plastic soul' man of his next album. It was also, he said, "my most difficult album".

Words: **David Sinclair** Photos: **Terry O'Neill**

Released in the summer of 1974, *Diamond Dogs* found David Bowie navigating the dog days of the glam-rock era – a hot and sultry period before the cultural weather broke. Having surfed and defined the pop zeitgeist about as well as any individual star since Elvis Presley, he was now cresting the last stretch of a wave as it came crashing into shore.

Diamond Dogs was a resounding commercial success – No.1 in the UK, No.5 in the US. But the album was marked down at the time. "A rather grandiose mood piece… It's okay, you know, but is it really necessary?" was the *NME*'s verdict. And, retrospectively, it tends to get brushed aside in the grand sweep of things as a transitional album, marking the point in Bowie's artistic timeline at which he was shedding his glam-rock skin and stepping into his role as the 'plastic soul' man of his next studio album *Young Americans*. (*NME* later revised its opinion and, in 2013, rated *Diamond Dogs* one of "The 500 Greatest Albums of all Time" – albeit ranked at No.447, a long way behind many of his other albums.)

Bowie himself was quick to recognise the record's limitations. "It was not a concept album," he told Robert Hilburn in September 1974. "It was a collection of things. And I didn't have a band. So that's where the tension came in. I couldn't believe I had finished it when I did. I had done so much of it myself. I never want to be in that position again. It was frightening trying to make an album with no support behind you. I was very much on my own. It was my most difficult album. It was a relief that it did so well."

Whatever the sense of "tension", both musically and personally, which overshadowed the making of *Diamond Dogs*, the album is nevertheless a remarkably pure distillation of Bowie's genius. Indeed, if you are looking for a collection of recordings that stands as a monument to Bowie's across-the-board prowess as a songwriter, singer, guitarist, saxophonist, keyboard player, producer and all-round media maven, there is no other album in his entire catalogue that compares to *Diamond Dogs*. Transitional or not, it remains as true an expression of his artistry on every front as anything he ever released.

"It was frightening trying to make an album with no support behind you. I was on my own."

David Bowie

The album was recorded in London, mostly at Olympic Studios, and Hilversum in the Netherlands, between December 1973 and February 1974. Having famously disbanded the Spiders From Mars live on stage at Hammersmith Odeon the previous July, Bowie's first challenge was to fill the guitar genius-shaped hole left in his musical life by the departure of Mick Ronson. In a defiant display of ambition and bravado, Bowie resolved to do the job himself. "I knew that the guitar playing had to be more than okay," he said, looking back in 1997. "That couple of months I spent putting [*Diamond Dogs*] together before I went into the studio was probably the only time in my life where I really buckled down to learn the stuff I needed to have on the album. I'd actually practise two hours a day."

Having also dispensed with the services of longstanding producer Ken Scott, Bowie's initial plan was not only to produce the album but also to play every instrument himself – perhaps reaching the point at which ambition gave way to hubris. Wiser counsel prevailed and he found a new rhythm section comprising session bass player Herbie Flowers (the man responsible for the swooping bass line on Lou Reed's *Walk On The Wild Side*) and drummer Tony Newman (best known for his stint in the Jeff Beck Group). Pianist Mike Garson and drummer Aynsley Dunbar, who had both contributed to *Pin Ups*, the album of cover versions which Bowie had somehow slotted into his schedule and released in October 1973, were also brought in.

All sorts of grand ideas were floated in the build up to *Diamond Dogs*. Bowie had spoken of his intention to mount a "full-scale rock musical" re-telling the story of Ziggy Stardust. He'd also let it be known that he was planning to write and direct a musical production for TV of George Orwell's *Nineteen Eighty-Four*, one of his favourite novels.

"I'd failed to obtain the theatrical rights from George Orwell's widow," Bowie told the *Mail On Sunday* in 2008. "And having written three or more songs for it already, I did a fast about-face and recobbled the idea into *Diamond Dogs*: teen punks on rusty skates living on the roofs of the dystopian Hunger City; a post-apocalyptic landscape." ➢

Left: In the studio during the album's recording.

Right: With William Burroughs in 1974. The novelist inspired Bowie to write lyrics as "ingredients lists".

The scene is set on the opening number, *Future Legend*, a brief, howling, growling, synthesised soundtrack with a voiceover from Bowie introducing us to a ghastly, ruined cityscape where '*Fleas the size of rats sucked on rats the size of cats/ And ten thousand peoploids split into small tribes…*' The recitation ends with the jarring proclamation: '*This ain't rock and roll. This is genocide!*'

The title track, which follows, actually sounds a lot more like rock'n'roll than mass murder – with an influence that owed a noticeable debt to Mick Jagger and Keith Richards. As chance would have it, the Rolling Stones were in Olympic Studios recording their album *It's Only Rock'n'Roll* at the same time as Bowie was working on *Diamond Dogs*. Olympic's in-house engineer, Keith Harwood, who engineered *Diamond Dogs*, had previously worked on several Stones albums. And if the general fraternising that went on during the course of the sessions wasn't enough to reinforce the connection, Bowie and his then-wife Angie (Angela Barnett) had recently moved into a grand terraced house in Chelsea where they were now near neighbours of Mick and Bianca Jagger, with whom they socialised.

Indeed, according to the American singer and model Ava Cherry, who stayed in the house for a time with David and Angie, there was a lot more than socialising going on. "Mick Jagger knew David, and I was friends with both of them," Cherry told Bowie biographer Dylan Jones. "So all three of us used to hang out a lot, and yes we did have some fun together." According to Cherry, at the end of one party in New York, everyone had left apart from her, Bowie and Jagger. "So it just ended up with the three of us sleeping together. That was it. And we had a wonderful time and we had a lot of fun."

Diamond Dogs performed disappointingly when released as a single in June 1974 (after the album was released) in the UK, where it peaked at No.21. Far more resonant and enduring as a flagship track for the album was *Rebel Rebel* – the song that

most clearly marked both the end of an era for Bowie and the jumping off point for *Diamond Dogs*.

Recorded on December 27, 1973, *Rebel Rebel* was the first song of the sessions and the last song that Bowie recorded at Trident Studios in Soho where he had recorded the majority of his work since 1968. Released as a single in the UK in February 1974, ahead of the album, *Rebel Rebel* reached No.5 and remains one of Bowie's touchstone songs. The lyric is as pertinent today – maybe even more so – as it was almost 50 years ago: '*You've got your mother in a whirl, cos she's not sure if you're a boy or a girl.*' And the riff is a masterpiece: simple, original and instantly recognisable in the way that only a handful of pop-rock riffs – *Sweet Jane, Jumping Jack Flash, You Really Got Me* – could ever truly claim to be. Did Bowie really come up with that and play it completely off his own bat?

"He had the riff about seventy-five per cent sorted out," recalled Alan Parker, a session

"*Diamond Dogs* was a weird period because everything that David had done up to that point suddenly exploded."

Earl Slick

guitarist credited for his contribution to one track (*1984*) on the album. "He wanted it a bit like a Stones riff and he played it to me as such, and I then tinkered around with it. I said: 'Well, what if we did this and that and made it sound more clangy and put some bends in it?' And he said: 'Yeah, I love that, that's fine.'" Whatever Parker's contribution to the sculpting and performing of the song behind the scenes, Bowie is the sole writer and guitarist listed on the credits.

While *Rebel Rebel* and the title track echoed the triumphs of Bowie's glam-rock past, the rest of the album offered a tantalising glimpse of the future-Bowie that was yet to fully materialise. At the heart of Side 1 is the three-piece song suite *Sweet Thing/Candidate/Sweet Thing (Reprise)*, which was originally intended to be the centrepiece for the would-be stage production of *Nineteen*

Eighty-Four. It is a yearning yet chilling sequence, with lyrics rendered as a collage of bittersweet images and ideas. '*I guess we could cruise down one more time, with you by my side it should be fine/We'll buy some drugs and watch a band, then jump in the river holding hands.*'

The sequence is notable for its intensely detailed arrangement – brought to life not least by Bowie's contributions on saxophone and guitar. The end of the *Reprise* section (which runs into *Rebel Rebel*) has him conjuring a screeching, crunching, overdriven guitar noise that prefigured the industrial sounds that Earl Slick would later develop on *Station To Station* and Reeves Gabrels would take to another level on the Tin Machine albums.

Bowie wrote the lyrics for these and other songs on *Diamond Dogs* using the 'cut-up' method popularised by the 'beat' writer and literary figurehead William Burroughs. "You write down a paragraph or two describing several different subjects," Bowie explained. "Creating a kind of story ingredients list, I suppose. And then cut the sentences into four- or five-word sections; mix 'em up and reconnect them. You can get some pretty interesting idea combinations like this."

While the mood and subject matter of the songs on Side 2 is clearly derived from the nightmarish gloom of Orwell's novel, it is impossible to know where and how these cut-ups might have been made or what the precise meaning is. '*We're today's scrambled creatures, locked in tomorrow's double feature, heaven's on the pillow, its silence competes with hell/It's a twenty-four-hour service guaranteed to make you tell…*' Bowie sings mournfully on *We Are The Dead*. It certainly sounds like a bad trip.

The comparatively jaunty music on tracks such as *Rock'n'Roll With Me* and *Big Brother* sounds like it should be part of a stage musical – as indeed it was originally intended to be. *The Rocky Horror Show*, which opened at the Royal Court Theatre in London in 1973, was on the way to becoming a cult phenomenon at the time Bowie was writing the album and there was a lot of musical theatricality in the air. There was also evidence of the looming switch of musical pace and persona that Bowie would effect on his next album, *Young Americans* – most obviously represented in the ▷

The *Diamond Dogs* album was Bowie letting himself off the leash, up to a point.

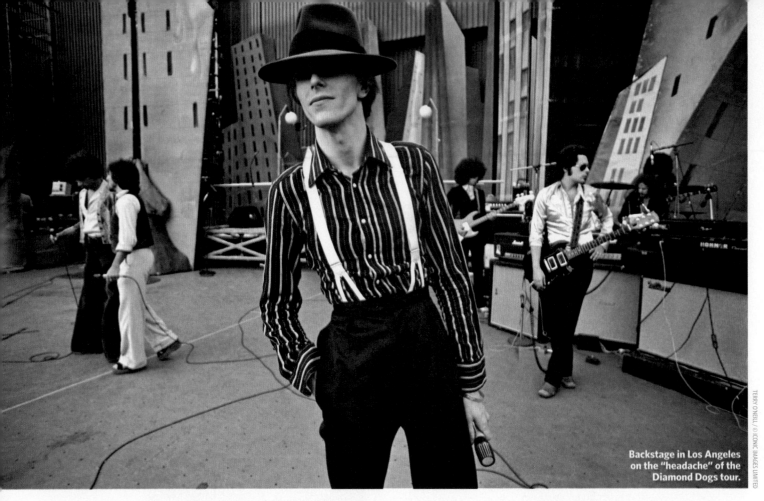

Backstage in Los Angeles on the "headache" of the Diamond Dogs tour.

track *1984*, which took its inspiration from the wah-wah guitar and string arrangements of Isaac Hayes's soundtrack to the 1971 film *Shaft*.

"When we worked on the song *1984* he was already referencing Barry White," said Ken Scott, who had produced an earlier recording of the song as part of the *Aladdin Sane* sessions in January 1973. "He wanted the hi-hat and the strings to sound like they would be on a Barry White album. He was already anticipating the sound of *Young Americans*."

The faintly shocking, sci-fi cover artwork by the Belgian artist Guy Peellaert, featuring a picture of Bowie with his lower body transformed into that of a dog complete with genitalia (airbrushed from most versions at the time) became instantly iconic. Bowie got the idea after Mick Jagger told him that Peellaert was designing the sleeve of the forthcoming Stones album *It's Only Rock'n'Roll*. "I immediately rushed out and got Guy Peellaert to do my cover too," Bowie admitted later. When *It's Only Rock'n'Roll* was released several months after *Diamond Dogs*, everyone assumed the Stones had copied Bowie. "He [Jagger] never forgave me for that!" Bowie said.

The spectacular and technically ambitious tour to promote *Diamond Dogs* set new standards for theatrical invention and sheer scale of endeavour.

According to the Bowie chronicler Nicholas Pegg the stage set "was more elaborate than any previously attempted for a rock tour and cost an unprecedented $250,000… A giant backdrop depicted the nightmarish Hunger City skyline, tilted in jagged perspective. To either side stood two massive aluminium skyscrapers, linked by a moving bridge which would rise and fall during the show. The specialist props, run by hydraulic

mechanisms and early forms of computer control, were to be built from scratch."

The early reviews were delirious. The reviewer from *Melody Maker* described it as "a combination of contemporary music and theatre that is several years ahead of its time… a completely new concept in rock theatre – the most original spectacle in rock I have ever seen."

According to Bowie: "It was truly the first real rock and roll theatrical show that made any sense." But he nevertheless remembered the tour as "quite an unbelievable headache".

At times, the sheer ambition of the staging threatened to outstrip the technical knowhow. With cranes and cherry-pickers and bits of staging flying around, there was little margin for error.

|||||||||||||||||||||||||||||||||||||||||||||||||||||||||||||||||

"*Diamond Dogs* scared me because I was mutating into something I just didn't believe in any more."

David Bowie

According to stage manager Nick Russiyan, "David was in great danger physically and could have gotten electrocuted or killed."

There was a disconnect too between the sophisticated musicianship of the new stage band – featuring guitarists Carlos Alomar and Earl Slick – and the rough edges of the original *Diamond Dogs* recording, played by Bowie himself. "That album had a quality of obsession with what I wanted to get over," Bowie later reflected. "They played it too well and with too much fluidity. So to me *Diamond Dogs* was never played well on stage, or at least never with the sensibility that the album had."

Despite the positive reaction, the production was scaled back dramatically after the first leg

and morphed into the so-called Soul Tour, with a set-list featuring material from Bowie's forthcoming album *Young Americans* (released in 1975).

"I threw the set away and came back with a completely different show," Bowie later recalled. "They were supposed to be selling the entire show on this spectacular set, and the kids would come and there was no set, no nothing, and there I was singing soul music."

"*Diamond Dogs* was a weird period because everything that David had done up to that point suddenly exploded," said guitarist Earl Slick. "It was like a nuclear explosion… Bowiemania… Then he decided to just abandon the whole thing. *Diamond Dogs* is probably one of the most iconic things he did in his entire career but… it [the tour] didn't even make the West Coast."

"It was pretty obvious that David was taking coke," recalled Jayne County, the American proto-punk glam-rocker who was signed to Bowie's management firm MainMan at that time. "He became very skeletal in his appearance and began rattling off speeches that sounded meaningless to the rest of us… He began to get paranoid… accusing people of ripping him off and stealing his drugs."

"*Diamond Dogs* scared me because I was mutating into something I just didn't believe in any more, and the dreadful thing was, it was so easy," Bowie said, looking back in 2008. "The *Diamond Dogs* period was just an extension of *Aladdin Sane*, which in itself was just an extrapolation of *Ziggy Stardust*.

"But by the time of *Diamond Dogs* that persona had started to feel claustrophobic, and I needed a change… *Diamond Dogs* was making me sick, both physically and creatively, and I was shifting into melodrama." ❶

Reborn In The USA

Glam rock was on its last legs when David Bowie fell hard for soul music, R&B and cocaine. The result was 1975's *Young Americans* – the "plastic soul" masterpiece that put him on the map in the US.

Words: **Chris Roberts**

've gone through some pretty interesting changes", Bowie told *NME*'s Andrew O'Grady in 1975. "Rock and roll certainly hasn't fulfilled its original promise… it's just become one more whirling deity, right? Going around that never-decreasing circle. Rock and roll is dead. It's a toothless old woman. It's really embarrassing".

What he was saying wasn't a million miles away from what punk rockers would soon shout. But this was 1975, and Bowie had become a soul man. His blue-eyed – or as he put it, "plastic" – soul switched a generation of white boys on to the joy and pain of black music. His alleged inauthenticity was of no significance. He sang it, felt it, transmitted it. The listener was moved by the result, never mind the process. The influence of the *Young Americans* album, the ripples and reassessments it initiated, were to prove incalculable, irreversible. Elton, Roxy and Rod soon embraced soul or disco; throughout the 80s everyone from Talking Heads and Japan to ABC and the new romantics chose this strain of Bowie as their infection. Rock may not have expired, but it knew it had to learn some new moves. Another Bowie risk, intuition, perverse gamble, had, by accident or design, paid off handsomely.

With the lurex lemon of glam rock squeezed dry, ch-ch-changes were necessary again, especially if you were the peripatetic, hyperactive Bowie. *Diamond Dogs* was the last great album of that era, its epic theatrics both taking the glam ethos of delirious decadence sky-high, and wilfully razing it to the ground. Yet even there, as is often the case within the Bowie narrative, one could discern the seeds of his next chapter. *1984* had flung itself into funk rock with a hint of Isaac Hayes; *Rock'n'Roll With Me* was like a soul torch song turned up to 11, referencing Bill Withers' *Lean On Me*. Bowie was asking himself, as the glorious song dropped from the original *Young Americans* tracklisting goes, *Who Can I Be Now?*

Lulu, of all people, played a part in *Young Americans*' origin story. At sessions in New York with her, Bowie met Carlos Alomar, who he snapped up as his new band leader. Alomar had not previously been aware of Bowie. He'd been a session player at the Harlem Apollo, working

> ## "I was not on this planet. I was just not aware of what was going on around me."
> **David Bowie**

with James Brown, Wilson Pickett and Chuck Berry. Bowie was a huge fan of Brown's *Live At The Apollo*, and so cranked up his charm offensive to make sure he and Alomar bonded. They'd work together on 11 Bowie albums.

As the first leg of the *Diamond Dogs* tour was ending in July 1974, Bowie visited Sigma Sound Studios in Philadelphia, owned by Kenny Gamble and Leon Huff, founders of Philadelphia International Records, to work on tracks for Ava Cherry, by most accounts, his paramour. He was dazzled, wooed. He came away with a list of classic black albums in which to immerse himself.

Gamble and Huff, as writers and producers, were, with Thom Bell, behind the "Philly soul" sound, which updated genre tropes with disco rhythms and heavy strings. Their house band, MFSB (an acronym for Mother Father Sister Brother), a collective of over 30 musicians, had backed the label's O'Jays, Billy Paul, Harold Melvin & The Bluenotes and The Stylistics. They'd even had a million-selling hit themselves, with The Three Degrees on vocals, with *TSOP (The Sound Of Philadelphia)*, also the theme for TV show *Soul Train*. Bowie, understandably, thought it would be a terrific idea to hire MFSB as his new backing band. But even being Bowie didn't automatically turn wishes to reality: MFSB weren't available, with the exception of percussionist Larry Washington.

He did however hold the winning card of Carlos Alomar. He already had sax wizard David Sanborn in his live band, but upon Alomar's advice hired Andy Newmark, former drummer with Sly & the Family Stone, instead of Tony Newman, and Isley Brothers bassist Willie Weeks instead of Herbie Flowers. Ruthless and cold? Or decisive and visionary? Hearing that his bass-player idol Weeks was in, Tony Visconti set off to join camp immediately. And for all these top-rank players, the master-stroke was the choice of backing vocalists as, alongside Ava Cherry, Alomar brought in his wife Robin Clark and a young unknown, Luther Vandross.

The Sigma Sound sessions began in August 1974. Bowie had to adjust to the engineers' un-British reluctance to use effects (prior to mixing) while recording. He was hearing his own voice undressed. But things moved apace, most tracks cut live in one take, including the vocals. The album, according to Visconti, boasts "about 85 per cent live Bowie". The star had no problem with long ⊳

With Yoko Ono and John Lennon –
who played guitar and sang vocals
on *Young Americans'* *Across The
Universe* and *Fame.*

sessions night and day over the two weeks: his cocaine addiction was rising to a peak. It should have affected his voice. It does, but only by giving his soulful testifying extra scorch and heart. His performances are a full-throated force of nature. Justice can be flaky.

"It was self-abuse", he told me when I interviewed him in 1999. "Drugs were not helpful in my life". What drove him to that? "Absolutely nothing original. I just took 'em. Ha! I had lots of money, I bought 'em, and I ingested 'em. Mr. President, I did inhale. I dived in with a vengeance."

It must have been strange being David Bowie at that time? "I wouldn't know! I was not on this planet. I was just not aware of what was going on around me."

A dozen or so local fans caught on and began hanging out outside the studio. Bowie liked them, and on the last day invited "the Sigma kids" in to hear rough versions. As a playback ended, there was a moment's awkward silence until one youth shouted, "Play it again!" This time, everybody, including Bowie, got up and danced.

So productive were these sessions that numerous out-takes – from *Lazer* to *Shilling The Rubes* to a stab at Springsteen's *It's Hard To Be A Saint In The City* – didn't make the cut (until, in most cases, later repackagings). Working titles for the whole album included, at various stages, *The Gouster, Dancin',* and *One Damned Song.* And then came the intervention from a Beatle.

The second half of the Diamond Dogs tour became soul-centric, and in December Bowie, Alomar and Visconti reconvened at the Record Plant in New York. *Win* and *Fascination* were nailed here. Believing that was a wrap,

> ### "David apologised for not including me. There just wasn't time to send for me."
> **Tony Visconti**

Visconti flew to London to mix, while Bowie and in-house engineer Harry Maslin worked on other mixes in New York. That's when the singer met up with John Lennon, who was recording his covers album *Rock'n'Roll* and was enjoying, perhaps too much, his "lost weekend" phase. The illustrious pair had previously met at an LA party thrown by Elizabeth Taylor. They drank together, sang together, an excited Bowie blitzing Lennon with his new sound. With Alomar – plus guitarist Earl Slick and drummer Dennis Davis – they recorded *Fame* and Lennon's *Across The Universe* at Electric Lady, with Maslin co-producing.

Impetuously, as the new year dawned, Bowie now insisted these collaborations with a hero had to take priority on the album. He informed

an ambivalent Visconti. *Who Can I Be Now?* and *It's Gonna Be Me* were benched. "Beautiful songs", sighed Visconti, "and it made me sick when he decided not to use them. I think it was the personal content of the songs which he was reluctant to use, although they were so obscure I don't think even I knew what he was on about in them."

Certainly their mountain-ranges of melodrama were more intriguing than the overblown Beatles cover, which strains and grunts as if Bowie's trying too hard to ingratiate himself with his new pal. "David apologised for not including me", recalled Visconti. "There just wasn't time to send for me. Oh well".

Fame, however, took on a life of its own, sparking a flame, giving him a first US No.1. Based on an Alomar riff, bashed out in an evening, it was a "nasty little song" (said Bowie), aimed partly at Tony DeFries. When James Brown later sampled it for *Hot,* Bowie felt vindicated. It gave him North America's seventh biggest seller of the year. Acceptance, coast to coast, for the limey weirdo.

Fame: what he
likes is in the limo.

GETTY X5

The Diamond Dogs tour in LA, 1974.

With wife Angie in Beverly Hills, 1975.

On The Dick Cavett show in 1974.

So many elements land just right to allow the alchemy of this album. Sanborn doesn't believe in "less is more", but his every note swings. Vandross, co-writer of *Fascination* (his first published co-writing credit), was a vocal superstar in waiting. Tracks flow indulgently but the gospel-tinged call-and-response refrains keep everything tingling with gorgeous sensuality. Bowie jumps half-octaves, smashes a falsetto like he's a Delfonic.

Young Americans, the track, for all its foggy feints at Nixon, came across to the US public, not paying much attention to the lyrics, as a celebration – we're young! We're American! You can, if you squint, discern the subtle influence of the rivers of rhymes which fuelled Springsteen's first two albums, which Bowie was ingesting. *"We live for just these twenty years/Do we have to die for the fifty more?"* feels, however, like the kind of stunning, luckily profound throw of the poetic dice which only Bowie pulled off repeatedly in the 70s.

He was vague about the sumptuous *Win*: "It's a "get up off your backside" song really…" He described *Right* as "a positive drone, a mantra." As for *Somebody Up There Likes Me*, he touched on his dodgiest of philosophical avenues of that period. "It's: 'Watch out mate, Hitler's on his way back.' It's your rock'n'roll sociological bit". It's safe to say *Young Americans* works better as transcendent in-the-zone pop-soul if you don't spend too much time analysing what the then coke-addled creator said about it as it made him a transatlantic superstar. His active, irrational response was to move to LA, develop an interest in the occult, and gut and rewire these soul mannerisms, deploying them in unanticipated, counter-intuitive ways on the next album, *Station To Station*.

Those dropped tracks returned, correctly, on legacy reissues. Their confessional edge – is he singing about his own sex life, without misdirection? – offers a buzzy frisson. His vocals are wild, windy, winged. *It's Gonna Be Me*, in

particular, is extraordinary, and makes you resent the Lennon link-up. Its huge, slow, misty-blue build and stop-start arrangement support a Bowie vocal of oceanic scale: on any other album it would be the centrepiece. Maybe he felt the words portrayed – revealed? – him as a heartless womanizer. But he could have pleaded genre tropes, or being in character. Then again, "loved her before I knew her name" and other florid swoons ring of a pretty undeniable romanticism. Soul love? Love is careless in its choosing.

In 1999, with rock and roll not dead, I asked David Bowie if it had been therapeutic to sing soul. "Hmm, it was more… just another way to write," he replied. "It added something. I still wanted to learn. I remember talking to John at the time – er, John Lennon – about people we admired, and he said, "Y'know, when I discover someone new, I tend to become that person. I want to soak myself in their stuff…" When he first found Dylan, he said he would dress like Dylan, until he understood how it worked. And that's exactly how I feel about it… In an awkward fashion, I did that too – I lived the life, whatever it was. I'd immerse myself. Method acting? I guess it was, in a way. It comes from having an addictive personality. Transform into the thing you admire, then hopefully you absorb that knowledge – and then you move on to something else."

Which he did in 1975, his "plastic" soul having rerouted music's march.

"But you don't leave it behind. I rarely did. R&B still comes through in my music. All the things I've been through on the way still come through".

Once again, he'd swooped like a song. 🔾

> "Method acting? I guess it was, in a way. It comes from having an addictive personality."
>
> **David Bowie**

David Bowie
Fame & Golden Years

Before his move to Berlin, Bowie got seriously funky on these two tracks, thanks to inspiration from Aretha Franklin, James Brown and his own 17-year-old mistress...

Words: **Richard Purden**

When David Bowie arrived in New York to play Radio City Music Hall on Valentine's Day 1973, Cupid's slender arrow was already in motion. On the second of a two-night stint he met Ava Cherry – the 17-year-old from Chicago with short, peroxide hair who would soon become his backing singer. Her first gig was at Ziggy Stardust's final appearance, *The 1980 Floor Show*, filmed at London's Marquee in October that year.

"When I met David he was infamous but not famous," she says. "I knew who he was. There was a party I helped organise at a place called Genesis. All the greats were there: Stevie [Wonder], Aretha [Franklin] and Gladys [Knight]. David walked in with his bright red hair and a stunning suit. He said: 'My name's David. I love your hair. It's very rebellious.' I said: 'Yeah, a lot like you.'"

There began an affair that would soon fan the flames of Bowie's creative hunger. When plans to hire Cherry as a backing singer for a Japanese tour floundered, she decided to track him down. "I followed him to Europe where he put me up in a hotel. I then lived at his house on Oakley Street in London for about two months. Angie [Bowie] freaked, but it was her idea – she said to just stay at the house."

Raised in a working-class neighbourhood on Chicago's South Side, Cherry provided Bowie with an authentic line into black experience, language, fashion and culture.

"In London we talked about the idea of a soul band, way before he became involved with Carlos [Alomar, guitarist]. He discussed wanting to record a soul record similar to the artists he loved, like Aretha. I showed him a picture of my dad, who was a trumpet player in the 1940s – his group played with Count Basie. David said: 'My God, that suit. Do you still have it?' I borrowed one from my father, and David had Freddie Burretti [the designer behind much of Ziggy's sartorial elegance] knock up the suit for him. He was then The Gouster, which was a Chicago term for the black

men who would slow dance with the ladies. They would wear zoot suits with the baggy pants and little jackets."

Cherry continued in her role as backing singer while Bowie toured *Diamond Dogs* in the States and recorded at Philadelphia's Sigma Sound Studios.

"David surrounded himself with the best there was. Luther Vandross [backing vocals] added a lot of flavour to the sound. David Sanborn [sax] was also one of the superstars of that time – he played like a bat out of hell."

Young Americans was a key breakthrough, with *Fame* delivering Bowie's first No.1 hit single. The song was a late addition from a session at Electric Lady with John Lennon that changed the direction of the album. Co-written with Lennon and Carlos Alomar, it emerged from an aborted attempt to record The Flares' *Foot Stompin*. Bowie salvaged something of Alomar's riff, adding more guitars and a melody, while Lennon played acoustic.

Bowie would admit it was an "angry" track and had no idea it would be a hit. "It really was about the bullshit of the industry," says Cherry. "His manager Tony Defries had been good for David in the early stages, but they were having some trouble. The high backing vocal at the end was me singing in the booth with David and John."

One of the inspirations for the *Young Americans* album was Aretha Franklin. Her influence on Bowie is clear during the BBC documentary *Cracked Actor* that shows him prior to the 1975 Grammy Awards, singing along to *Natural Woman* in the back

of a limo while high on cocaine. James Brown's *Live At The Apollo* also left its mark. It seemed the influence was now cutting both ways. "James Brown tried to claim the riff for *Fame* was his," says Cherry. By the end of the year, Brown would produce a rip-off with his 1975 single *Hot (I Need To Be Loved, Loved, Loved, Loved)*.

Bowie once revealed that his follow-up single, *Golden Years,* was written for Elvis Presley. It continued in a similar funky vein to recent work, suggesting little of the true direction of his next album, *Station To Station*. The riff was provided by Earl Slick.

"I have to say thank you to Eric [Clapton] for that one," the guitarist admits. "It came from Cream's *Outside Woman Blues,* and there was a little of *Funky Broadway* by Wilson Pickett."

Carlos Alomar, who helped flesh out the track, suggested that Bowie had banged out some chords on the piano that reminded him of The Drifters' classic *On Broadway,* a song he had referenced during the *Diamond Dogs* tour, and steered him away from making it sounding too close. For the lyrics, it appears Bowie drew upon his recent break-up with Cherry.

"As soon as I heard that song, I knew it was about me," she says. "I wasn't with David in the period before he left for Berlin, but I know things were dire. He had some serious financial problems and was heavily into the drugs phase. I felt destroyed by the whole experience. I didn't know how to piece it all together, and that was really the end of the relationship.

"When I heard *Golden Years* I was in a supermarket and broke down. I was having some trouble launching my own career. David was involved in a project that had been shelved. It seemed to be his way of saying 'Don't lose faith, and keep going', even though we wouldn't be together any more.

"He was a creature that had to keep moving through experience after experience, and mine was beautiful and unique. But then he had to move on. I was blindly in love and lost in his aura." ●

Bowie with Ava Cherry, watching Rod Stewart and the Faces in 1975.

MAIN: GETTY. INSET: ALAMY

Golden years: Bowie during the filming of *The Man Who Fell To Earth* in 1975.

"Golden Years will always be my favourite Bowie song because he wrote it at my house. It's such a beautiful piece."

Glenn Hughes

"We were both out of it, all the time"

He's the guitar hero who connected a milk and cocaine-fuelled David Bowie with rock'n'roll during the Thin White Duke period. **Earl Slick** recalls the making of *Station To Station*, Bowie's experimental masterpiece.

Words: **David Sinclair**

Y ou probably would not recognise Earl Slick if you saw him in the street. But you would know he is a rock star. With his spiky, jet-black hair and elegantly undernourished physique, the 63-year-old guitarist has a look somewhere between Ronnie Wood and Derek Zoolander. We met in 2016, face to face in a rehearsal complex in North London in a room with no exterior windows. But I never saw his eyes, which remained encased behind big, black shades.

He was summoned to the capital under conditions of strict secrecy, to perform in a special tribute to David Bowie at the Brit Awards. As we talked, the sound of various Bowie tracks drifted through the studio walls. At one point, Bowie's voice intoning the familiar message *'Ground control to Major Tom,'* seems to have got stuck on a tape loop, lending a ghostly backdrop to our chat.

Slick was the most longstanding of Bowie's many decorated guitarists. The New Yorker, who was born Frank Madeloni in Brooklyn, first joined Bowie as a young hotshot for the *Diamond Dogs* tour of 1974 and last played with him on 2013's *The Next Day*. In between, he played on the albums *David Live*, *Young Americans*, *Station To Station* and *Reality* and took a key role in the *Serious Moonlight Tour* in support of the *Let's Dance* album. He has also worked with Ian Hunter, John Lennon and Yoko Ono, as well as releasing his own albums both as a solo act and in bands including Dirty White Boy and Phantom, Rocker & Slick.

Slick couldn't talk beforehand about the 2016 Brits tribute (which turned out to be an overture of Bowie's signature riffs – *Rebel Rebel*, *Ziggy Stardust*, *Heroes* and others – followed by a glorious version of *Life On Mars* sung by New Zealand pop star Lorde). But he did talk about his time with Bowie, and in particular his part in the making of Bowie's landmark 10th album *Station to Station*, released in early 1976.

S lick was first recommended to Bowie by the late conductor and composer Michael Kamen, who knew that Bowie was looking for a guitarist to replace Mick Ronson on the forthcoming *Diamond Dogs* tour, which Kamen also played on. At the audition, the then 22-year-old Slick was ▷

"You're asking me to get together with DB in the middle of the night and make some out-there shit? I'm right on it!" Earl Slick

"We're lucky we didn't kill ourselves. But it never would have been the same if we'd been in a different frame of mind." Earl Slick

understandably nervous. "I wasn't really sure what DB was going to want, because I never did a job for somebody else before. I thought, 'Oh my God. Have I got to copy all Mick [Ronson]'s stuff, note-for-note? This is going to be a nightmare.' Even to this day, I don't take direction very well. I can't read music and I don't like being told what to do note for note, because if I do that it doesn't sound like me. So why am I there? I'm a stubborn sonofabitch. David picked up all of that. And he said to me: 'You learn the song and then do it the way you do it.' I always loved Mick's playing, but I couldn't be Mick and I didn't want to be. Nobody's going to sound exactly like him, ever."

The full scale of the challenge – and how incredibly well Slick rose to it – is there for all to hear on *David Live*, the double-album recorded during the *Diamond Dogs* tour. It was Bowie's first live album and became a big hit in both America (No.8) and the UK (No.2). On track after track, Slick proved himself a lead guitarist with a surefooted touch and a buccaneering spirit. From the spiralling outro of *Moonage Daydream* to the breathtaking solo in *Candidate* and the monumental totality of *The Width Of A Circle*, Slick dished out sounds and solos that marked him out as a world-class performer. But making the album almost led to an insurrection among the band.

"We were not told that they were recording an album at the live shows,"

Slick recalls. "But back then if you were recording something live you would have two sets of microphones: one for the live sound and one for the recording. I was still inexperienced, but the other guys in the band noticed the two sets and figured out what was going on. When they questioned it, we all got a bit of paper under the hotel door offering us a pathetic fee for recording an album. It turned into a dispute between us [the band] and DB's management. Herbie [Flowers, bass] and some of the others negotiated a decent fee. The management then didn't pay the money. So we sued and eventually we got paid."

Bowie's manager at the time was Tony DeFries, and soon after this and other incidents, Bowie fired him and began legal action to free himself from his contract. "DeFries fucked David over really bad," Slick says. "He fucked us all over. He was a creep. You can print that."

While *David Live* was a tremendous showcase for Slick, he played a subsidiary role to Carlos Alomar on the *Young Americans* album in 1975. "I'm playing guitar on a lot of the record, but it's really background stuff," Slick says. "That's really a Carlos album. I think he did a great job. When you make records you got to do what works. What does the song need? If it doesn't need me on it or it just needs me to be in the background, fine. You play for the song."

In the back of a dream car 20 foot long: the infamous Victoria Station limo incident in 1976 when Bowie was vilified in the press for making a Nazi salute when he was actually just waving at fans.

The emphasis shifted decisively, however, on *Station To Station*, an album which found Bowie at the crossroads between his rock/R&B background and the experimental pop/ electronica sounds of the future. Slick whose playing style combined old-school lead guitar references with a natural taste for the wilder frontiers of sonic experimentation now found himself at the heart of the creative process. The 10 minute title track, with its opening blizzard of feedback, set down a marker at the beginning of the album.

"That happened at about five in the morning. That was just me and David in front of Marshall stacks in the studio both feeding back at the same time. It was spontaneous. When those kind of things came along, I was ready. We fucked around a lot with the guitars and messed around with ideas. You're asking me to get together with DB in the middle of the night and make some out-there shit? I'm right on it!"

Station To Station was recorded at Cherokee Studios in LA at a time when Bowie's personal excesses had escalated to a point where he could remember very little about making the album. "I know it was in LA because I've read it was," Bowie later remarked of the sessions. It is said that his diet at this time consisted of red peppers, cocaine and milk.

"The red peppers, I don't remember,"

Slick says. "But I remember all he ate and drank was milk. And all I ate and drank was beer. We were both out of it, all the time. I remember being in a bar in Hollywood one night and around two in the morning I got a call. There's a car waiting outside. David wants to go in right now and cut some songs. So I jump in the car and off to work. Another time I remember finishing a session at 4am [after] 36 straight hours in the studio."

Bowie was deep into his Thin White Duke character at this time. Did this spill into his personal relationships?

"Hell, yes," Slick says. "Everything did. Everything any of us did spilled over. Whenever you're in a situation like that your habits and your thinking spill into the work. And sometimes that's a really good thing and sometimes it's not. Christ, we almost killed ourselves with all this shit. We're lucky we didn't. But that record never would have been the same if we'd been in a different frame of mind.

"I don't condone that people need to get fucked up and take a lot of drugs and shit to make cool music. But I think that the whole environment at the time – the 1970s, the drugs – had a major impact on what that record sounded like. It had a major impact on everything. And actually I think that record benefitted from the insanity that ensued while we were doing it."

Less beneficial was the effect that this snowstorm of cocaine and sleepless nights eventually had on communications between Bowie and Slick. Although the guitarist had been at the very heart of creating and recording *Station To Station*, somehow, when the tour to promote the album began in Canada in 1976, he had been replaced by untried and largely unknown Toronto native Stacey Heydon.

"There were malevolent people behind the scenes that pitted me and David against each other," Slick says, without naming names. "We were maybe a bit compromised in our mental states and didn't realise what was happening. We both thought that we'd been fucked over by each other. The fact of the matter was that the powers-that-be had played some manipulation games, and me and David

not really having our eye on the ball didn't see what was going on. Later [in 1983] when I came into the *Serious Moonlight* tour, we knew we had to clear the air. Once we sat down and talked, it all made sense. Basically I got fucked out of a gig and he got fucked out of a guitar player, because there was just nasty people who had agendas. This wasn't Tony DeFries. I don't even want to give you these guys' names. They don't deserve the recognition. If you're really curious and you want to go into the archives, you'll see the names."

In 2016, Slick embarked on a run of dates to mark the 40th anniversary of *Station To Station*, during which he played the album in its entirety. When the shows were in the planning stage Slick, like most people, was unaware Bowie was ill. The guitarist was adamant that he did not want a Bowie clone to sing the album and so he decided to join forces with Bernard Fowler, best known as backing vocalist with the Rolling Stones. Also in the line-up for some of the UK dates was Lisa Ronson (daughter of Mick), linking the tour with an earlier chapter of Bowie's career.

Slick has always been a fierce advocate of *Station To Station* and now he has become positively evangelical about it. "I think it is one of the most important records anybody has ever made," he says, sitting forward, voice rising. "Tell me anything that was even close to sounding like that, up until that point in the rock era. There's nothing. I would call it the first really sonically experimental record by a major artist – barring Frank Zappa. The writing, the production, the lyrics. Who the hell put a 10 minute title song as the opening track? Nobody did. I don't think there was any conscious effort to make a ground-breaking new thing. I think it just happened. And that's why it's so good. It wasn't contrived. I just went in there and David was writing and it just happened. That's when shit is cool. When it just happens."

Despite his contributions to the songs, Slick received no share of

Above: on the *Reality* tour, 2003.

Left: with Lorde and Mike Garson performing their tribute to Bowie at The Brits, 2016.

Earl Slick: the "go-to guy if the house is on fire".

the writing credits, a subject that he doesn't care to dwell on. "It's a very grey area. I'm not sure that writing a lick means that you wrote the song," he says. "Maybe I should have got a credit for something. I don't know. That's really up to the artist to do that. Or up to me to demand it. But then it's all passed down in the end. I can tell you that the *Golden Years* lick is a combination I ripped off from Clapton's *Outside Woman Blues* and Wilson Pickett's *Funky Broadway*. I had both those songs in my head when David wanted a lick for the chord sequence he'd got. So thanks, Eric."

Slick rejoined Bowie's touring band after Stevie Ray Vaughan – who played guitar on the *Let's Dance* album – jumped ship on the eve of the *Serious Moonlight* tour.

"I came to save the day again," Slick says, recalling that he only got the call two days before the tour began. "I'm the go-to guy if the house is on fire!"

Slick never set out to be a firefighter. In a long and illustrious career, he has put out half-a-dozen or so albums under his own name and embarked on a string of collaborations in groups including Silver Condor, Phantom, Rocker and Slick, and late-80s glam rockers Dirty White Boy.

After performing again with Bowie on his *Heathen* tour and his *Reality* album and tour, Slick reconnected with DB for the last time for *The Next Day*. Had Bowie changed?

"He really wasn't any different," replies the guitarist. "He just wasn't working as many hours. There were no health issues that I was aware of. He looked fine. I couldn't tell you anything that was happening in David's life outside of music because he was very private – as I am. It's not that I want to hide anything, it's just that it's none of your fucking business."

Bowie, nevertheless went to remarkable lengths to keep secret the fact that he was even recording an album, requiring Slick – along with everyone else involved – to sign a non-disclosure document.

"Why not?" Slick says. "It's his record. He wants it quiet, he gets it quiet. It was a one-page document that just said 'Shut up'.

"As a sideman, your whole thing is to make sure that guy that's in front of you, you've got his back. You've got it on stage and you've got it in the studio. 'Cause it's not your name on the marquee. It's his name and you've got to do everything you can to make sure he's got the band behind him. That's your fucking gig, man." ●

ACHTUNG, BABY!

Holed up in Germany with partner-in-crime Iggy Pop, David Bowie released three albums between 1977 and 1979 that redefined him entirely – *Low*, *"Heroes"* and *Lodger*. This is the story of the Berlin Trilogy.

Words: **Ian Fortnam** ||||||||||||||||||||||||||||||||||||

L ife in Los Angeles was killing David Bowie. He'd moved to the city to begin work on Nicolas Roeg's science fiction drama movie *The Man Who Fell To Earth* in July 1975, but a cocaine addiction he'd developed the previous summer had caused him to develop a series of damaging obsessions, not least with the occult.

Not sleeping for days, paranoid and delusional, he'd avidly read texts on religion, magic, the Third Reich, Nietzsche, Crowley and then habitually coke-babble half-considered concepts to a grateful press. He was teetering on the brink of losing everything.

Despite Bowie's chemical-induced fall-out with reality, he retained a degree of self-awareness and a desire to get clean. To this end he made a decision to relocate to Europe. Having remade the acquaintance of ex-Stooge Iggy Pop he was determined to record with him, and where better than away from temptation at the Château d'Hérouville in France?

After all, he was suddenly in need of a project upon which to focus his mind, as he'd just abandoned work on *The Man Who Fell To Earth* soundtrack. When informed he'd have to present his work alongside other composers just like any other candidate, he'd chosen to abandon the project, retaining *Subterraneans* for later use on *Low*, the first of three albums latterly corralled as The Berlin Trilogy. Upon *Low*'s eventual release, Bowie sent it to Roeg with the note: "This is what I wanted to do for the soundtrack. It would have been a wonderful score."

As Bowie's Isolar tour progressed from the US to Europe in the Spring of 1976, Iggy joined the entourage as Bowie's constant companion and on arrival at Wembley, the singer bumped into Brian Eno. Turning on the charm, Bowie revealed he'd been avidly listening to Eno's ambient album *Discreet Music*, released the previous year. "Naturally, flattery always endears you to someone," Eno admitted, "I thought, God, he must be smart."

Bowie had long been an admirer of Eno, especially *Another Green World* (1975) with its short pastoral instrumentals and inspired guitar interjections from King Crimson's Robert Fripp. Bowie and Eno had an enormous amount in common, not least a shared fondness for krautrock, and vowed to keep in touch.

I n June 1976, with the Isolar tour behind them, Bowie and Iggy arrived at the 18th century Château d'Hérouville on the outskirts of Paris (where Bowie had recorded *Pin-Ups*), and set to work on recording Iggy's new album, *The Idiot*.

While the album would provide an experimental bridge between Bowie's *Station To Station* and its follow-up *Low*, its recording was relatively haphazard, and the fruits of Bowie and Iggy's Château-based labours more demo-level ▷

> "I like the friction. I can't write in a peaceful atmosphere at all."
> **David Bowie**

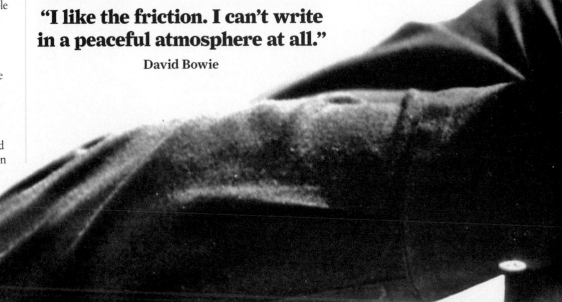

GETTY

"Poor Iggy became a guinea pig for what I wanted to do with sound."

David Bowie

recordings than releasable product. The album would ultimately constructed in post-production at Berlin's Hansa Tonstudio by Tony Visconti. Bowie's long-time producer, who'd been absent from *Station To Station* due to scheduling difficulties, had returned to the fold after ringing Bowie and boasting of a device that "Fucks with the fabric of time". It was this Eventide Harmonizer that would give *Low* its signature snare sound.

In its final incarnation, *The Idiot* proved to be something of a classic, though it wasn't so much an Iggy album per se, as a dry run for a sound, or perhaps more accurately, a mood which Bowie latterly perfected in his Berlin Trilogy.

"Poor [Iggy] became a guinea pig for what I wanted to do with sound," Bowie admitted, "I didn't have the material at the time and I didn't feel like writing at all. I felt much more like laying back and getting behind someone else's work, so that album was opportune, creatively."

Work on *The Idiot* concluded in August 1976, but Bowie was determined to get his own album recorded and released first, so it remained on ice until March 1977.

*L*ow (working title *New Music: Night And Day*) was recorded between September and October 1976. Completed at Hansa, its groundwork took place at Château d'Hérouville.

Brian Eno arrived late for the sessions (after backing tracks for the album's first side were almost done), so while he can't be credibly credited as *Low*'s co-producer, his influence on the album's second side is incalculable.

While the first side's material seems fragmented, the work of a distracted mind, *Low*'s Eno-influenced flip, four near-ambient impressions of Bowie's surroundings, comes across as more complete, rounded, stylistically assured.

Opening with a swift fade into a scene-setting vocal-free *Speed Of Life*, it's immediately clear *Low* is no ordinary David Bowie album. He finally makes his presence felt on the intriguingly brief *Breaking Glass*, six-lines of cinematic jump-cuts offering insight into the actuality of Bowie's coke madness: *"Don't look at the carpet/I drew something awful on it."* Bowie chalked out the Kabbalistic Tree Of Life at the peak of his occult obsession. *"See!"* he demands, revelling in his madness, before coldly concluding, *"I'll never touch you."*

Low continues with the lust-driven alienation of *What In The World*, before the

Above: With Iggy in West Germany, 1977.

Right: Playing live in Tokyo during 1978.

album's lead *Sound And Vision* single – an admission of the creative bankruptcy that hastened *Low*'s drastic change of tack. Visconti's then wife Mary Hopkin's 'Doo-Doo-Doo' backing vocals were the album's only real concession to traditional pop and recorded as part of the musical backdrop rather than as counterpoint to the lyric. As with the rest of the album, lead vocals were written and recorded at the tail end of the production process.

There are only two more 'songs' on *Low*, and they're hardly inspired: *Always Crashing In The Same Car*'s tarted-up anecdotage (Bowie had recently crashed his Mercedes in Switzerland) and *Be My Wife*'s short, sharp, normality-craving cry for help.

The central reason why *Low* and follow-up *"Heroes"* are largely instrumental is that Bowie was suffering with a writer's block in the lyric department. He wasn't writing songs like he used to, because he couldn't. He could use Iggy as lyricist in the context of *The Idiot* and *Lust For Life* (and would again circa *Tonight* when suffering another bout of block), but when push came to shove, he had to find another way of working around his on-going inability to spew out lyrics in quite the same inspired way he had previously.

At root of Bowie's problems was a short attention span: he'd done the rock poet bit, and was heartily sick of it, as he revealed in 1978: "(Eno) got me off narration which I was intolerably bored with. Narrating stories, or doing little vignettes of what at the time I thought was happening in America and putting it on my albums in a convoluted fashion. Singer-songwriter askew… And Brian really opened my eyes to the idea of processing, to the abstract of communication."

Unbound from the constraints of poetry, where carefully contrived words could get in the way of pure emotional expression, Bowie was free to communicate solely via musical impressions (*Warszawa*'s coldly oppressive funeral doom), with human voices used only as lyric-free ornature (the evocative phonetic murmurings of *Subterraneans*).

He'd attempted to escape the demanding role of lyricist and partially automate the poetic process as far back as *Diamond Dogs* by adopting William Burroughs and Brion Gysin's cut-up method. He'd sometimes even randomise composition, get musicians to improvise over a drumbeat, then pick those parts which worked best in tandem (irrespective of key) as a track's basis. It's a technique that positively reeks of Eno, whose boundary-breaking production concepts were often suggested by Burroughs-ian 'Oblique Strategies' cards. Printed with vague gnomic instructions ('use an old idea', 'what would your best friend do?'), Eno's cards were deployed to a far greater extent during the recording of *"Heroes"* and *Lodger*.

U pon delivery, Bowie's record company RCA didn't like *Low* anymore than they had liked (the still unreleased) *The Idiot*. Tony Visconti recounted an incident where, upon hearing *Low*, an RCA executive told Bowie: "If you make *Young Americans II* instead, we'll buy you a mansion in Philadelphia".

Somehow, Bowie's former manager Tony DeFries, who still had a 16 per cent stake in Bowie's output until 1982, heard a copy of the album and, because it 'didn't sound like a David Bowie record' decided to protect his 'investment' by lobbying contacts at RCA to block its release. DeFries found sympathetic, like-minded ears at RCA, and *Low*'s original pre-Christmas release was delayed until January 14. It reached No.2 in the UK charts, while the single *Sound And Vision* hit No.3 – his biggest British hit since *Sorrow* four years earlier (the US was less receptive – the album and single peaked at No.11 and No.69 respectively).

RCA remained unconvinced of *The Idiot*'s commercial potential, and only grudgingly released it in the wake of the chart success of Bowie's *Sound And Vision*. Iggy had returned to the road two weeks prior to its release with Bowie on keyboards, and while Bowie's low-profile presence may not have distracted the audience's attention

Above: At London's Dorchester Hotel, 1977.

Right: performing on a Christmas TV special with Bing Crosby in 1977.

> ## "He wrote *Lust For Life* in front of the TV on a ukulele."
> ### Iggy Pop

from Iggy, his involvement certainly sold a lot of tickets.

Variously described as 'dark', 'morbid' and 'disturbing' at the time of its release, *The Idiot*, a touchstone for post-punk, goth and electronica, was on Ian Curtis's turntable when the Joy Division vocalist committed suicide.

Following the Iggy tour, work commenced on *Lust For Life* in Berlin, but Bowie's influence is nowhere near as obvious as on *The Idiot*. Retaining Hunt and Tony Sales on drums and bass respectively from the tour, Ricky Gardiner joined on guitar. Bowie co-wrote material, but left the arrangement to Iggy and musical director, Carlos Alomar, his mind clearly on *"Heroes"*.

While *The Idiot* had provided a handy sketchbook with which to try out rough

drafts of the new Bowie sound, Iggy had served his purpose, and Bowie's mind was mostly elsewhere. The American later admitted Bowie co-opted most of the basic structures for *Lust For Life* co-writes from existing rock standards – he was clearly saving his best for himself.

The album's title track was, according to Iggy, written by Bowie, "in front of the TV on a ukulele… He cribbed the rhythm of this army forces network theme, which was a guy tapping out the beat on a morse code key."

But the album itself, with the riff-driven *The Passenger* at its core, was significantly more Iggy than Bowie: loose-limbed, groove-based and steeped in Detroit-born brink-dwelling rock'n'roll.

Work on *"Heroes"* (described by Visconti as "a very positive version of *Low*") ▷

commenced in July 1977. The existing *Low* band – Carlos Alomar (guitar), George Murray (bass), Dennis Davis (drums) and Eno – remained in place, but were augmented by King Crimson's Robert Fripp, whose own band had split two years earlier and who laid down his distinctive and complementary lead guitar parts in just three days.

The vocal material on *"Heroes"'* first side finds Bowie more confident in his new sound. He knows what it is, and having identified an optimum template, delivers the Berlin Trilogy's defining moment in style. *"Heroes"'* title track is an emotional epic, a towering triumph, the apogee of the Berlin period. Aside from Bowie's gloriously histrionic vocal performance. It's a basic two-chord trick save for the odd vocal crescendo but, when powered by Eno's trio of oscillating VCS3 drones and three simultaneously soaring guitar arcs from Fripp, it's simply irresistible.

Released in three languages (as *"Héros"* in France and *"Helden"* in Germany),

this simple love song, inspired by Bowie watching a pair of lovers (latterly revealed to be Visconti and nightclub singer Antonia Maas) kissing in the shadow of the Berlin Wall is widely held to be David Bowie's magnum opus, though, when released in the UK as a single in September 1977, three weeks prior to the album, it only managed to peak at No.24.

Every element of *"Heroes"* was recorded in Berlin's Hansa Tonstudio. Bowie, Eno and Visconti were on a roll, but while it should be better than *Low*, it falls somehow short. The wall's oppressive influence is just too strong. It's bleak without being playful, there's an all-pervasive gloom (the chilling *Sense Of Doubt*), a wallowing doom (the robotic, melodrama of Anthony Newley-channeling *Sons Of The Silent Age*, the only song Bowie brought to the studio at the start of recording) and an industrial chill (the wilfully teutonic *V-2 Schneider*).

With Iggy absent, Bowie's extra-curricular activities were not quite so tightly focused on getting hammered in

nightclubs. He was going to art galleries with Visconti, stroking his chin over Oblique Strategies with Eno. His move to Berlin had been successful on both an artistic and personal level. He was living a reasonably normal life, had grown a moustache, excised the dye from his neatly cut hair and mooched about the place in checked shirt and jeans. He was able to be David Jones again, even pass for a native. But, aside from the joys of anonymity, the city's essential edge offered an ample portion of grit for his creative oyster: "I like the friction… I can't write in a peaceful atmosphere at all. I've nothing to bounce off. I need the terror."

"Heroes", released at the height of UK punk's first wave, was marketed under the bullish slogan: 'There's old wave, there's new wave, and there's David Bowie…'

Touring throughout 1978, the Isolar II tour, commemorated in the double live *Stage* album, proliferated the new Berlin-era Bowie persona with an unbroken block of selections from the instrumental backsides of *Low* and *"Heroes"*, though cannily offsetting them with a collection of songs from *The Rise and Fall of Ziggy Stardust and the Spiders from Mars*.

Eternally progressive he may have been, but he still knew how to please a crowd, and he wasn't about to turn his back on commerciality anytime soon, as financially speaking, he was still suffering the effects of early 70s MainMan excess and mismanagement.

Despite the fact the Berlin spell was broken when Bowie set out on the nine-month Isolar II tour in March 1978, *Lodger* (working title: *Planned Accidents*) is still considered to be the third instalment of the Berlin Trilogy, when arguably *The Idiot* is a far better fit stylistically. While *Lodger* had a great deal in common with its two most recent predecessors – Eno randomising, Visconti producing, fashioned in Europe (Mountain Studios, Switzerland), Isolar II tour sideman/future King Crimson frontman Adrian Belew on hand to provide Fripp-alike stunt guitar – it's a far more conventionally-structured, if still doggedly experimental, Bowie album.

Rather than seeking to refine what had gone before, *Lodger* comes across as a feet-finding exercise in advance of the coming decade, a post-punk, position-reassessing mishmash of styles, and is only considered to be the third instalment in the Berlin Trilogy because Bowie said it was during

> ## "Eno really opened my eyes to the idea of processing, to the abstract of communication."
> ### David Bowie

Above: Pictured in a scene from his 1978 film *Just A Gigolo* during its West Berlin shoot.

Left: Iggy Pop playing on tour for *The Idiot* in 1977 with Bowie on keyboards.

its promotion. And he probably only said it because he had to say something. It was a handy handle for journalists to grab onto, and it certainly worked; we've been dutifully trotting out the same line ever since. Presenting *Lodger* as the final instalment of a Trilogy (or 'Triptych' as Bowie preferred to define it) served to legitimise its haphazard combination of styles, though rather than being *Low Part III* it's possibly better, more accurately, described as *Scary Monsters Part I*.

While Eno's influence on the album was outwardly minimal by comparison to *Low* and *"Heroes"* – there were no ponderous instrumentals on *Lodger*, let alone an entire second side of them – his Oblique Strategies often held sway in the studio. Hence Alomar, Davis and Murray swapping instruments to record *Boys Keep Swinging* (which shared its chord structure with *Fantastic Voyage*), reversing *All The Young Dudes*' chords for *Move On* and revisiting *The Idiot's Sister Midnight* with a new lyric (*Red Money*).

Eno's Oblique Strategy cards were designed to 'instruct random actions in order to bypass creative blocks', but there's very little suggestion of such stasis on *Lodger* (working title: *Planned Accidents*).

Elsewhere, *D.J.* deftly deals with the vacuity of celebrity, *Look Back In Anger* documents an encounter with the Angel Of Death, and *Repetition* tackles the horrific mundanity of routine domestic violence. An influential precursor of much of the appropriated world music to come in the 80s (*Yassassin*'s Turkish/Middle Eastern-reggae, *African Night Flight*'s deployment of pidgin Kiswahili), *Lodger* was a wide-ranging musical travelogue with Berlin only one of its many destinations. If there was a conceptual link between *"Heroes"* and *Lodger*, it's *The Secret Life Of Arabia*, *"Heroes"'* half-hearted, yet over-sold, shape-of-things-to-come afterthought.

Low's influence reached the mainstream by the time of *Lodger*'s arrival two years later (a long time in 70s pop), its May 1979 release coincident with that of Tubeway Army's *Are 'Friends' Electric?*, which rose to the UK No.1 in the following month.

Obviously, Bowie was no stranger to reinvention as he sought to reboot his coke-hobbled career in 1976, but why the Berlin Trilogy? Why the embrace of Brian Eno's quasi-classical instrumental ambient tropes at this particular time and stage of his career?

Bowie was about to turn 30. No age now, but at the time a very big deal indeed. This was the age at which, as punk dawned, one became a 'boring old fart'. He'd seen it happen to Jagger, and while no one had actually aimed that particular epithet at Bowie yet, it was surely only a matter of time.

It's therefore possible that with *Low*'s, and *"Heroes"'*, post-Kosmische, Eno-ised instrumentals the steadily ageing pop idol was endeavouring to create more adult-targeted Bowie music. Music that would take him out of the generational rock market, where youth was still seen as the most important, if not essential, asset of any serious contender, and ultimately redefine him as the biggest star in his own particular musical firmament.

That said, *Low*'s first side was incredibly punk-friendly. Very 1977. Its songs were the antithesis of rock cliché and boasted an en vogue brevity, while Bowie himself sounded gloriously bored, even to the point of nihilistically *"Breaking Glass in my room again"*.

How punk was that?

Brian Eno, meanwhile, presents a far simpler reason for Bowie's drastic mid-career volte face: "He was trying to… duck the momentum of a successful career."

But the juggernaut of stardom is not the easiest entity to bring to a halt. ❼

David Bowie

"Heroes"

Although Bowie's Berlin-period anthem was initially something of a commercial failure, it became his most life-changing single.

Words: **Bill DeMain**

One afternoon in July 1977, David Bowie was looking out of the window of Hansa Studio in Berlin when he noticed a couple kissing near the Berlin Wall.

"I always said it was a couple of lovers by the Wall that prompted the idea for *"Heroes"*," Bowie tells *Classic Rock*. "Actually, it was [Bowie producer] Tony Visconti and his girlfriend. Tony was married at the time, so I couldn't talk about it. But I can now say that the lovers were Tony and a German girl [Antonia Maass] that he'd met while we were in Berlin. I think possibly his marriage was in the last few months. And it was very touching because I could see that Tony was very much in love with this girl, and it was that relationship which sort of motivated the song."

The basic track had already been started by Bowie and Brian Eno in the weeks before, with Visconti behind the mixing desk. Their working method during Bowie's so-called 'Berlin period' was to build layered tracks that would later inspire lyric and melody, like making the frame before the picture. And using Eno's 'oblique strategies' cards (aphorisms that encouraged lateral thinking), they would often give themselves creative dilemmas within that frame.

"Maybe I'd write out five or six chords," Bowie explains, "then discipline myself to write something only with those five or six chords involved. So that particular dogma would dictate how the song is going to come out, rather than me and my sense of emotional self."

On a broader level, living in Berlin itself was an oblique strategy for Bowie. As he said at the time: "I find that I have to put myself in those situations to produce any reasonably good writing. I've still got that same thing about when I get to a country… I have to put myself on a dangerous level, whether emotionally or mentally or physically, and it resolves in things like that: living in Berlin, leading what is quite a spartan life for a person of my means, and in forcing myself to live according to the restrictions of that city."

Bowie threw his restricted chord progression out to the band, and they ran with it, building an eight-minute groove into a triumphant crescendo. The underlying riff of *"Heroes"* came from guitarist Carlos Alomar, with the hypnotic pulse provided by bassist George Murray and drummer Dennis Davis. "With such great musicians the notes were never in doubt," Bowie later said. "We looked at 'feel' as being the priority."

From the start, Eno described the music as "grand and heroic", and said he had "that very word, 'heroes', in mind." After the basic track was done, he overdubbed shuddering atmospherics by twiddling knobs on his EMS Synthi, a mini-synthesizer built into a briefcase.

The final touch was added by guitarist Robert Fripp. What the King Crimson leader later called "hairy rock'n'roll" was more a soaring series of aria-like feedback loops. Fripp marked with adhesive tape the spots on the studio floor where he could lock into certain singing tones. For a guitarist known for playing while seated, it's interesting that one of his most enduring performances came from stepping and swaying.

The finished track sat for weeks. There have been rumours that *Heroes* was intended as an instrumental (hence Fripp's wall-to-wall soloing). But Bowie says he was just waiting for the right lyrical spark, which eventually came from the lovers by the Wall.

Delivered in one of his greatest vocal performances, the us-against-the-world theme of his lyric was full of odd poetic touches, like the lines about the dolphins. As Bowie says, he often used a William Burroughs-inspired cut-up method of writing, taking random text from a book or magazine and reshuffling it.

"I'll use that idea to provoke a new set of images for me," he explains, "or a new way of looking at a subject. I still find it incredibly useful as a writer's tool. And I'm amazed these days at the amount of cut-up sites that are now on the internet. It's quite phenomenal. There are at least ten, and two or three of them are excellent. I've used them too. I've put a bunch of pieces

of text into the thing, then hit the 'cut-up' button and it slices it up for me."

"Heroes" was released as a single in September 1977. It only reached No.24 in the UK, and didn't chart at all in the US. But the emotional power of the song would continue to resonate, as it became one of Bowie's theme songs, along with the likes of *Space Oddity* and *Changes*.

Its most memorable moment would come 10 years later, when he performed it live at the Platz der Republik Festival, right across from the studio in Berlin where it was conceived.

"I'll never forget that," he recalls. "It was one of the most emotional performances I've ever done. I was in tears. They'd

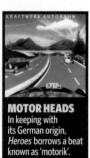

MOTOR HEADS
In keeping with its German origin, *Heroes* borrows a beat known as 'motorik'. Associated with Krautrock bands such as Can, Kraftwerk and Neu!, the word is a combination of 'motor' and 'musik'. And indeed motorik has a kind of relentless, forward-feeling motion to it, almost like driving down an open motorway. Other motorik songs include *Autobahn* by Kraftwerk, *Hallogallo* by Neu! and *I Can't Stay Long* by Ultravox.

Bowie during recording at Hansa, with Robert Fripp (left) and Brian Eno (right).

CORBIS

backed up the stage to the Wall itself so that it was acting as our backdrop. We kind of heard that a few of the East Berliners might actually get the chance to hear the thing, but we didn't realise in what numbers they would. And there were thousands on the other side that had come close to the wall. So it was like a double concert, where the Wall was the division. And we would hear them

cheering and singing along from the other side. God, even now I get choked up. It was breaking my heart. I'd never done anything like that in my life. And I guess I never will again.

"When we did *Heroes* it really felt anthemic, almost like a prayer," Bowie continues. "I've never felt it like that again. However well we did it later, it was almost like walking through it

compared to that night because it meant so much more. That's the town where it was written, and that's the particular situation that it was written about. It was just extraordinary.

"In 2002 we did it in Berlin again. This time, what was so fantastic – it was in the Max Schmeling Hall, which holds about ten to fifteen thousand – is that half the audience had been in East Berlin that time way before. So now I was face-to-face with the people I had been singing it to all those years ago. And we were all singing it together. Again, it was powerful. Things like that really give you a sense of what a song and performance can do." ❶

"[By the Wall] was one of the most emotional performances I've ever done. I was in tears... God, even now I get choked up."

THE FACTS
RELEASE DATE
September 1977
HIGHEST CHART POSITION
UK No.24
PERSONNEL
David Bowie
Vocals, saxophone, piano
Robert Fripp
Lead guitar
Carlos Alomar
Rhythm guitar
George Murray
Bass
Dennis Davis
Drums
Brian Eno
EMS Synthi synthesiser, treatments
WRITTEN BY
David Bowie & Brian Eno
PRODUCERS
Tony Visconti & David Bowie
LABEL
RCA

'I've Never Done Anything Out Of The Blue...'

After the minimalism of his 'Berlin trilogy', in 1980 **David Bowie** and his long-time producer Tony Visconti went all out for a kitchen-sink art-rock album. "We wanted to make our *Sgt. Pepper*!" The result: *Scary Monsters*.

Words: **Bill DeMain**

B y the end of the 1970s, Major Tom had been 'sitting in a tin can' for 10 years, his circuits all but dead. Meanwhile, back at ground control, his alter-ego had turned into a succession of slightly more terrestrial sorts: Ziggy Stardust, Aladdin Sane, the Thin White Duke.

Then, just when it seemed that everyone's favourite rock'n'roll astronaut would remain marooned in space for ever, he re-entered our orbit. First there was the stark '79 remake of *Space Oddity*. Next, the following year, came *Ashes To Ashes*, the hypnotic and funky update and centerpiece of *Scary Monsters (And Super Creeps)*. Not only did both song and album carry David Bowie back to the top of the charts, establishing his 80s artistic reputation, it also served as a powerful look back that mourned, mocked and sampled his own mythology.

"*Scary Monsters* always felt like some kind of purge," Bowie told me in 2003. "You think: 'How do you distance yourself from the thing that you're within?' I felt I was on the cusp of something absolutely new. There were no absolutes. Nothing was necessarily true, but everything was true. It was this sense of: 'Wow, you can borrow the luggage of the past, you can amalgamate it with things that you've conceived could be in the future and you can set it in the now.'"

If that seems like a heady vision for an album, there was some precedent. "David and I had ➤

"*Scary Monsters* was a new awakening. The intention was up-tempo, high-energy songs. It was to hit them right between the eyes."

Guitarist Carlos Alomar

a running joke," producer Tony Visconti tells *Classic Rock*.

"It was: 'Let's make this next record our *Sgt. Pepper!*' The Berlin records – *Low*, *"Heroes"* and *Lodger* – were all done in five weeks each. You can't exactly make a *Sgt. Pepper* in that time frame. On *Scary Monsters* we decided to give ourselves the luxury to think of every possible thing we could do. That was the premise. And we took ourselves very seriously."

Carlos Alomar, Bowie's guitarist and key collaborator, tells *Classic Rock*: "*Scary Monsters* was a new awakening. The intention was up-tempo, high-energy songs. It was to hit them right between the eyes."

At the start of the 80s, Bowie was dividing his time between a home in Switzerland and a flat in London. He'd finalised the divorce from his wife Angie, and having spent the previous three years in relative anonymity in Berlin he wanted to plug into a different energy. New York City was, as Alomar says, "the shot of adrenaline that he needed", so he rented a midtown apartment at 26th & 8th, next door to the guitarist's. "Our building was right behind the Fashion Institute of Technology," Alomar says. "When they found out that David lived there, oh my god, they would just ring the buzzer night and day."

Manhattan at the time still had a late-70s hangover of drugs, crime, experimental art and punk. Bowie, both mentor and friend to bands like Talking Heads, Blondie and Television, loved the "sense of urgency about the place. Wherever I'm writing, that place tends to make itself very known," he told me. "Either in the atmosphere or sound. New York feels very *street*."

But the Power Station, where they recorded, was anything but street. "Out from the cave of Berlin, David wanted a studio that was bigger-than-life, with all the bells and whistles," Alomar says.

"There was nothing like it," Visconti says. "It was built by a musician/producer. He'd modelled it after Motown's Hitsville studio, where he'd worked. It was twenty-four-track, and every

GETTY

Bowie with key *Scary Monsters* collaborator Carlos Alomar on the Serious Moonlight Tour, in support of *Let's Dance*, in '83.

Clown Prince

The making of the video for *Ashes To Ashes*.

"The discussion for *Ashes To Ashes* was: 'I want to be a clown, I want to be on the beach and I want some modern romantics with me,'" director David Mallet said of what was then the most expensive pop video ever made.

Featuring Bowie in the Pierrot costume (a nod to his apprenticeship with mime artist Lindsay Kemp) that became the visual representation of *Scary Monsters*, the beach scenes were shot in East Sussex. Among his clown posse was Steve Strange, the New Romantic face of the Blitz Kids, named after the London club where they hung out. There were also scenes of Bowie as Major Tom, in a padded cell and some kind of HR Giger-like space womb. Through

a very early use of computer graphics, the video's color palette was rendered in jarring reverse negatives, all pink ocean and black sky.

As ground-breaking as the clip was (it set the bar for big-budget videos by Madonna and Michael Jackson), Bowie would remember it for a different reason. Filming was interrupted by an old man walking his dog, looking for driftwood on the beach. Mallet asked him if he would mind moving, and pointed to Bowie sitting outside the catering van. "Do you know who this is?" Mallet asked. The old man looked, then said: "Of course I do. It's some c**t in a clown suit." Bowie later said: "That was a huge moment for me. It put me back in my place and made me realise: 'Yes, I'm just a c**t in a clown suit.'"

else was sketches with working titles."

Working "strict hours", from 11am to 7pm, Bowie and Visconti put the core band of Alomar, drummer Dennis Davis and bassist George Murray through their paces, developing those sketches into finished tracks, while Bowie improvised vocal ideas.

"I wanted to make sure that this album had me, George and Dennis being totally forceful," says Alomar, who was Bowie's musical director. "I wanted songs with defined beginnings and endings that had signature lines, with complexity. But we also left holes for other players, and for David to shape his melodies. We might present him with five different arrangement ideas. He would accept all our offerings, then choose. When we heard what he liked, he gave you that smile and nodded. When it was wrong, he'd say: 'Um, it's okay.' And that 'okay' was the death knell. It meant: "Right, on to the next attempt."

Among the first wave of guest musicians brought in to give *Scary Monsters* its otherworldly vibe was Chuck Hammer, who had been making waves with his guitar synthesiser playing – which he dubbed 'guitarchitecture' – in Lou Reed's band.

"On my first day," Hammer recalls, "David called the studio to tell me he was going to be ten minutes late. Which was the opposite of Lou Reed, who could leave you waiting for hours. David was so polite. And he was only five minutes late. He walked in and really put me at ease, telling me how much he loved the tape of demos I'd given him. He was drinking a carton of milk and holding a clipboard, and dressed in a full-length leather coat with wooden Japanese sandals."

Hammer's first order of business was overdubbing on the track that would become

Ashes To Ashes, which Visconti remembers by its "working title *People Are Turning To Gold*".

"I love Tony, but he doesn't know everything about the background of the songs," says Hammer. "Bowie kept certain things from him. *Ashes To Ashes* started with a demo tape that I'd given to David of an instrumental piece called *Guitargraphy*. It had a descending chord structure. He appropriated it for *Ashes To Ashes*, in a much more brilliant manner than I ever would've envisioned it. I have no complaints. David appropriated art from other young artists in a totally positive way. I just started layering on guitar tracks, trying to make it sound like a choir. When I came in the control room, David said: "That's really beautiful, Chuck!" It was one of those moments where you knew you were part of something magical. I think the 1980s started with *Ashes To Ashes*."

Ashes To Ashes is, along with *"Heroes"* and *Life On Mars*, one of Bowie's greatest songs, and key to understanding his collage-like creative process. Getting at its true inspiration, Bowie told me: "It really came from *Inchworm*, by Danny Kaye. It was a song that he sang for the film of Hans Christian Andersen. I loved it as a kid and it's stayed with me forever. You wouldn't believe the amount of my songs that have sort of spun off that one song. *Ashes To Ashes* wouldn't have happened if it hadn't have been for *Inchworm*. There's a nursery rhyme element in it, and there's something so sad and mournful and poignant about it. It kept bringing me back to the feelings of those pure thoughts of sadness that you have as a child, and how they're so identifiable even when you're an adult."

After five weeks in New York, Bowie and Visconti had captured on tape what ▷

> ## "Scary Monsters always felt like some kind of purge... I felt I was on the cusp of something absolutely new."
>
> **David Bowie**

channel went through a tube amplifier. So we would get these warm, fat sounds, which thrilled us to no end.

"The other thing, which made us kind of antsy, but in a good way, was that Bruce Springsteen was recording next door," Visconti continues. "There was no cafeteria, just a small lounge shared by the two studios. So quite often we were having lunch with the E Street Band. And that's how Roy Bittan, Bruce's piano player, came to play on *Scary Monsters*. The Power Station was really a good place to make our *Sgt. Pepper* album."

Yet for such an ambitious endeavor, Bowie initially seemed under-prepared, arriving with song snippets and bits rescued from the past. "I've just got some chord changes," he told Visconti. "You know what I'm like."

"He only had lyrics for *It's No Game*, which was a song he supposedly wrote when he was sixteen," Visconti recalls. "So we only had one song on the album with a clear lyrical direction. Everything

David Bowie in concert in New York City in '81. But a tour in support of *Scary Monsters* was scrapped following the death of John Lennon.

Trusted partner: Tony Visconti at the mixing desk of his recording studio, Good Earth, in London, 1979.

sounded like the Sgt. *Pepper*-style future they'd had envisioned.

"David was overwhelmed with how great the tracks turned out," Visconti says. "He wanted to take three months off so he could write proper lyrics. We then reconvened at my studio, Good Earth, in London to record vocals."

"David had many tools in his vocal tool box," says Visconti. "He was just about the best singer I've ever worked with. He sings from his soul, from his spirit. My job was to step to the side when he was doing great, but I wasn't afraid to step in if I felt he could do something better. Sometimes he would challenge me and say: "Why?" And I'd give my reasons. Then he'd do another take. We were friends since 1967. The reason that we lasted so long together is because he trusted me."

With the vocals complete, they brought in King Crimson guitarist Robert Fripp. His squalling, dissonant blasts coloured seven songs, most notably *Fashion* and *Teenage Wildlife* (Fripp called his playing "very out"). Visconti: "David and Fripp would kind of grin at each other, as if to say: 'Let's dare each other how far out we can go!' And Fripp was always a joker. He'd crack the most obscure jokes, where it took a second or two for the penny to drop. He was a total joy to work with. He called David 'Mister B'. One thing you never called Bowie was 'Dave'. He would never let anyone call him that. But I think he liked Fripp calling him 'Mister B'."

Then there was Pete Townshend, who added power chords to *Because You're Young* and brought a darker vibe to the studio.

"This was in Pete's drinking days," says Visconti. "He just dropped by the studio, and then he said: 'Okay, I'll play guitar on a song.' David and I were afraid of him, because he was already slightly drunk. And he said: 'I'd like a bottle of wine.' I said: 'Red or white?' And he shouted at me: 'There's no such thing as white wine!' So we got him the best bottle of red we could find. He looked at us defiantly, wearing his guitar, and said: 'What do you want me to play?' And we obviously wanted him to play his windmill chords, but we were afraid that maybe he thought that was too cliché. Finally, I said: 'Um, we want you to play Pete Townshend chords.' 'Oh, okay!' Then he spent about forty-five minutes playing windmill chords."

Scary Monsters (And Super Creeps) was released in September 1980, and charted at No.1 the UK and No.12 in the US. *Ashes To Ashes* and *Fashion* were not only ubiquitous radio hits, but also video favorites on the newly launched MTV.

Bowie with his friend John Lennon in 1975. Bowie was deeply affected by Lennon's murder in 1980.

Although Bowie had plans to tour the album, with a satellite link to cinemas for select shows, he scrapped the idea after his friend John Lennon was shot dead in New York on December 8. Eerily, the killer, Mark David Chapman, reportedly had a front-row ticket to see Bowie in *The Elephant Man*, the Broadway play he was starring in, the following night. Also, in Chapman's hotel room police found a program for the play with a circle drawn around Bowie's name, and a photo of Bowie at the Booth Theatre stage door.

"We were living next door to each other, and he was just destroyed by John's death," Alomar recalls. "Destroyed. You must understand that David was living in New York with his son. He had just gotten to a great place in his life where he was coming back. He felt comfortable walking around the city. And then you find out that your friend, who also felt comfortable walking around, got shot – and you were supposed to be next? I can't put words in David's mouth about why he didn't tour. But in mourning someone dear to him, he had to have considered all precautions and cautions. It was necessary."

Three years later, Bowie turned towards the commercial sound of his *Let's Dance* album and a decade of increasingly conventional material. *Scary Monsters*, often called his last great album, seemed to end the experimental chapter of his career, until his mid-90s resurgence.

When we spoke, Bowie contemplated the idea of how isolation might have affected that change: "I probably reached a peak of a certain kind of writing at that time, where it worked for me being sort of pulled back from things in a bemused fashion. But what started off as more of an arty exercise ended up, because of my addictions, with me almost ostracizing myself from the rest of whatever society I was in. It became more of a mental health concern. And I think it led to a depression in my writing during the eighties. When I reemerged as being part of something or willing to have more of an affinity with the people around me, and obviously with my marriage, my writing improved beyond belief.

"It's the culmination of both my career and David's entire career up to then."

Tony Visconti

From the late eighties into the nineties, and onwards, I really like what I've written. I can't say that about the eighties."

Chuck Hammer, who has gone on to have a successful career doing TV and film soundtracks, says: "David Bowie is like an artistic portal, somebody people have to absorb in order to do any kind of current kind of art, whatever century we're in. You work your way through the masters to be knowledgeable. David is one of the masters. And *Scary Monsters* is a masterpiece."

Carlos Alomar, now a professor at Stevens Institute of Technology, and pre-Covid-19 pandemic was planning a 2020 tour of a show called The Soulfulness Of David Bowie, says: "I'm a collaborator, but I'm also a David Bowie fan. So when *Scary Monsters* came out, I bought the album and was just as excited as everybody else to hear it: 'Did my parts make the final cut?' 'Oh my god, I forgot I played that riff.' David always knew that he could throw a million things at me and I'd play my parts and it didn't matter to me if he used them or not. It heightened my anticipation of receiving David's new record and finding out if I did well in the overall outcome. To David's credit, he was a great listener, and had an innate sense of which pieces would fit together, like a jigsaw puzzle. When you put that puzzle together, you end up with *Scary Monsters*."

"*Scary Monsters* is my favorite record we made together," says Visconti, who produced Bowie's final two albums *The Next Day* and *Blackstar*. "It was the first one where we had the luxury of time on our side. We only signed off on it when we felt it was absolutely finished. It is dense. Not so much the amount of instruments, but everybody was playing complicated parts. It's like a Swiss watch. If you open up a Swiss watch you see all those tiny little wheels and hammers going. But no matter what's going on, it has to tell the time in the end. There was so much Swiss watch business going on in those tracks. That's why I love it. We did everything we could to make our *Sgt. Pepper*. It's the culmination of both my career and David's entire career up to then." ♦

For David Bowie in 1983, art rock and clown suits were in the past. He wanted to become a bona fide superstar – and he would recruit the man nicknamned The Hitmaker to help him achieve that ambition.

Words: **Scott Rowley** • • • • • • • • •

F••K ART LET'S DANCE

A new David Bowie was born on a beach near Hastings in the summer of 1980. Bowie was on location filming the video for *Ashes To Ashes*, the song that would become his second No.1 single when something happened, he said, that profoundly changed him.

Director David Mallet was filming Bowie as he walked up the beach dressed in the pierrot outfit he wore on the cover of *Scary Monsters (And Super Creeps)* when an old man and his dog walked into shot. The director and the crew yelled at the old guy, asking him to get out of the way. The man – who probably walked there every day – was unfazed: "Screw you," he said, "this is *my* beach".

So Bowie took a seat next to Mallet and waited for it to blow over. Eventually, the old guy is walking past and David Mallet says to him, "Do you know who this is?"

The old guy looked Bowie up and down. "Of course I do," he said. "It's some cunt in a clown suit."

Bowie thought it was hilarious ("That was a huge moment for me," he said later. "It put me back in my place and made me realise, yes, I'm just a cunt in a clown suit") but it had a wider impact. When he told the story years later, Bowie said that the incident "profoundly changed" him. The "whole facade," he said, "came crumbling down".

T hings were changing in the world of David Bowie. His relationship with manager Tony DeFries and Mainman finally ended in 1982 after a protracted split. *Scary Monsters* had been his last album for RCA, the label that had been his home since *Hunky Dory* in 1971. The label was milking his back catalogue with compilations – *Changes One, Changes Two, Rare* – and a new multi-million dollar deal with EMI offered a fresh start.

In an interview with *The Face* magazine before the release of *Let's Dance*, writer David Thomas suggested that EMI would be banking on *Let's Dance* repeating the success of the Rolling Stones' *Some Girls* album, a hugely successful record inspired by New York's disco scene.

"Absolutely," said Bowie. "The kind of enthusiasm they've shown is peculiar for me. I mean, I've never had that kind of thing shown to me for years!"

He talked about his older albums as sounding like historical artefacts. "I want something now," he said, "that makes a statement in a more universal international field."

A year earlier he'd bumped into Nile Rodgers in New York. "To me," Rodgers wrote in his autobiography *Le Freak*, "Bowie was on the same level as Miles and Coltrane, James Brown and Prince, Paul Simon and Jimi Hendrix, Joni Mitchell and Nina Simone. In other words, he was a genuine, creative artist, doing what I called 'that real shit'."

The two men bonded over a love of jazz. Rodgers had been brought up in a bohemian household where he'd come home to find "Thelonious Monk, Nina Simone, Miles Davis hanging at our apartment". As a guitar player he had been infatuated by jazz legends like Wes Montgomery and Django Reinhardt, and later the guitarists of Motown, and funk players like Eddie Hazel, Jimmy Nolen, Willie 'Beaver' Hale. Like Bowie, he was a walking musical encyclopedia and loved it all: rock, pop, soul, R'n'B, blues, jazz.

The meeting was a coincidence, but a lightbulb must have flickered in Bowie's head. Nile's band Chic – formed with bandmate and bass player Bernard Edwards – had become one of the most influential bands of the late 70s and early 80s. They had huge international hits – slick, funky, stylish tracks like *Good Times, Everybody Dance, Le Freak* – and, with their astonishing basslines and mercurial guitar playing, had inspired everyone from Queen to the Sugarhill Gang, from The Clash to the Blockheads. Elegant and cool, with grooves that could raise the dead, Rodgers was fresh from producing and co-writing Diana Ross's biggest album, 1980's *Diana*. People were calling him The Hitmaker.

The pair set about making a record together, Rodgers excited at the prospect of pushing boundaries with a big star who was plainly

> **"I wasn't very familiar with David's music when he asked me to play on the sessions."**
> Stevie Ray Vaughn

unafraid of experimenting. They listened to records they might take inspiration from. Bowie told *The Face* that he listened to "much older stuff" before making *Let's Dance* because he wanted to avoid modern trends. He wanted, he said, "things that I wasn't going to pull apart… Things like the Alan Freed Rock'n'Roll Orchestra and Buddy Guy, Elmore James… Albert King, Stan Kenton."

"We searched around listening to all these different records," Niles told the *Rolling Stone* podcast, *Music Now*. "We were just looking at everything from Hapshash and the Coloured Coat, Mott the Hoople, Peanut Butter Conspiracy. Like ridiculous stuff, from the hippiest hippie stuff to The Ventures."

Eventually, Nile played Bowie some material for a solo album he was working on. He explained how he had been trying to innovate and experiment, how he believed artists had to push boundaries, when Bowie stopped him.

"I want you to do what you do best," he said. "I want you to make hits."

T he first song they worked on was *Let's Dance*. Bowie strummed it on an acoustic to Rodgers who says it sounded like "Donovan meets Anthony Newley. And I don't mean that as a compliment."

"I felt that a lot of his songs were lacking in ear candy," he told *Rolling Stone*.

The song was so basic that Rodgers wondered if it was a test: "I just thought that he was [testing] me to see if I was a sycophant." He asked Bowie is he could try and arrange it differently. In video interviews since, Rodgers has demonstrated how he took the folk song, made it first jazzy ("I knew that he liked jazz") before making it brighter and choppier – into the weird mutant funk song we know today.

"I explained to him that every song I've ever written starts with the chorus," says Rodgers. "He says, 'Really? That's crazy – you build to the chorus'. I said, 'Yeah, well, if you're white, you build to the chorus.'"

Rodgers' theory was that radio stations gave black records less time to impress them, so ⊳

you had to cut to the chase: don't bore us, get to the chorus. He won the argument: After the Isley Brothers/Beatles *Twist And Shout*-inspired build-up, the chorus and the title are the first words out of David Bowie's mouth.

Bowie had another secret weapon up his sleeve. At the 1982 Montreux Jazz Festival he'd caught a performance by an up-and-coming blues guitarist called Stevie Ray Vaughan, whose Albert King-inspired playing was in sync with Bowie's listening at the time. "He completely floored me," Bowie said. "I probably hadn't been so gung-ho about a guitar player since seeing Jeff Beck with his [pre-Yardbirds] band, the Tridents."

Was Stevie Raynma Bowie fan? "To tell you the truth, I wasn't very familiar with David's music when he asked me to play on the sessions," he said later. "David and I talked for hours and hours about our music, about funky Texas blues and its roots. I was amazed at how interested he was."

Nile Rodgers had been tasked with putting together the band for the album. Worried that his Chic bandmates – Bernards Edwards and drummer Tony Thompson – were too deep into their drug use, he brought in Omar Hakim, at that point famous for Weather Report and Carly Simon, and bassist Carmine Rojas (then with Rod Stewart). Recording in New York's The Power Station, they nailed the title track in two takes.

In Rodgers's eyes, he'd been trusted to put the band together, "And then [Bowie] brings in this guy Stevie Ray Vaughan, who none of us had ever heard of."

The two guitar players soon became friends – Vaughan broke the ice by having barbecue from Texas flown in for all the musicians; Rodgers would later produce SRV's final album before his untimely death in 1990. Vaughan laid down fiery guitar parts on *Let's Dance*, reworkings of two older tracks: *China Girl* (co-written with Iggy Pop for Iggy's album *The Idiot*, 1977) and *Cat People* (co-written with and produced by Giorgio Moroder in 1981). His playing is the highlight of cover version *Criminal World*. It was a perfect collision of sounds, Vaughan bringing

With *Let's Dance* bassist Carmine Rojas (left) and Serious Moonlight tour musical director and longtime guitarist/band leader, Carlos Alomar.

passion and grit to a project that could sometimes have seemed slick and clinical.

The finished album divided Bowie fans. At just eight songs long, tracks like *Ricochet, Shake It* and *Criminal World* seemed like filler. On *Without You* – backed by Bernard Edwards and Tony Thompson of Chic – they channel *Avalon*-era Roxy Music. The new version of *Cat People* was more muscular. The singles did all the heavy lifting. As well as the title track, there was Rodger's reworking of *China Girl*, transformed from Iggy's muddy-dirge into a widescreen romance. *Modern Love* was a rock'n'soul pastiche with an infectious call-and-response structure.

> ## "It was great in its way, but it put me in a real corner in that it fucked with my integrity."
> David Bowie

All three singles featured large on MTV. The TV channel was changing the landscape of pop and and the video for *Let's Dance* unveiled the new Bowie. No longer "a cunt in a clown suit", he was tanned, with a blonde quiff and dangerous white teeth, singing an accessible, dance-able pop classic. The David Bowie of *Let's Dance* was a world away from the guy in the *Ashes To Ashes* video. Clean-cut, healthy, handsome, he was also unambiguously hetero: the video for *China Girl* featured him shagging on the beach in a nod to *From Here to Eternity*.

To the disappointment of many, in an interview with *Rolling Stone* he disavowed his past in no uncertain terms: "The biggest mistake I ever made [was saying] that I was bisexual," he said. "Christ, I was so young then. I was experimenting."

A generation of gay fans had felt liberated by Bowie's claim to be bisexual a decade earlier. Now, it started to look like a PR stunt, or like he was moving back into the closet to appease middle America. In 2002, he admitted as much to *Blender* magazine: "America is a very puritanical place, and I think [being known as a bisexual] stood in the way of what I wanted to do," he said. "I had no inclination to hold any banners or to be a representative of any type of people."

It was there on the record itself. Album track *Criminal World* was a cover version of a song by British art-rockers Metro. Released as a single in 1977, it had been banned by the BBC for its 'sexual content': allusions to cross-dressing and gay sex. Bowie's cover made plain his nervousness about his image.

The original's lyrics *"I'm not the queen so there's no need to bow/I think I see beneath your mink coat/I'll take your dress and we can truck on out"* are changed to *"I guess I recognize your destination/I think I see beneath your make-up/What you want is sort of separation"* and Metro's later reference *"I saw you kneeling at my brother's door/That was no ordinary stick up"* was changed to *"You caught me kneeling at your sister's door."* In the words of Bowie expert Chris O'Leary, he had "turned a gay-themed line into one that Vince Neil could've written."

The Serious Moonlight tour played three nights at Wembley in June 1983.

With all those sexual ambiguities out of the way, the door to the mainstream was kicked open. *Let's Dance* became Bowie's only single to go no.1 in the US and UK. The parent album went on to sell 11 million copies and turned Bowie into the international star he had wanted to be. By the end of 1983, it's estimated that he earned around $50 million.

Nile Rodgers didn't appear in the video for the title track or any of the follow-ups – *China Girl*, *Modern Love* – and Bowie didn't invite him on the road for The Serious Moonlight Tour. In fact, as Nile pointed out, "If you notice all the interviews that he did, very few of them talked about me."

Stevie Ray Vaughan had a similar experience. Originally, he explained later, he was just brought in for the album. "And then he asked me to do the tour, with Double Trouble opening up. It stopped because Double Trouble was really never ever included on the shows. He just wanted me to play with him."

Bowie had form, of course. In 1970, he had been a struggling singer-songwriter with two novelty hits behind him – *The Laughing Gnome* and *Space Oddity* – watching with envy as his friend Marc Bolan reinvented himself as a glam rock superstar. Mick Ronson and the Spiders From Mars reinvented Bowie musically and created some of rock's best-loved albums, only to be fired after an argument over money. Bowie was an amazing talent spotter, but he could be cold and callous when it came to the people who helped make him.

"I don't think that David had anything against me," Nile Rodgers told *Music Now*. "I think that he had what I would call survivor's guilt. Like: you're so successful you might be defined by this one record when your body of work is so vast.

"Looking at it from my perspective: that record [*Let's Dance*], I made. Period. End of story. I mean, yes, David sang. Yes, he wrote songs, but basically, the way we made the album? Here's what we did: We had a brand new studio and it had a really nice lounge. He went into the lounge, I made the record. He would walk in after we cut the track and he would listen and give a nod of approval. I never once had him say, 'Do that song again'. He never said that. If you look at all the years that have gone by, you've never heard any outtakes from *Let's Dance*."

Bowie had worked the same way previously on *Ziggy Stardust* and *Aladdin Sane*, revealing sketches to the band on an acoustic guitar, leaving them to work them up into the rock songs we know and love. *Jean Genie*, for example, "was knocked out in an hour on the second or third take," according to bassist Trevor Bolder.

"He didn't know one musician on that album," said Rodgers. "Other than me and Stevie Ray Vaughan. He had never heard Omar Hakim, didn't know anybody."

Maybe some of the critical responses to the album stung Bowie a little. From being the arty outsider, he was now a global superstar. Critics

Let's Dance guitarist Stevie Ray Vaughan in 1983.

With songwriter Otis Blackwell and *Let's Dance* producer, Chic's Nile Rodgers, at the Urban Contemporary Awards in 1983.

sniped that he had sold out, as though Nile Rodgers had forced him into making some terrible disco album. Back then, the mostly white music press was sceptical about pop music and dance music, which meant a genuine talent like Nile Rodgers, could struggle to be taken seriously. Pop geniuses could look like Brian Wilson or Phil Spector, but not Nile Rodgers.

In fact, *Let's Dance* helped break down divisions between black and white music. Famously, Bowie gave MTV a hard time for not showing enough black music on the channel. *Let's Dance* was at the vanguard of that, pioneering a post-punk dance music sound that defined the 80s.

In fact, as Bowie himself commented, "At the time, [*Let's Dance*] was not mainstream. It was virtually a new kind of hybrid, using blues-rock guitar against a dance format. There wasn't

> "David said to me in no uncertain terms that he wanted me to make a hit album."
> Nile Rodgers

anything else that really quite sounded like that at the time. So it only seems commercial in hindsight because it sold so many.

"It was great in its way, but it put me in a real corner in that it fucked with my integrity!" he said. "It was a good record, but it was only meant as a one-off project. I had every intention of continuing to do some unusual material after that. But the success of that record really forced me, in a way, to continue the beast. It was my own doing, of course, but I felt, after a few years, that I had gotten stuck…"

But it was his own doing. And it's revisionism to suggest that Bowie hadn't looked for hits in the past: *Space Oddity* was designed to cash-in on the Moon landing. From *Starman* to *Fashion* and *Ashes To Ashes*, Bowie wrote hits. He wasn't some avant-garde artist with no interest in the mainstream.

"David said to me in no uncertain terms that he wanted me to make a hit album," Nile said later. "Let's be very clear. A hit album, meaning he wanted every song to be popping like a Chic record or Sister Sledge."

He got what he wanted and more. ⊘

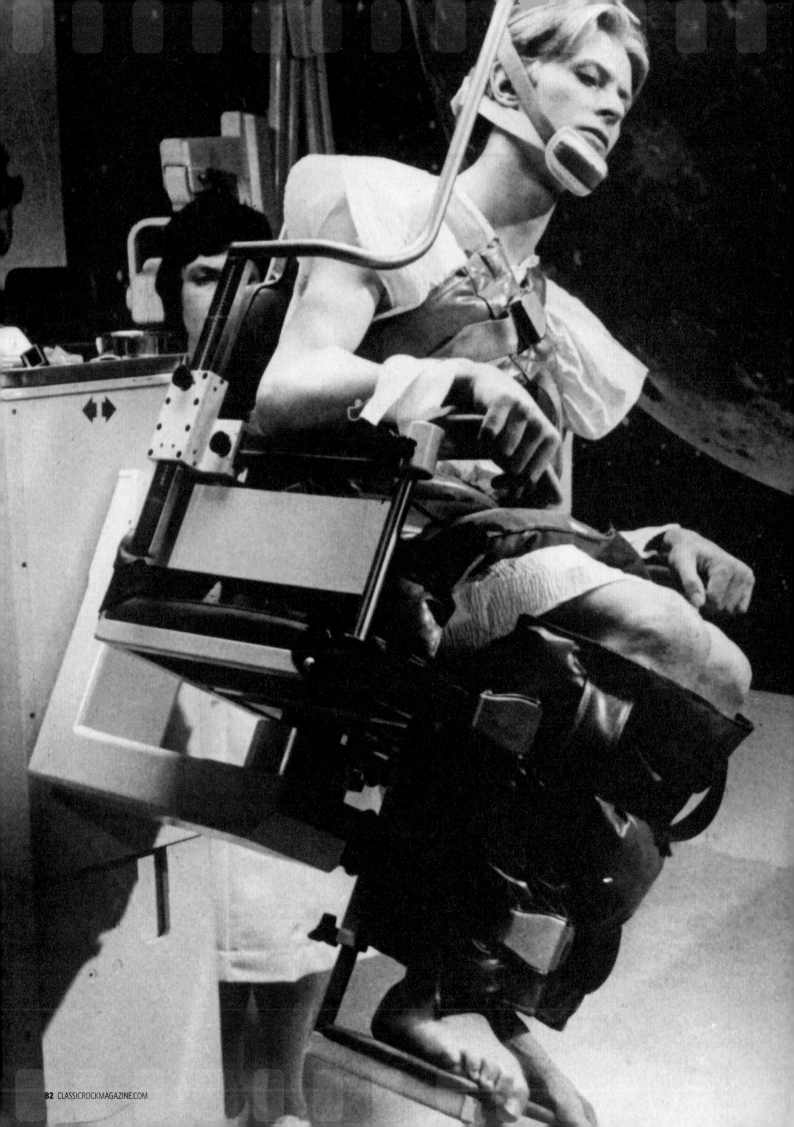

BOWIE ON FILM

FROM PASTY-FACED EXTRA-TERRESTRIALS
TO SPIKY-HAIRED GOBLIN KINGS,
THESE ARE BOWIE'S MOST MEMORABLE
SCREEN APPEARANCES.

Words: **Stephen Dalton**

The Man Who Fell To Earth (1976)

Bowie's first major screen role, as an extra-terrestrial tourist lost in the alien weirdness of America is rich in autobiographical echoes. Director Nicolas Roeg was a perfect fit for Bowie: both were visionary English mavericks who enjoyed a fertile imperial phase of creative originality and critical acclaim across the 1970s, each bringing avant-garde methods into the mainstream.

Bowie arrived for the New Mexico shoot during a period of heavy cocaine use, and reportedly struggled to keep his promise to Roeg not to use drugs on set. "I was stoned out of my mind from beginning to end," he later claimed.

Even if true, he still gives a radiant and magnetic star turn as Thomas Jerome Newton, a homesick alien trying to save his native planet from disaster, only to be sidelined by malign foes and earthly temptations. Bowie downplayed the film's space-travel angle, preferring to read the fable-like plot in more mythic terms. He told *Creem* magazine that Newton represents "man in his pure form who's corrupted or brought down by the corruption around him. But it's never definitely said where he comes from, and it really doesn't matter. I mean, he could come from under the sea, or another dimension, or anywhere. The important thing is what happens between the people. It's a very sad, tender love story that evolves over a long period of time."

Cryptic, hallucinatory and luminously beautiful, *The Man Who Fell To Earth* remains a landmark in cerebral science fiction cinema. It clearly struck a deep personal chord with Bowie, who revisited Newton at the end of his life in his hit stage musical, *Lazarus*.

Cracked Actor (1975)

The stars aligned in the summer of 1974 when Alan Yentob flew out to the US with a BBC film crew to shoot a documentary profile of Bowie around his Diamond Dogs tour. The pale, skeletal Englishman abroad they encountered was jittery and fragile, wired on cocaine and drowning in American pop culture. But they also caught an embryonic superstar on the cusp of morphing from alien glam rocker to chart-topping, zoot-suited plastic soulman with the *Young Americans* album.

Almost half a century later, *Cracked Actor* is firmly established as an essential piece of the Bowie canon. It is also one of the finest rock documentaries ever made, from its endlessly quotable druggy ramblings to its teasingly rare glimpses of Bowie's early 70s tours, which he would later regret failing to immortalise capture on film. Crucially, the striking image it projected of the exiled rocker as a milk-skinned, flame-haired stranger in a strange land, cruising America's desert hinterlands in the back of a limo, would inspire Nicolas Roeg to cast him as an actual alien.

"That was basically his screen test for *The Man Who Fell To Earth*," Yentob told the BBC in 2013. "The notion of this Martian let loose in America is of course what Nic Roeg was thinking of as well."

Just A Gigolo (1978)

Cementing his late 1970s love affair with Berlin, Bowie followed his triumphant starring debut in *The Man Who Fell To Earth* with this ill-fated period piece set in the German capital during Hitler's rise to power. Actor-director David Hemmings cast Bowie as Paul Ambrosius von Przygodski, a former Prussian officer traumatised by the Great War, who becomes a gigolo in 1920s Berlin.

An uneven mix of black comedy and serious drama, *Just A Gigolo* was released in 1978 to hostile reviews, and dropped out of circulation for decades. But critics who attacked Bowie's wooden performance "missed the point," according to Hemmings. "The whole point about that character is that he is a sponge," the director told me decades later. "He is supposed to be cold and somewhat thick. You don't get Ziggy Stardust if you want to see someone playing a German soldier who survived the war."

The film's poor reception sabotaged Bowie and Hemmings, whose planned concert film of Bowie's 1978 Stage tour was subsequently shelved and remains buried even today. Viewed through modern eyes, *Just A Gigolo* remains a mess, but a richly ambitious mess full of fascinating ingredients, including German screen legend Marlene Dietrich in her final role.

Ziggy Stardust And The Spiders From Mars (1979)

Bowie and his team summoned feted American documentary maker DA Pennebaker – director of the classic Bob Dylan tour chronicle *Don't Look Back* – to shoot Ziggy's rock'n'roll suicide farewell show at London's Hammersmith Odeon in July 1973.

The film was initially planned as a promotional short, but Pennebaker was sufficiently impressed by Bowie's electric charisma and theatrical vision to push for a full-length feature, blending live performance with backstage glimpses of the off-duty glam messiah and his entourage, including wife Angie and Ringo Starr.

The climactic shock announcement of Ziggy's symbolic death feels almost incidental now, but the raw footage of Mick Ronson and the Spiders in their proto-punk prime is exhilarating, with storming versions of *All The Young Dudes, Changes, Cracked Actor, Time,* a cover of VU's *White Light/White Heat,* and more.

Hampered by muddy sound, murky visuals and Bowie's reluctance to revisit his past, the film then spent almost a decade in limbo before its theatrical and video release. Later anniversary editions, digitally remastered and remixed, finally restored this historic velvet goldmine to its full flawed glory.

Merry Christmas, Mr. Lawrence (1983)

Drawing poise and stillness from his early mime training with Lindsay Kemp, Bowie gave one of his most refined acting performances in Japanese director Nagisa Oshima's elegant literary adaptation. Adapting Laurens van der Post's semi-autobiographical novel, *The Seed and The Sower*, Oshima cast Bowie as self-sacrificing British prisoner-of-war, Major Jack Celliers after seeing his role as Joseph Merrick in *The Elephant Man* on Broadway, noting that the star displayed "an inner spirit that is indestructible".

Set in a Japanese prison camp on Java in 1942, *Merry Christmas, Mr. Lawrence* is a poetic ruminaton on national honour, hidden shame and the unspoken homoerotic sadism of war. Bowie spent a month shooting the film on the Polynesian island of Rarotonga alongside co-stars including Tom Conti, Ryuichi Sakamoto and cult actor-director 'Beat' Takeshi. He later called Celliers "the most credible performance" he had given to that point. Many critics would agree that he never bettered it.

The Hunger (1983)

Tony Scott, brother of Ridley, made his directing debut with this stylish soft-porn vampire thriller set in contemporary New York. Bowie ages by several centuries as John Blaylock, a suave bloodsucker entangled in a bisexual love triangle with Catherine Deneuve and Susan Sarandon.

Memorably opening with a sinister nightclub seduction, superbly intercut with Bauhaus performing *Bela Lugosi's Dead*, the film was widely panned as glossy trash on release. But it has since amassed a cult reputation, not least as a rare big-screen document of the post-punk, goth, and new romantic subcultures that Bowie helped inspire. Life imitated art when Bowie and Sarandon began a brief off-screen romance, though she later declined his marriage proposal.

Bowie spoke fondly of *The Hunger* for years afterwards. "It really is a great opening," he told *Rolling Stone* in 1987. "It loses its way about there, but it's still an interesting movie."

Decades later, Scott said: "I loved Bowie in *The Man Who Fell To Earth*. One director who I've always looked up to, and stolen from, is Nic Roeg. *The Hunger* was a total rip-off of *Performance* with Mick Jagger."

Labyrinth (1986)

Bowie spent most of the late 1980s in creative limbo, later dismissing this period in his career as "simply dreadful". Signing up to play Jareth in *Labyrinth* – a goblin king who kidnaps a human baby in order to gain sinister power over his teenage sister Sarah (Jennifer Connelly) – could be dismissed as just another bizarre wrong turn in this lost decade.

Yet *Muppets* mastermind Jim Henson's fairytale puppet fantasy has endured over time, partly because of its feminist message about a young woman defying the authority of a controlling, entitled, older man. But also because the singer's playful, mischievous performance as a malevolent charmer with glam-metal hair and prominent trouser bulge made him a sex symbol to a whole new generation. Bowie contributed five songs to the soundtrack, claiming on official press notes that the role appealed because he wanted to be involved in a child-friendly film.

"The script itself was terribly amusing without being vicious or spiteful or bloody," he said, "and it had a lot more heart in it than many other special effects movies."

Absolute Beginners (1986)

Renowned today as a veteran punk-scene chonicler and rockumentary maestro, director Julien Temple almost destroyed his embryonic career with this over-hyped, patchy pop musical based on the feted Colin MacInnes novel about 1950s Soho. Temple had already tested Bowie's acting skills in 1984 with dual comedic roles in the Grammy-winning extended promo clip *Jazzin' For Blue Jean*. For *Absolute Beginners*, he cast the singer as oily advertising mogul Vendice Partners alongside a cast including Patsy Kensit, Ray Davies, James Fox, Robbie Coltrane and more.

The film was a critical and commercial bomb, but today it plays more like an admirably ambitious folly than total train wreck. And while Bowie's performance is stilted and stiff, his soaringly romantic title track for the film became one of his most beloved and successful singles, clothed in a stylish Temple-directed video. Speaking to *Empire* in 2017, Temple recalled Bowie's fondness for vintage British cinema: "he loved Tony Hancock and the Ealing comedies. He could watch Tony Hancock's *The Rebel* on a weekly basis and he would laugh and laugh."

Judging the walk-off scene in *Zoolander*.

Basquiat (1996)

As somebody who moved in the same arty-party circles as Andy Warhol, and even wrote a song about him on *Hunky Dory*, Bowie proved a good fit to play the iconic modern artist in this heartfelt biopic. Artist turned film director Julian Schnabel plays posthumous homage to his former friend Jean-Michel Basquiat, played here with panache by Jeffrey Wright. *Basquiat* was a charismatic, charming, volatile and self-absorbed heroin addict who embraced both success and excess in equal measure.

But Schnabel's film was also a fond tribute to Warhol. Comparing Bowie's affectionate, camp, wobbly-wigged performance to earlier portrayals, longtime Warhol associate Paul Morrissey told *People* magazine: "Bowie was the best by far. You come away from *Basquiat* thinking Andy was comical and amusing, not a pretentious, phony piece of shit, which is how others show him."

Bowie was even allowed to borrow Warhol's actual wig, glasses and jacket from the Warhol Museum for the shoot.

Moonage Daydream (2022)

Freewheeling through Bowie's vast pop culture legacy, Oscar-winning director Brett Morgen's sprawling audiovisual collage documentary pays lavish IMAX-sized tribute to the late avant-rock icon. Drawing heavily on live performance footage and archive interview clips, all densely layered with psychedelic visual treatments, *Moonage Daydream* contains stylistic echoes of Morgen's previous rock films, notably *Crossfire Hurricane* (2012) and *Kurt Cobain: Montage of Heck* (2015).

It adds little new to the overcrowded canon of posthumous Bowie releases, but it does features rare and thrilling performances of classic numbers including *Space Oddity, All The Young Dudes, Oh! You Pretty Things, 'Heroes', Absolute Beginners, Let's Dance, Hallo Spaceboy, Blackstar* and more. For all its high-minded intentions, Morgen's mixtape marathon is a hit and miss affair. But as a high-gloss video jukebox of some of the greatest art-pop songs ever written, this sense-swamping spectacular is a crash course for the ravers.

"HE WAS UNIQUE"

Rounding up Bowie's cameos and blink-and-you'll-miss it appearances...

Beyond his modest portfolio of starring and co-starring credits, David Bowie's screen career is also peppered with striking cameos and eccentric supporting roles. He played himself on multiple occasions, whether recreating a late 70s Berlin concert on a New York stage for the gritty teenage drug drama *Christiane F* (1981) or gatecrashing Ben Stiller's clownish fashion-show catwalk antics in *Zoolander* (2001). Bowie's off-beat acting choices often mirrored his love of comedy and friendship with comedians: he played a shark alongside Peter Cook and a boatload of Monty Python members in the flop pirate spoof *Yellowbeard* (1983), and a bumbling hit-man for John Landis in the comic thriller *Into The Night* (1985).

But more impressive than these goofy comic turns were Bowie's high-profile cameos for major directors like Martin Scorsese, David Lynch and Christopher Nolan. He may occupy barely four minutes of screen time in Scorsese's *The Last Temptation of Christ* (1988), but his finely rendered snapshot of a haughty Pontius Pilate condemning Jesus to death is a chilling dramatic highlight. "He left behind a remarkable body of work," Scorsese told *Entertainment Weekly* in 2016. "His music and his image and his focus were always changing, always in motion, and with every movement, every change, he left a deep imprint on the culture."

As an early champion of David Lynch's work, it was perhaps inevitable that Bowie would end up working with his fellow inner-space explorer. Their paths finally crossed when the rocker made a strikingly surreal appearance as rogue FBI agent Philip Jeffries in *Twin Peaks: Fire Walk With Me* (1992). "He was unique, like Elvis was unique," Lynch told *Pitchfork* in 2017. Bowie was increasingly reclusive in his autumn years, initially declining Christopher Nolan's offer to play maverick genius inventor Nikola Tesla in the sumptuous historical magic-trick thriller *The Prestige* (2006). But Nolan persisted and ended up capturing one of the late rocker's most memorable, mirthful shorter roles. "Tesla was this other-worldly, ahead-of-his-time figure," the director told *Entertainment Weekly* in 2016, "and at some point it occurred to me he was the original Man Who Fell To Earth."

"Full establishment acceptance meant that I started to strangle myself artistically."

David Bowie

On stage during the Glass Spider tour at Giants Stadium in New Jersey, on October 3, 1987.

HANG ON TO YOURSELF

With *Let's Dance,* David Bowie had undergone his most successful reinvention – into a truly global pop star. But that sucess brought its own problems – ones that would carry through to the start of the next decade.

Words: **David Sinclair**

The massive success of *Let's Dance* turned David Bowie into a global superstar. As a songwriter and performer, Bowie had repeatedly proved himself to be a supremely adaptable creature. But he found this transformation to be the most difficult of all to manage.

"Before *Let's Dance* I had always felt quite happily balanced on the edge of mainstream popular music," Bowie told journalist Robin Eggar in 1991. "But full establishment acceptance meant that I started to strangle myself artistically.

"I really liked the money I was making from touring, and it seemed obvious that the way that you make money is give people what they wanted, and the downside of that is that it just dried me up as an artist completely, because I wasn't used to doing that."

This "drying up" of Bowie's creative inspiration initially manifested itself most obviously in a lack of new songs. *Tonight,* the follow-up album to *Let's Dance,* released in 1984, included just two new songs written by Bowie alone (*Loving The Alien* and *Blue Jean*) and another two written with Iggy Pop (*Dancing With The Big Boys* and *Tumble And Twirl*). The rest of the songs were all covers. And not very distinguished covers at that. His version of the Beach Boys hit *God Only Knows* – a leftover from the *Pin Ups* sessions in

1973 – was a cartoonish performance that found Bowie over-emoting as if he were his own tribute act, while the reggae stylings of *Don't Look Down* and the title track (a duet with Tina Turner) found him travelling in the slipstream of The Police, whose producer Hugh Padgham engineered/co-produced the album.

Whatever its shortcomings, *Tonight* was a big transatlantic hit – No.1 in the UK, No.11 in the US – and Bowie remained at the peak of his commercial powers when he was asked to appear at the Live Aid charity concert at Wembley Stadium in 1985. Bob Geldof and others who organised the show have credited Bowie as one of the key figures in getting the ball rolling.

"A lot of the bigger artists were wary of getting involved," recalled the event's press officer Bernard Doherty. "But as soon as Bowie said he was in, it all started to roll. It shows you just how much influence he had."

Despite having to go on stage accompanied by a scratch band straight after Queen (who stole the show), Bowie gave a supremely resonant performance which included a spine-tingling version of *Heroes*. His impromptu duet, recorded beforehand, with Mick Jagger – a chart-topping version of *Dancing In The Street,* and its gay-spirited accompanying video – symbolised the spontaneous energy of the whole event and further cemented Bowie's populist superstar status, while doing rather less to bolster his "serious" artistic credentials.

The scene was thus set for a blockbuster when Bowie released *Never Let Me Down* in April 1987. But pride comes before a fall. Although boasting a bunch of brand new songs and a crack session band featuring the guitarists

Peter Frampton and Carlos Alomar, *Never Let Me Down* was not the sensation that had been hoped and planned for. It sold respectably, reaching No.6 in the UK and No.34 in the US, but posterity has not judged the album kindly, with even Bowie himself describing it in retrospect as "a bitter disappointment".

A string of singles – *Day-In Day-Out, Time Will Crawl* and *Never Let Me Down* – failed to gain long-term traction as Bowie set off to promote the album on the Glass Spider tour. This monstrous production found the star, his band and a cast of spangled dancers literally upstaged by the towering presence of a glowing 60-foot-high spider with long illuminated legs which bestrode the complicated split-level staging beneath.

Described by Bowie biographer Nicholas Pegg as "a non-stop blitzkrieg of crazed routines" the show was "outrageous and utterly unprecedented". And although Bowie was again his own fiercest critic – "It was so big and so unwieldy and... I was under so much pressure... which is not a great way of working" – the Glass Spider tour was an overwhelming commercial success. As a theatrical experience it raised the bar ➤

Tin Machine in 1988.

The style! The glamour! That 80s era in full effect...

for stadium show excess to new heights, which big name acts from Michael Jackson to the Rolling Stones and U2 were quick to capitalise on.

Bowie had reached the very top of the music business mountain when he met guitarist Reeves Gabrels in Switzerland in May 1988. "He was at a crossroads," Gabrels later recalled. "Either he became Rod Stewart and played Las Vegas, or he followed his heart." Gabrels told Bowie that "The only barrier between you doing what you want, and you doing what you think you should do, is you."

What Bowie wanted to do was to find someone with whom he could share the burden (and rewards) of being fixed so firmly in the spotlight. The grass is always greener on the other side, and the end of a decade when Mick Jagger, Freddie Mercury, Sting and Roger Waters were all attempting to launch solo careers of one sort or another, Bowie decided he wanted nothing more than to be the singer in a rock'n'roll band.

That band was Tin Machine, a quartet named featuring Bowie and Gabrels alongside Tony Sales (bass/vocals) and Hunt Sales (drums/vocals). Bowie had previously worked with the Sales brothers when he played keyboards in Iggy Pop's touring band in 1977. Their approach as a rhythm section was loud, aggressive, high energy and hardcore. Gabrels' playing embraced the outlandish extremes pioneered by Jimi Hendrix and developed by Robert Fripp and Adrian Belew. The chemistry between the four of them – both musically and personally – was vigorous and volatile. "Playing together was so exhilarating that within the first 36 hours or so, we knew we were a band," Bowie said.

Clockwise from top: the Wembley 1985 Live Aid finale, comparing 80s suits with Fab Macca backstage at Live Aid, hanging with Tina Turner at Birmingham NEC in 1989, performing with Mick Jagger at Wembley for The Prince's Trust 10th Birthday Party in 1986.

Tin Machine was a big roll of the dice for all four musicians. For Gabrels and the Sales brothers, the band offered a guest place at rock's top table, while the experience of being first among equals granted Bowie fresh perspective and a creative lifeline. The group's debut album, *Tin Machine*, provided a clear vindication of the quartet's fierce commitment to the project. From the opening salvo of *Heaven's In Here* with its striding bass line, screeching, scattergun solos and suave vocal delivery, it established itself as a rock album of rare distinction, ushering in a formula which Gabrels memorably described as "pinstripes and *Purple Haze*".

The album charted at No.3 in the UK (No.28 in the US) and Tin Machine went on to record a second album, *Tin Machine*

II (1991) and a live album *Oy Vey, Baby* (1992) extending the franchise with more fearless and extravagantly performed variations on the theme. The project was then retired, with Bowie citing "personal problems within the band" making it "physically impossible for us to carry on".

Various live recordings of Tin Machine have surfaced in recent years, most notably *Live At Cigale, Paris, 25th June, 1989*. Released in 2019, it's an outstanding recording of a simply incredible performance when the whole band, but most notably Hunt Sales and Gabrels, were on fire.

Tin Machine wound down just as grunge was getting firmly established in America and the resurgence of guitar bands that heralded the Britpop revolution was getting underway in the UK. So although the suits and ties weren't the right image, Bowie had yet again shown his uncanny ability to switch direction in an unexpected way that prefigured the coming changes in the musical and cultural landscape. ❼

"As soon as Bowie said he was in, Live Aid started to roll. It shows how much influence he had."
Bernard Doherty

Who Can I Be Now?

Art-funk experimentalist, industrial music enthusiast, drum'n'bass dabbler, internet pioneer, loving husband – the 1990s saw David Bowie trying on countless different hats.

Words: **Chris Roberts**

I f the 80s had seen David Bowie sacrifice credibility and mystique to cash in as a stadium-pleasing, bouffant-haired mainstream pop star who took his eye off the ball when his albums were being recorded, the 90s saw him claw back much prestige with a series of diverse, experimental records and a realignment of his personal and creative lives.

"By the time the 80s was over, nobody could put their finger on what I was any more", he told me when I interviewed him in 1999. "It was: "What the fuck is he doing?' I've been finding my voice, and a certain authority, ever since".

The venting, one-of-the-boys rock-out of Tin Machine may have been deemed his musical nadir, but it achieved his objective of scorching his Earth so he could rebuild afresh. "I look back on the Tin Machine years with great fondness", he said. They charged me up, I can't tell you how much".

He left EMI but mustered the business savvy to undergo the seven-month-long Sound + Vision tour, wherein he smartly trotted out the hits to remind flagging audiences of why they loved him in the first place.

In a twist which played against many of the radical social ripples his 70s personae had championed, marriage seemed to give him a more contented foundation from which to work. He was introduced to Somali-born supermodel Iman in LA in October 1990, and gushed, "It was absolutely immediate – I was naming the children from the night we met".

They married in April 1992 at a private ceremony in Lausanne, Switzerland, with the wedding solemnized in Florence in June. Heartwarming development though this was, the photo sessions of the latter gathering for *Hello!* magazine, with everyone from Bono to Yoko to Eno in attendance, emphasised how far Bowie had wandered from his subversive, alien-bisexual-in-green-jumpsuit breakthrough days. The same thought occurred when he elected to recite *The Lord's Prayer* at Wembley Stadium during the April 1992 Freddie Mercury Tribute Concert (as well as performing *Heroes, All The Young Dudes* and – with Annie Lennox – *Under Pressure*).

He tried to move to LA with Iman only to find the LA riots in full flow. They settled in New York instead, a default move which turned out decidedly well for the new couple: they effectively lived there for the rest of Bowie's life. Iman, along with those LA riots, inspired much of 1993's *Black Tie White Noise* album, an underrated, genre-hopping construct. It flirted with electronica – as Bowie was to do for much of the decade – and was co-produced by Nile Rodgers, a reunion which, while delivering less obviously commercial sounds than *Let's Dance* still gave him a UK No.1 and yielded the hit *Jump They Say*, which referenced Bowie's late half-brother Terry.

Mike Garson and even Spiders From Mars guitarist Mick Ronson (who died soon after its release) guested, as did trumpeting namesake Lester Bowie. Covers of Cream, Walker Brothers and Morrissey numbers might suggest flailing, but the album's restless jackknifes– from house and Euro-soul to jazz and *Pin-Ups* style homages, from musings on racial harmony to blissed-out cooing over his marriage – make for an exhilarating ride. The American label Savage's bankruptcy blew its Stateside chances, but in the UK, posing with touted heir-to-the-throne Suede's Brett Anderson for the *NME* cover, Bowie was regaining higher ground.

There he stayed for *The Buddha Of Suburbia*, part soundtrack album, part spin-off reverie regarding the BBC's adaptation of Hanif Kureishi's 1970s-set novel. Kureishi claimed the book "reminded Bowie of his own life" as a teen in South London. With no promotion, the album tanked – a peak of No.87 for a Bowie release seems implausible now – but with hindsight, critics clamber over each other to hail it as neglected treasure. (In 2003, Bowie called this personal work, which ➢

"Let's just say I'm taking the bull by the horns and expressing myself."

David Bowie

In Concert at Roseland during 1996, New York.

> ## "My past has given me such a fantastic life. Negatives, positives, an incredible learning process."
> **David Bowie**

UK Top 10. Bowie told a press conference: "I was always far more interested in the periphery of life's matters than what was happening in the centre."

"Let's just say I'm taking the bull by the horns and expressing myself," he told me. "By any means necessary. I can do it, so I'm gonna flaunt it. I'm really not very self-judgmental anymore. I feel, psychologically, in a safe place. It's publish and be damned, it really is." (In the next breath he was eulogising Dylan, Hendrix, Pearl Jam, Nirvana, Tricky and PJ Harvey).

While reviews were all over the shop, from "intriguing" to "rubbish", its legacy has seen some rank it up alongside *Low* and *Heroes*. Bowie toured the album, at first reluctantly, under pressure from Virgin, with Nine Inch Nails in the US and (initially) Morrissey in the UK. Nine Inch Nails' Trent Reznor and Bowie bonded creatively, confusing both fan bases, with Bowie refusing to play "the hits". The crowd threw stuff at him.

Less fractious was the meeting of Bowie and PM-in-waiting Tony Blair as the latter presented him with a Brit Award for Outstanding Contribution to Music in February '96. "A source of inspiration for practically everybody – he's always at the cutting edge," gushed Blair. Oasis taunted Blur; Jarvis Cocker waved his bottom at Michael Jackson; Bowie the evergreen, dressed as a raunchy vicar, performed *Outside*'s break-out single *Hallo Spaceboy* with the Pet Shop Boys, *Moonage Daydream* and *Under Pressure*.

Still the sultan of charm, Bowie had plenty of cool friends and hip fans anyway. He celebrated his 50th birthday in January '97 with a show at Madison Square Garden, joined onstage for songs and grins by luminaries both time-honoured and topical – Lou Reed, Foo Fighters, Sonic Youth, Robert Smith of The Cure, Billy Corgan of Smashing Pumpkins, Black Francis of Pixies. If that line-up indicated Bowie had paused the esoteric studio boffin phase of *Outside* and was immersed chiefly in contemporary headbanging rock, once again, inevitably, he was to confound expectation. "An absolute truth seems so hard to get to in this… fragmented age and all that," he told me.

Earthling, largely self-produced, bore a too on-the-nose title: look everyone, Alien Dave is just like you, grooving to those drum-and-bass sounds the kids of today enjoy! Released in February 1997, it dabbled in techno, jungle and a blast of industrial (*I'm Afraid Of Americans* was remixed by Reznor). Bowie appeared on the cover in a Union Jack coat designed by Alexander McQueen. Again, this appeared a little premeditated, focus-grouped. The reception was perplexed, from praise for an ageing rock god keeping in touch with musical

flickers with ideas he'd investigate more explicitly on subsequent pieces, his favourite album).

The ideas he explored on 1995's often bewildering, sometimes bewitching *Outside* (subtitled *The Nathan Adler Diaries: A Hyper-Cycle*), his 20th album, were received as, at best, challenging, at worst, pretentious. Yet again the passage of time has emphasised how prescient Bowie's butterfly mind could be, his early obsession with the internet – its paranoia, its untetheredness – tapping into at-the-time nebulous future legends. He'd conceived the work as the first in a run of narratives nosing into a conceptual linking of art and murder, or the motivations beneath them.

It brought Brian Eno (co-producing) and him together again, and was an uncompromising attempt at outsider music.

"The strength in my work is when there's as much room for multi-interpretation as possible", he told me. "I've always had an orientation toward combining contradictory information, and just seeing what happens. Messing about with structures, taking them apart. That's one of the fascinations of writing, for me. I think we as a culture embrace confusion".

Defiantly inaccessible, going full Dada in an era when Britpop was bringing back jingoism and laddism, it's a miracle *Outside* scraped into the fashion to snipes pointing out that these genres had been around for longer than ageing people realised. Bowie, doubling down, toured through the second half of the year, at first playing two sets – one of established songs, another of zeitgeisty experimentation. This was ditched after audiences took to leaving during the second set. I saw people at the small venue Hanover Grand slumping from excitement at being in such close proximity to Bowie to shuffling bashfully to the exits as he delved into marathon avant-jazz wig-outs.

If turning 50 had supercharged Bowie's desire to be unpredictable, he seemed to focus a touch more, allowing himself involvement in projects which made sound sense. Some seemed bonkers then but proved remarkably clairvoyant. Bowie bonds – the first security backed by a performer's cash flow potential – were used as collateral royalty streams from his then and future album sales and live profits, and raised him $55 million. With that, he bought rights to his music catalogue from his former management, in turn generating more income to shareholders. If this seemed calculating at the time, it's since informed many comparable music industry deals (and maximised his stock just before streaming wounded record sales). Then there was BowieNet, which in 1998 launched his own internet service provider (subscription required). Mocked by some then, it now highlights that he was once again an early bird in seeing a revolution coming in art and commerce, in culture and the means of distribution. His ideas of how the 21st century would shape up were bang on.

There were scattergun shots too. A star on the Hollywood Walk Of Fame. Contributing *I'm Deranged* to the soundtrack for David Lynch's *Lost Highway*. Recording a track, *Safe*, for *The Rugrats Movie*, which was removed (later appearing as a b-side). Singing his bit on the BBC Children In Need charity cover of Lou Reed's *Perfect Day*, alongside everyone from Bono and Elton to Lesley Garrett and Heather Small (what a long way that song – originally produced by Bowie on *Transformer* – had travelled).

In 1999, he added vocals to a single from latest best pals Placebo, *Without You I'm Nothing*, and was made a Commander of the Ordre des Arts et des Lettres by the French government. He composed (with Reeves Gabrels) the soundtrack to computer game *Omikron: The Nomad Soul*. Some *Omikron* music was reworked for his next album proper, his last with Gabrels, as keen on reflecting on ageing as *Earthling* had been on staying young.

Iman and David in New York, 1994.

With Brian Eno in 1994.

> "I personally think my work in the 90s has been the best that I could possibly do."
>
> **David Bowie**

Hours (styled as *'hours…'*) kissed goodbye to what's imperfectly called his "electronic era" and offered more conventional, soft, warm, meditative songcraft. With a kind of this-is-me-behind-the-mask approach, it explores mortality, and drops references to John Donne and the Bible, probing the gap between memories and reality, haunted by *Hunky Dory*, obsessed with the number seven. The lyrics from one song, *What's Really Happening?*, were chosen from fans' entries on a Bowienet competition be).

"It is a more personal piece", he told me, "but I hesitate to say it's autobiographical. The progenitor of this piece is a man who is fairly disillusioned. He's not a happy man. Whereas I am an incredibly happy man! My wife and I are extremely happy: I'd like to state that quite publicly! I'm much too jolly. I'm inwardly jolly.

"I'd say, broadly, it's songs for my generation. There's not much concept behind it, but I guess the one through-line is that they deal with a man looking back over his life… but me, I don't have regrets. If I'm cajoled into looking at the past, I tend to look on at it not so much as luggage as wings. My past has given me such a fantastic life. Negatives, positives, an incredible learning process. Arriving now at a situation where I… know far less than I knew starting out Nobody knows more than a young person knows. I knew so much when I was about 25. I knew all the answers…

He spoke with great enthusiasm of New York, of his passion for art and involvement with *Modern Painters* magazine, even of his jogging routine. And of how marriage had made him realise how great company and conversing could be, how it had opened him up, first privately, then publicly.

"I personally think my work in the 90s has been the best that I could possibly do. I'm very proud of it all. My only real ambition now is to feel I don't waste a day. I like reality a lot! I'm hungry for it." ●

HEROES, JUST FOR ONE DAY

For one night only in 1997, **David Bowie** and personally invited stars celebrated his 50th birthday with a show at Madison Square Garden. Here's how the stardust was sprinkled...

Words: **Niall Doherty**

Throughout the 90s, David Bowie embarked on an era of course correction. He had come dangerously close to comfort zone territory in the previous decade, and the thought of playing out the classics as a nostalgia act for the rest of his days sprang him into action. Over five albums from 1993 to 1999, Bowie got back to his forward-thinking, progressive best, experimenting with drum 'n' bass, jungle, industrial soundscapes, jazz, electro-rock and more. He was the king of reinvention once more.

Amid the audacious march forward, though, there was one night when he allowed himself to revel in his triumphant legacy. It was January 9, 1997 when Bowie, his band and some stellar guests assembled for a huge show at New York's Madison Square Garden for his fiftieth birthday celebration (his birthday was actually the day before). The show had the Starman sharing the stage with Foo Fighters, Robert Smith, Billy Corgan, Frank Black, Sonic Youth and Lou Reed for a set that took in some oldies and some newies, some classics and some soon-to-be classics.

"I wouldn't have expected to have such an appetite for life at this point," Bowie remarked to the *New York Daily News*. "I had assumed, like romantic poetic heroes, that I would burn it all out. But nothing has been quenched. I'm still feeling fiery."

> ## "The guest artists all grew up listening to David, right? It was all very respectful and very uncompetitive."
> **Mike Garson, pianist**

Billed as 'David Bowie And Friends: A Very Special Concert', the sold-out show was broadcast on Pay-Per-View television in the US, with proceeds from both ticket sales and Pay-Per-View going to the charity Save The Children. Looking back at it now, 25 years later, it seems too good to be true: a bill of multi-generational, era-defining stars all coming together to honour the biggest multi-generational era-defining star of them all. But, as those who were there on the night recall, it happened. All of it.

Reeves Gabrels (guitarist/musical director): David said he wanted to have a bunch of guests that were newer artists who were – he didn't say this, but I'll say it – like his spawn. That was pretty much it.

Tim Pope (film director): David had asked me to film a variety of live shows across the years, and he seemed to like what I brought to them. It was the natural progression that he asked me to film his special birthday party. It was all put together by him, I have to say. He was very detail-oriented, but he wanted me to be his eyes and ears in the development of the show.

Reeves Gabrels: From the late spring of 1996, I had become a musical director for the touring band, which I always hated. But I took the title and took the money and did the job. David is the guy at the top of the pyramid, he's got other things he's gotta do. There's only so many hours in a day, so someone has to organise sound-check.

Tim Pope: I went to New York pre-Christmas and spent some time with him. David had this model theatre made of cardboard, and he had this little version of himself. He said: "This is me, right," and he had this little character. And I was lighting it with a hand-held projector on this scrim, along with images of him from *Space Oddity*. He played the CD of *Space Oddity* and I sang along in harmony with him, which was hilarious because I can't sing. After Christmas, more and more bands came into town to rehearse with him.

Kim Gordon (bassist/guitarist/vocalist, Sonic Youth): We felt very flattered and honoured to be asked. I always feel a little bit out of place in those

THE STORY TELLERS

Reeves Gabrels
The guitarist worked with Bowie from 1987-1999, forming the group Tin Machine with him, and becoming his musical director in 1996. Since 2012, Gabrels has been a member of The Cure.

Mike Garson
One of Bowie's longest-standing collaborators, pianist Garson was a member of his iconic Spiders From Mars backing band, in the 70s, and brought his avant-garde jazz style to a series of classic Bowie records. He reunited with Bowie in 1993 and played with him throughout the 90s.

Brian Moloko
The frontman with Placebo. Despite them having only just released their debut album, Bowie had requested that Placebo open the show. It ignited a friendship between the two artists, and in 1999 they would collaborate on a version of Placebo's *Without You I'm Nothing*.

Kim Gordon
Bassist, guitarist and vocalist Gordon was a founding member of Sonic Youth, who Bowie requested join him at the show for a version of his song *I'm Afraid Of Americans*.

Nate Mendel
Foo Fighters bassist. The group were in the middle of recording their second album, *The Colour And The Shape*, when the call came from Bowie to take part in the show.

Tim Pope
Famed for his work with Bowie, The Cure, The The and more, British film director Pope was enlisted to capture the live event and be, as Bowie told him, his "eyes and ears".

---

situations. It was kind of a boost psychologically, because we didn't consider ourselves part of the mainstream. We admired him, so it was very flattering that he liked us enough to ask to play his birthday celebration.

Brian Moloko (vocalist, Placebo): I remember David being charming and affable. A bit like when you meet a president – they make you feel like the most important person in the room. That was another of David's talents. It didn't really matter if you were Bono or a bricklayer.

Nate Mendel (bassist, Foo Fighters): It was kind of a milestone for us, because it ended up being the last time William Goldsmith, our first drummer, played with the band. It was our first time in Madison Square Garden, first time we met

Bowie, first time that we probably played a stage anywhere near that big. We were about halfway through the recording of *The Colour And The Shape*, so it was pulling us out of the studio, going to New York, meeting a legend and just having all these firsts. It was pretty monumental. We were excited to be there.

Reeves Gabrels: My job was to teach all of the guests the songs, or make sure that they knew the songs, or at least make sure they knew what songs they were expected to know when they showed up. So I had been in touch with everybody. Robert Smith and I were faxing back and forth and calling, and he was sending me chord diagrams for *The Last Thing You Should Do* and *Quicksand* because he wanted to make sure he had the chord voicings correct.

Nate Mendel: I don't recall exactly how the songs we ended up playing came down. I assume, based on where we were at the time, that it was probably more of an assignment; they weren't gonna ask the Foo Fighters what they wanted to play!

Reeves Gabrels: We had two days of run-through rehearsals. Robert Smith was the last one that I actually got together with. It was pretty obvious he had done his homework.

Mike Garson (pianist): The guest artists all grew up listening to David, right? So he's the king. And these guys are future kings and princes, but they were all a little nervous, all very flattered to be there. It was all very respectful and very uncompetitive, almost like: "We're a team, let's make this a great show." ▷

Some of Bowie's birthday concert collaborators: (l -r) Robert Smith, Lou Reed, Brian Moloko, Billy Corgan, Dave Grohl.

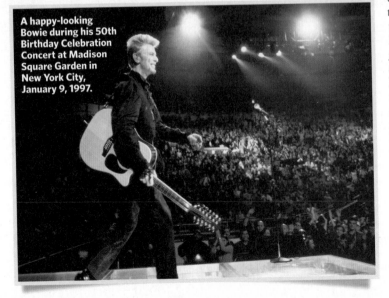

"Everyone was intimidated by Lou Reed. Not David. But all of us youngsters were like: 'Don't piss off dad!'"

Reeves Gabrels, guitarist/musical director

Reeves Gabrels: The only thing that was odd to me was that Billy Corgan couldn't make it for the run-throughs. He did show up for sound-check on the day of show, but the night before, his guy called me and he wanted to know if we could change the key on *All The Young Dudes*. And I was like: "Yeah – if we'd talked about it a week earlier."

Mike Garson: Frank Black was great. He epitomised cool. Just did his thing and walked off.

Reeves Gabrels: The day that Frank Black showed up to rehearsals, David had said to me: "I'm not going to sing every verse or every song." He wanted to save his voice for the show. So we start playing *Scary Monsters (And Super Creeps)*, and Frank Black takes the first verse and just destroys it in the best possible way. Before the first chorus is done, David is out at his mic to sing the next verse. I think it was a little bit of wanting to join the pre-party party, but also a little competitive in the best possible sense.

Mike Garson: Everybody had done their homework. Any of those singers could have sung the song without him. They knew the words and they were ready to go.

Nate Mendel: In comparison to what we would do now, which is

listen to a song on an iPhone in a car on the way to whatever we're going to do, we'd rehearsed a bit. We were doing *Hallo Spaceboy*, and we came in having prepped a little.

Tim Pope: I remember watching David and Robert Smith performing together for the first time, and Bowie said: "Oh, Smith and Jones back together again!" David also said to me: "Madonna is probably coming. But we won't know until the night."

Reeves Gabrels: We didn't know if Madonna was going to show. Or Courtney Love. The idea of Madonna singing *The Jean Genie* didn't really

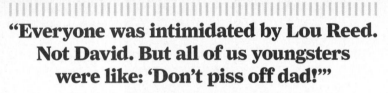

A happy-looking Bowie during his 50th Birthday Celebration Concert at Madison Square Garden in New York City, January 9, 1997.

connect for me. That's just my opinion, of course. But Madonna didn't make it, and Courtney didn't show up.

Tim Pope: One day Bowie said to me: "Oh, Lou's coming in today."

Reeves Gabrels: Everyone was kind of intimidated by Lou Reed. Not David. But all of us youngsters were like: "Don't piss off dad!" Lou was kind of surly. Not ridiculous, just a little New York grumpy. I had to sit with Lou and teach him *Queen Bitch*. So we're playing it, and he keeps doing this one chord that's not right. I'd written the chord changes down, and I said to him: "There's one chord there that you're having trouble with?" And he goes: "Yes, this one," and points to it. And I said: "Well, that's a D chord." He goes: "That's not a D chord – that's an awfully weak spine for a D. It looks like an O chord." So I took my Sharpie out, made the spine straight, and said: "That should do it, right Lou?" And he goes: "Yeah." I don't know if he was doing it just to be funny.

Mike Garson: We used a metronome to keep it totally steady, but the only one we didn't use the click with was Lou, because David said: "He can't play in time. Just follow him and it'll be great." And it was.

GETTY x4

Nate Mendel: The day of the show, I remember seeing everybody backstage and being kind of intimidated but feeling the positive vibe in the room. Everybody was very supportive. I was quickly able to kind of get over those nerves of having been asked to do this thing. Bowie was so gracious and kind and approachable, so I just remember good vibes. And seeing my first rock legend snorting cocaine in the bathroom also. Like: "Oh, I've heard about this, I've read about this in books, and there you are doing it." Who was it? Yeah right!

Reeves Gabrels: There was a backstage electricity. It was palpable. It was the first time everybody was together. It really felt like a birthday party – almost like a surprise party, when you're trying to keep it a secret but everybody's bubbly and excited. But in this case the surprise was really for the audience, because David knew what was going on.

Brian Moloko: It was celebrity central backstage. Prince in high heels, Christopher Walken looking scary. I gave Moby a beer from our cool box, and accidentally head-butted Naomi Campbell's chest while enthusiastically turning a corner. I also snogged Dave Grohl. As you do.

Nate Mendel: Then we took that photo where everyone's in black and looking like they're in a rock band. And I get seated directly behind Bowie for the photo, which is unfortunate because I'm in a white button-up short-sleeve shirt that's like ten times too big for me. It's a bad look, and it's a very prominent look due to the scope and the sizing and the colour. Every once in a while my wife will pull up the photo and just have a good laugh.

SET-LIST

LITTLE WONDER
THE HEARTS FILTHY LESSON
SCARY MONSTERS (AND SUPER CREEPS) *(with Frank Black)*
FASHION *(with Frank Black)*
TELLING LIES
HALLO SPACEBOY *(with Foo Fighters)*
SEVEN YEARS IN TIBET *(with Dave Grohl)*
THE MAN WHO SOLD THE WORLD
THE LAST THING YOU SHOULD DO *(with Robert Smith)*
QUICKSAND *(with Robert Smith)*
BATTLE FOR BRITAIN *(The Letter)*
THE VOYEUR FOR UTTER DESTRUCTION (AS BEAUTY)
I'M AFRAID OF AMERICANS *(with Sonic Youth)*
LOOKING FOR SATELLITES
UNDER PRESSURE
"HEROES"
QUEEN BITCH *(with Lou Reed)*
I'M WAITING FOR THE MAN *(with Lou Reed)*
DIRTY BLVD. *(with Lou Reed)*
WHITE LIGHT/WHITE HEAT *(with Lou Reed)*
MOONAGE DAYDREAM
ALL THE YOUNG DUDES *(with Billy Corgan)*
THE JEAN GENIE *(with Billy Corgan)*
SPACE ODDITY

Bowie blows out the candles while pianist Mike Garson plays Happy Birthday.

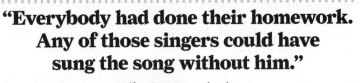

"Everybody had done their homework. Any of those singers could have sung the song without him."

Mike Garson, pianist

Brian Moloko: We [Placebo] were basically the band that played as the audience took their seats. We played to a mixture of indifference and confusion.

Tim Pope: Bowie asked me to introduce the show, so I went on and said something like: "I'm from Enfield, he's from Bromley." I don't think they knew who I was.

Reeves Gabrels: When the show started, it was like strapping yourself into a rocket. Occasionally I'd look across the stage, and [bassist] Gail Ann Dorsey would look at me and widen her eyes like, "Oh, fuck!"

Mike Garson: We were an amazing band at that point in time – Reeves, myself, Gail and [drummer] Zack Alford. I'd played in thirteen bands with David since 1972, and that was my favourite band. I was having a ball. That night was just like any other night, except that it had the magic of his birthday. We brought out a birthday cake and I played *Happy Birthday*. He was relaxed. He's David Bowie. He's like King Midas, whatever he touches it just turns into magic.

Nate Mendel: I was a little nervous, but I remember it going well, actually being fun in the moment. I was able to focus on the fact that: "I'm twenty feet away from Bowie and we're playing a song together, and it's actually fun and it's ⯈

With a little help from my friends: Bowie with his birthday concert collborators.

working." As opposed to: "What am I doing here?" and "Let's not fuck up!"

Reeves Gabrels: *Hallo Spaceboy* was a surprise, with three drummers. I didn't realise just how thunderous that was gonna be.

Mike Garson: You want to hear something interesting that David wanted for *Hallo Spaceboy*? So it was Dave Grohl and his other drummer from Foo Fighters at the time [William Goldsmith], and David wanted me on drums instead of the other drummer that played with Foo Fighters, together with Zack, our regular drummer. I thought to myself: "This is ridiculous. I can play a little drums, but these guys need to have a real drummer." So I said: "Let me go back to the keyboards", and it was those three drummers.

Tim Pope: I had some roving cameras, including David's son Joe [aka film director Duncan Jones]. I said to him: "Go film your dad at the office," which I thought was great. I said: "You'll get stuff that no one else will get." So Joe was doing stuff as well.

Reeves Gabrels: To finish, David went out and played *Space Oddity* by himself. The after-party was immediately after the show. I remember running around backstage and seeing all these people crowded in the hallway waiting to get into the VIP area. I saw this sea of faces, like

Vanessa Williams, the singer and former Miss America, and Beck.

Tim Pope: There was a wrap party at [artist] Julian Schnabel's house. It was the best queue for

||||||||||||||||||||||||||||||||||||||||||||||||||||||||||||||||

"He was relaxed. He's David Bowie. He's like King Midas – whatever he touches, it just turns into magic."

Mike Garson

a loo I've ever been in – something like Christopher Walken, Lou Reed, Iman, me and so on.

Brian Moloko: I don't recall what happened after the show… I think I peaked early.

Playing with the man: Lou Reed and Bowie.

Nate Mendel: It was just like you'd imagine a Bowie party to be – super-stylish, in a loft, everybody famous in the world is there.

Kim Gordon: Matt Dillon was there. At that time Matt Dillon could be seen in many places, so I kind of knew him. He was going to get food at the buffet, and was standing next to Julian Schnabel. Matt said hi to me and he goes: "Hey, Julian, do you know Kim?" And then Julian Schnabel said: "Oh, yeah, you're a real artist." And then he said: "Can I give you my CD?" That was funny."

Nate Mendel: David said to us: "Nice job, kids. Keep at it and maybe you'll figure this shit out in a few years." I'm kind of paraphrasing, I'm sure he said it more artfully than that.

Tim Pope: I think he knew he'd pulled it off. He'd phone me in my cutting room and go: "It's rock'n'roll Dave for cinema Tim." He pretty much let me have free rein. I think once he saw that I got it how he wanted he was happy. He said: "I was really clever to get you to do this, wasn't I?" Which I thought was quite a compliment.

Mike Garson: The day after the gig, he said: "Maybe we'll do this every year, Mike, and maybe we'll have Beck next year." I said: "I'm in!" But David had a million ideas, and one out of every thousand would come through. His mind was always in 'create' mode. ⏻

GETTY x2

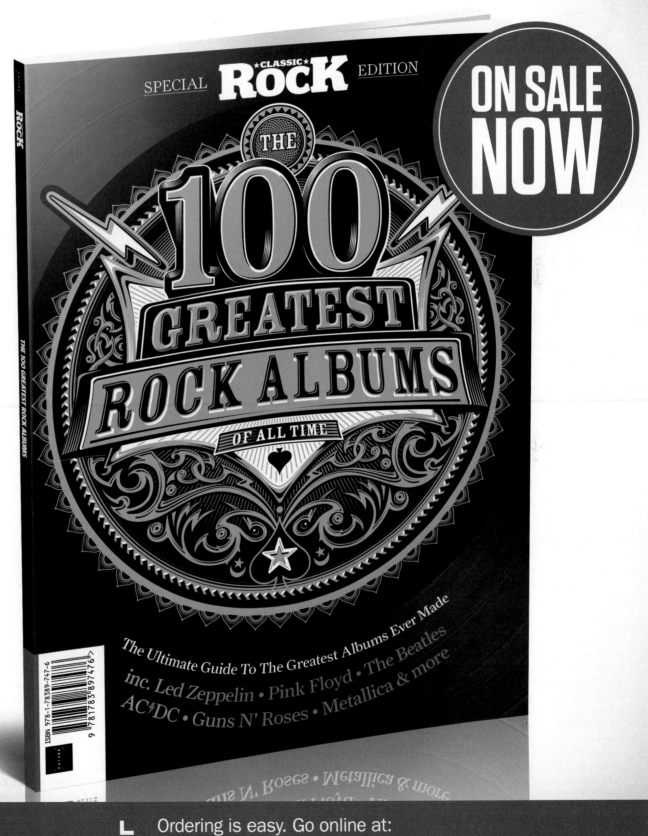

It started with a triumphant Glastonbury appearance and was curtailed by a mid-tour heart attack. But the early 00s saw David Bowie closer to the peak of his powers than he'd been in years.

Words: **David Sinclair**

Glastonbury 2000 was a watershed in the life and times of David Bowie. His presence as the headlining act at this most significant of English festivals at the turn of the millennium marked a moment in time when rock music was balanced on the tipping point between counter-culture and heritage industry.

Bowie's performance somehow straddled both sides of the divide as he appeared – now aged 53 – with a new, long-haired, pre-Raphaelite look that echoed the original, "dress" image of him that adorned *The Man Who Sold The World* album on its first UK release in 1971. With a calm, imperious authority, he performed a set of greatest hits that stretched back to some of his most cherished early songs including *Changes*, *Life On Mars* and *The Man Who Sold The World*. The performance was eventually released posthumously, in its entirety, as a live album and DVD in 2018 – providing a glorious summary of his career up to that point.

Bowie had long endured a love-hate relationship with his old songs and had vowed at the time of the Sound + Vision greatest hits tour in 1990 that he would never perform them again, a promise he had kept, to a greater or lesser extent, up until Glastonbury.

"I didn't know if my [new] songs were any good," Bowie later told journalist Paul du Noyer in 2003. "I didn't want to be intimidated by my own catalogue, so I thought I would really have to begin again... build a new catalogue and see where it takes me... I now feel very confident about touring and putting new songs against old songs. I don't feel intimidated. It's as simple as that."

For his fans, Glastonbury was a timely reminder of Bowie's towering achievements and of just how precious he still was to them. Coming after a long stretch of swimming against the populist tide, this one, partly-televised performance rehabilitated him as a superstar with enduring mainstream appeal. For Bowie, having at last made peace with his past on such a momentous occasion, it was as if he had liberated himself to pursue his artistic muse with complete freedom for the rest of his recording career.

That said, he was forcefully reminded of the commercial imperatives that still applied when, at the end of 2001, he was dropped by Virgin Records – with whom he had signed only three years previously – having released just one album on the label, *Hours*, in 1999.

A lot was thus at stake when in 2002, Bowie released *Heathen* on his own ISO label via a new deal with Columbia/Sony.

Live in 2002 at London's Hammersmith Apollo.

"I wanted to create a timeless piece that didn't owe to the past, present or future, but just floated in its own autonomous kind of place," Bowie airily explained to *Interview* magazine. *Heathen* marked the return of producer Tony Visconti to the camp and with guitar contributions from Carlos Alomar, Dave Grohl and Pete Townshend, the album benefitted from a renewed sense of purpose in Bowie's songwriting. "*Heathen* is the sound of a man who has finally worked out how to grow old with a fitting degree of style," said *The Guardian*.

The album charted at No.5 in the UK (No.14 in the US) and went on to sell more than two million copies worldwide. It was also short-listed for the prestigious Mercury Music Prize, making Bowie the oldest pop musician – at the time – to have received such an honour.

The album's tour was a brief swing through Europe and North America comprising two legs in each territory between June and October 2002. "Touring has become harder and harder for me," Bowie said in the summer, about midway through the dates. But the success of the shows – many of which incorporated a near-complete performance of his 1977 album *Low* along with songs from *Heathen* and a smattering of hits – proved invigorating for Bowie and his audiences alike, and far from tailing off, his career now entered a spectacular Indian summer.

Bowie's vision for his next album *Reality* was, he explained, for it to be "a collection of songs with no through line, no narrative undercurrent of any kind, no concept of tying it all together." Or to put it another way, the plan was simply to write a bunch of songs and get an album out.

Recorded at Looking Glass Studios in New York with Tony Visconti again producing, *Reality* was in the shops by September 2003, just 15 months after *Heathen*, a work rate that he hadn't accomplished since the 1970s. The studio band, which featured Earl Slick and Gerry Leonard on guitar, Sterling Campbell on drums and Mike Garson on piano was a tight, focused group of musicians he could depend on, and the album again won plaudits for its coherence and contemporary charm.

"That's two good ones in a row," chirped the Miami Herald. The album charted at No.3 in the UK (No.29 in the US) and earned Bowie a Brit Awards nomination for Best British Male Artist.

A world tour in support of the album – dubbed A Reality tour – kicked off in Denmark in October 2003 and reached the UK the following month. "C'mon kids, wake up! Your grandad's here," Bowie yelled at the start of the show at the MEN Arena in Manchester, where he performed not only with complete authority but also a newfound charm – as if all the battles with his myth and the baggage of his past had now been resolved. *"I've been right and I've been wrong/Now I'm back where I started from,"* he sang on *Reality*'s title track as a patchwork of abstract swirls and patterns flickered across the giant screens behind him.

The touring band featuring Earl Slick and Gerry Leonard on guitars, Gail Ann Dorsey on bass and vocals, Sterling ➤

GOLDEN YEARS

At the BBC's Maida Vale studio in October 1999. Bowie suffered a heart attack in 2004 despite having stopped smoking and drinking.

With Paul, and daughter Stella, McCartney.

Campbell on drums, Mike Garson on piano and Catherine Russell on keyboards, percussion and vocals had grown into one of the strongest and most established line-ups in Bowie's entire performing career. Greeted with rave reviews at every stop on the itinerary, it was by some distance the longest tour that Bowie had ever undertaken and also the most warmly received since the 1970s. "The Thin White Duke can still lay claim to the title of rock & roll's greatest showman," said the *Irish Independent*.

On June 13, 2004 Bowie headlined the final night of the Isle of Wight Festival. No mention of grandads this time but rather a cheery "Hello Isle of Wight, you crazy motherfuckers! How are you? Old songs, new songs, songs I haven't written yet. See what comes up."

What came up was a set that soundtracked a lifetime of changes: from

"I think he loved the last tour. But it was way too long. He got tired."

Mike Garson

swirling anthems such as *All The Young Dudes*, *Heroes* and *Under Pressure* to the harsh avant-rock sounds of *Station To Station* and *Hallo Spaceboy*. A final, ringing encore of *Suffragette City* and *Ziggy Stardust* brought the curtain down on the festival and – unbeknown to anyone at the time – marked the end of the last show that Bowie ever played in the UK.

The tour ended prematurely less than two weeks later when Bowie suffered a heart attack following a performance at the Hurricane Festival in Scheebel, Germany. He was helicoptered to a hospital in Hamburg where on June 26, 2004 he underwent emergency surgery to relieve an arterial blockage.

"Obviously he had a time bomb going on," guitarist Earl Slick told Bowie biographer Dylan Jones. "First of all he wasn't even smoking. We'd both been sober for many years. So it wasn't drugs and alcohol. I spent every day with him and he ate well. And when I was out the back of the hotel smoking, he was in the gym. He was taking good care of himself."

"I think he loved the last tour," said pianist Mike Garson. "But it was way too long... What happened is he got tired. He stopped smoking around 1999, and thank God he did, because he was always smoking. We were on the bus in 2002 or 2003, and he was very pissed off because the doctor had put him on cholesterol pills... And I said, 'What, you don't think the last 25, 35 years has taken a toll on your body?'"

Bowie made just two further live appearances. In May 2006 he joined David Gilmour on stage at the Albert Hall in London for an encore of the Pink Floyd songs *Arnold Layne* and *Comfortably Numb*. And in November 2006 he sang *Wild Is The Wind* at a benefit concert at the Hammerstein Ballroom in New York, before joining Alicia Keys and her band to perform *Fantastic Voyage* and *Changes*.

Despite recurring rumours that he was about to return to performing live, Bowie never did. "He does not want to tour," Visconti told *The Times* in 2013. "He's been doing it for more than 30 years and he's tired of it." ●

GOLDEN YEARS, GOLDEN GREATS

BOWIE'S BEST SONGS, AS CHOSEN BY THE STARS.

Words: **Ian Fortnam** Interviews: **Dave Everley**, **Dave Ling**, **Henry Yates**

The London Boys
B-side of Rubber Band, 1966

The most sophisticated of all Bowie's early recordings, this frank portrait of a 17-year-old's attraction – like a moth to a flame – to the capital's burgeoning mod scene and its strutting peacock 'faces' was first recorded back in 1965. A live favourite with a compelling lyric, it was originally passed over for release after producer Tony Hatch raised concerns about its references to drugs (specifically pills). Redolent of The Kinks, but with the bite of kitchen-sink drama, *The London Boys* nearly saw its verses repurposed as linking passages between *Pin Ups'* tracks in 1973, but was ultimately revisited for 2021's *Toy*.

Space Oddity
Single, 1969

TONY IOMMI, Black Sabbath
"It's such a timeless song. The concept is brilliant, and it was put together in an exceptional manner. Once you heard that song, it stuck in your head for days."

JOEY TEMPEST, Europe
"This was one of the first singles I ever bought and it had a great impact on me. The lyrics for *The Final Countdown* were sort of lifted from *Space Oddity* – the idea of the song, anyway. I love most of Bowie's catalogue, but for me *Space Oddity* stands out as a little different. The arrangement and the producing are both so inspiring – the way the guitar comes in. As a songwriter and a lyricist, it really fuelled my inspiration."

JIM LEA, Slade
"I first heard *Space Oddity* while I was sitting in Slade's band van parked outside Dave Hill's house, waiting for him to finish preening himself. It was a slightly fuzzy reception on Radio Luxembourg, I think, as we'd made an aerial out of an old coat hanger. When the song came on, Don [Powell, Slade drummer] said: 'Listen to this. I think it sounds like the Bee Gees.' Which it did at the time. It had such an impact on me, but Bowie disappeared after that.

"The second time I heard anything by him was on [radio DJ] Annie Nightingale. We were picking Nod [Holder] up this time, and by this time we were starting to become successful. Annie was reviewing new single releases on a show on Radio 1 called *What's New*, and she played this song called *Changes*. She was saying how pleased she was that David Bowie was emerging as an artist. As soon as I heard her say his name I got really excited, and of course, the record was just fantastic.

"I think his golden era was the Ziggy Stardust days. We shared the same tour promoter, Mel Bush. I was friends with Mel, and I went to see Bowie twice in the Spiders From Mars days. David asked me to go backstage both times because he wanted to meet me, but seeing how he was on stage, I found it a bit disconcerting. Slade were really hot by then, with number one records, so I used to make excuses not to go backstage, saying things like, 'I've just got back from America. I'm very tired.'

"I met him at Olympic Studios in 1973 when I was writing part of *Everyday*. I looked around, and there was a clown standing in the doorway. I didn't really want to look at him, but then he said: 'You'll be Jim Lea of Slade, won't you?' I look around, and this guy had an Ecky Thump-type hat on, big shirt and great big baggy trousers on – like MC Hammer –all in the same material. I said: 'Yeah.' He said: 'I'm David Bowie.' I said: 'I know you are.' "He then asked me if I fancied a cup

ALAMY

"*The Bewlay Brothers* is haunting and dark – you're inside the Bowie persona a bit more."

Pete Trewavas

of coffee. I told him: 'No, I've got to write a song and it's got to be done now.' He said: 'I write songs too, and I have a cup of coffee, so come on, let's go and have a cup of coffee.'

"Bowie was quite some distance away, never once stepping over the threshold of the doorway, so he knew something was up. He then said: 'Look, you came to see me play a couple of times and I asked Mel Bush for you to come backstage. I really wanted to meet you. Come on, let's go and have a cup of coffee. I think we'll get on.' I said: 'No, I've got to go.' As I was walking off, Bowie cupped his hands and shouted: 'Mel told me what you were like!'

"I never saw him again after that. But that's what I was like back then – I wasn't bothered about meeting famous people."

DON DOKKEN, Dokken

"The word 'oddity' is appropriate. What an unexpected song. Quite honestly, the first time I heard it, I didn't understand it at all. It took me by surprise that it became such a huge hit, but now, of course, I get it. I needed to open up my mind. It's a work of genius. Bowie was a genius. I especially love the early stuff – *Diamond Dogs* – but his catalogue is pretty much flawless, even that last record he made [2016's *Blackstar*]."

TOM JOHNSTON, The Doobie Brothers

"It was very different for the time, and such a unique song. Nobody has ever done anything that was remotely comparable, so far as I know."

The Width Of A Circle
The Man Who Sold The World, 1970

With an ostensibly Buddhism-inspired, labyrinthine lyric that combines self-analysis with the occult, Nietzsche with Kahlil Gibran, surrealistic Lewis Carroll whimsy with evocative Dylan imagery, *The Man Who Sold The World* highlight *The Width Of A Circle* was originally meant to be an acoustic piece until guitarist Mick Ronson got hold of it and turned it into Bowie's most unashamedly heavy recording of the 70s – even bordering on metal

But it was in the live arena that it always took flight. During the Ziggy Stardust-era, Bowie would disappear offstage for a cigarette break and costume change while Ronson would wig out, Jeff Beck style, for up to 15 minutes. Back at the dawn of the 70s, absolutely everybody boogied, and Bowie was no exception.

Saviour Machine
The Man Who Sold The World, 1970

STEVE McDONALD, Redd Kross

"I'm a really huge fan of the album *The Man Who Sold The World*, and Redd Kross started covering *Saviour Machine* – it's on our record *Teen Babes From Monsanto* [an EP from 1984]. I love the whole sci-fi trip, and it's so redolent of the year 1970. It's an incredibly evocative piece of music."

All The Madmen
The Man Who Sold The World, 1970

Musically schizophrenic, *All The Madmen* was, as Bowie clarified in 1971, "written for my brother and it's about my brother". In 1969, Bowie's half-brother Terry Burns, who'd been an enormous formative influence, introducing young David to modern jazz and 'beat' writer Jack Kerouac, was confined to South London's Cane Hill asylum, and his predicament marked *The Man Who Sold The World*. Here Bowie's narrative reflects on the parallels between the 'mad' and the nonconformist before concluding that *'all the madmen'* are *'just as sane as me'*. Dramatic, intense, full of nagging themes, *Madmen*, complete with its nonsensical coda, nodded toward imminent brilliance.

The Bewlay Brothers
Hunky Dory, 1971

PETE TREWAVAS, Marillion/Kino

"There's a bit of a tenuous connection between Marillion and Bowie, and that's Aylesbury [where Marillion were based at the start, and where Bowie played many of his seminal early concerts]. My sister, who was about 17 at the time, went to the show at Friars where he turned up for the first time with a band. This was his new band, and they were going to be called the Spiders From Mars. She had a poster of that concert. I was too young, I was never allowed to go!

"My choice is so old that I can't even remember which album it was on, but I really, really love it. Bowie's voice was staggeringly good at the time, and I also love the stanza thing at the end. Above all, I love what *The Bewlay Brothers* stands for. It's quite haunting and dark. The better-known songs on *Ziggy Stardust* are all well and good, but with this one it's like you were inside him – the David Bowie persona – a bit more. Although the lyrics are quite impenetrable, it still manages to paint an amazing picture. I love songs that take the listener to a different place."

Life On Mars?
Hunky Dory, 1971

JOE ELLIOTT, Def Leppard

"Sorry to be predictable, but I'm not going to be clever-clever and go for something from the *Hours* album [1999] – it's got to be *Life On Mars?* The history behind that song is so fascinating. Bowie wrote a song called *Even A Fool Learns To Love* that was set to the music of a song [*Comme d'habitude*] originally written by a couple of French guys [Claude François and Jacques Revaux]. The American singer Paul Anka later rewrote it as Sinatra's *My Way*, and Bowie responded with *Life On Mars?* as his own parody of Frank's song. Listen to them back to back and the first 20 seconds of each are almost identical. That's why on the back cover of *Hunky Dory* it says '*Life On Mars?* – inspired by Frankie', as in Sinatra. I heard that from the mouths of [Spiders From Mars] Trevor Bolder and Woody Woodmansey.

"Bowie was maybe 21-years-old when he wrote *Life On Mars?*, and it was Mick Ronson's first attempt at a string accompaniment. Both of those statements are beyond unbelievable because it's so brilliantly done, so mature and understated. And yet 50-odd years later it still sounds as though it was recorded last week. Rick Wakeman's piano

part is also simply amazing. And I love those great, obscure lyrics, yet at the same time they were completely believable.

"It was a beautifully melodic, well-constructed and great-sounding song. Whenever I hear it on the radio I always think: 'Good. A few thousand people will be hearing that for the first time.' Somewhere in the back of a car in Lincolnshire, a kid will say: 'Mummy, mummy, what's that song?' That's what good music is – it spreads good feelings."

LENNY KRAVITZ

"*Hunky Dory* is one of my favourite albums, not only for the writing but also the production by Ken Scott. That record is such a brilliant document of the era; those amazing, deep songs. And there were none more deep then *Life On Mars?*, with its surreal words.

"As a teenager I auditioned for Spike Lee's movie *School Daze* [1984] by singing that song. Most people were bringing in tapes of a piano backing track that they would sing along to – *The Greatest Love Of All* [Whitney Houston] was popular at the time. I walked in, no tape, and sang *Life On Mars?* a cappella. The production crew were all African American and had no clue what that song was about [laughs]. They may have heard *Fame*, but they didn't know David Bowie. I'll never forget the looks on their faces: 'Who is this crackhead and what is he doing here?' Of course, I didn't get the part."

BENJI WEBBE, Skindred

"I still recall being a small boy and the day that song entered my life – Bowie was that ginger-haired, weird-looking guy wearing a blue suit and with those eyes. I'd never seen or heard anything like it before. The tone of his voice stunned me, and the lyrics are so incredible. He conjures up all these wonderful images with his words. And Rick Wakeman is on the piano – what more could you ask for?

"Fast-forward to *Blackstar* and he did deserve to win all of those awards. It was a brilliant record. They didn't honour him that way just because he had died."

DEVON ALLMAN

"I've always loved the combination of the orchestration and those otherworldly lyrics. It's just a really mystical song. It always transports me to the first time I heard it. I bought it on vinyl at the age of around 19 and I played that thing right into the ground."

JOHN OTWAY

"I didn't follow Bowie's later work anywhere near as avidly as I did the early years, and I was lucky to see him in Aylesbury just as he'd got the Spiders From Mars together and before they really cracked it in terms of success. When I was much

younger I always used to play that song. Lyrically and melodically it was so good… I found myself singing it all the time."

MIKE PORTNOY, Sons Of Apollo

"It would be in my top five songs of all time. It's so perfectly written – just listen to the chord changes and the melody. Bowie had a style that was so unique. The production is also amazing. I love Rick Wakeman's piano, and when that cello comes in on the first pre-chorus it always gives me goosebumps. I've even got those right now from talking about the song."

CONNY BLOOM, Electric Boys

"As a piece of music, that one is on a level with Paul McCartney working with [producer] George Martin. It's like they [The Beatles] wrote it and he [Martin] produced it. It's so good. And it's just one of the many all-time greats written by Bowie."

Changes
Hunky Dory, 1971

With benefit of hindsight, *Hunky Dory*'s opening track has been identified as Bowie's defining statement, a catchy manifesto for an ever-evolving career of risk-taking, assimilation and staying one step ahead of the competition. With Bowie, new sounds and new styles always coexisted. He was as much an ever-on-trend fashion icon as he was a musical innovator, and, complete with the hubris of youth, *Changes* was his statement of intent. "I guess it was me being arrogant," Bowie admitted in 2002. "It's saying: 'I'm going to be so fast you're not going to be able to catch up with me.'"

Queen Bitch
Hunky Dory, 1971

Without the benefit of Rick Wakeman's piano, *Queen Bitch* stands out as an unambitious riff-driven anomaly by comparison to *Hunky Dory*'s more sophisticated material, but it marks a crucial moment in Bowie's metamorphosis into Ziggy. Musically and stylistically, it owes everything to the Velvet Underground; its lyrics venture tentatively into Lou Reed territory. More Brit camp than NYC dark, it soundtracked Bowie's dramatic "I'm gay, and always have been" pronouncement to *Melody Maker* as 1972 dawned. *Queen Bitch* was a game-changer, and its pivotal *Old Grey Whistle Test* incarnation – alongside *Five Years* – marked the moment the 60s finally ended and the 70s truly began.

Starman
The Rise And Fall Of Ziggy Stardust And The Spiders From Mars, 1972

TOMMY SHAW, Styx

"*Starman* came out 50 years ago but it still sounds so current. It starts one way and goes off in another direction. It's typical Bowie – it could have been released yesterday. He was a guy of so many different flavours."

LUKE MORLEY, Thunder

"It still resonates with me because it was the first Bowie song I heard. I saw that legendary appearance on *Top Of The Pops*, seeing him and Ronson and thinking: 'Fucking hell, what's that? Is it an alien?' My mind was completely fused by it and I knew he would be absolutely enormous. It made me into an enormous fan."

Rock 'N' Roll Suicide
The Rise And Fall Of Ziggy Stardust And The Spiders From Mars, 1972

The climactic closer to one of the most iconic and acclaimed albums of the rock era certainly doesn't disappoint. It's nothing other than epic, from the opening intimacy of *"Time takes a cigarette"* through to the raw, intensely personal emotional connection of *"You're not alone"* to the life-affirming, hackle-raising call-and-response crescendo of the *"Gimme your hands, you're wonderful"* coda – not to mention Mick Ronson's skyscraping final guitar motif and a final chord to match The Beatles' *A Day In The Life*.

Deployed as the dramatic finale to Bowie's 1973 Hammersmith Odeon 'farewell' show, it left not a dry eye, nor indeed seat, in the house. Rock theatre par excellence.

Ziggy Stardust
The Rise And Fall Of Ziggy Stardust And The Spiders From Mars, 1972

PAUL SAYER, The Temperance Movement

"We covered that song at the Forum in London in January 2016, a few nights after he died, as a tribute. It opened our set that night and the place went wild. We wanted to mark the event somehow. I love it because it's Bowie at his most rock'n'roll. It's immediate and exciting."

Moonage Daydream
The Rise And Fall Of Ziggy Stardust And The Spiders From Mars, 1972

PHILIP LEWIS, LA Guns

"Those lyrics and the song's whole imagery were so seductive. That song was such a big part of what was going on at the time. I was a kid and very much on the coat-tails of it all, but I used to go down to Biba [classic fashion store] in Kensington High Street and would try to dress like Mick Ronson. His wailing guitar solo at the end of that song, it still gives me chills just thinking about it. The guy was a genius."

➢

Hang On To Yourself

The Rise And Fall Of Ziggy Stardust And The Spiders From Mars, 1972

ROSS THE BOSS

"I was at Bowie's show at Radio City Music Hall in New York in 1973 and, being a guitar guy, I was very, very impressed with Mick Ronson. He was such an incredible player. He had a Les Paul through a 200-watt Marshall amplifier and he blew me away. It was The Spiders From Mars, with Trevor Bolder and Woody Woodmansey. That song has everything: the heaviness, the rock'n'roll and the glamour. It's just awesome."

Five Years

The Rise And Fall Of Ziggy Stardust And The Spiders From Mars, 1972

BEN HARPER, Innocent Criminals

"Without a doubt it would be in my all-time top ten. *Five Years* is just absolute startling, for numerous reasons. The song structure, the voice and the rhythmic instrumentation all speak for themselves, but I find the whole subject matter of five years – half a decade – so mysterious. Whether we know it or not, a five-year period can be pivotal to our lives. Those five years can give us a golden glow or kill us all – you know, *"My brain hurts a lot… Five years, that's all we got."*

"It's such a powerful statement. Think of the first five years of your life and how pure they were, and then think of your most recent five years – or the best or the worst. I love the way he encapsulates it all in that arc of life. That song works on so many different levels."

Suffragette City

The Rise And Fall Of Ziggy Stardust And The Spiders From Mars, 1972

ANDY SCOTT, Sweet

"Sweet and Bowie were on the same label, RCA, at the time, and there was a guy who used to play us Bowie's rough mixes. I heard that Bowie offered *Suffragette City* to Mott The Hoople as a single before *All The Young Dudes*. He wrote that song with them in mind, but ended up recording it himself. I remember talking to Mick [Tucker, Sweet drummer] and saying: 'If he's not going to fucking do that song, we'd love to do it.'

"It came from the area we really wanted to move into. The guitar sound is what makes it for me – a Les Paul with a wah-wah pedal slightly backed off. Later the following decade, after I became a producer, a well-respected Swedish guy told me: 'The guitar sounds of you and Mick Ronson defined the 1970s.'"

LEE AARON

"I first heard *Suffragette City* on the yellow transistor radio I'd got for my 10th birthday. It was captivating. It made me look up 'suffragette' in the dictionary. I was taken with the idea that David Bowie would write a song centred around an independent, strong-minded woman. That really resonated with me. It also had every element

of a perfect rock song. From the opening bluesy riff, that distorted guitar, the gritty piano, sax and full-on lyrical and melodic hooks, it was fierce. Listening to it today it's still as badass as ever."

LIPS, Anvil

"It's an awful thing to say thing, but to me it's the only song of Bowie's that's redeemable. I'm not a fan – he's one of those artists I've never really got. *Suffragette City* was heavy enough to enter my scope – as close as he ever got to Black Sabbath."

TUK SMITH

"I do an awful lot of DJ-ing these days. When that song goes on, it's hard to better it. Everyone screams out the *"Wham bam thank you ma'am"* part. The weird effect on the lead vocal… Nobody can fuck with that song. It's fucking awesome."

All The Young Dudes

Released by Mott The Hoople, 1972

GRAHAM BONNET

"Only an artist like Bowie could write such a wonderful song and give it away. Ian Hunter is

an old friend of mine, and Mott did such a great job with it. As we all know, it saved their career. It was instantly singalongable, like the first time you heard *When A Man Loves A Woman* [by Percy Sledge] or *That's The Way God Planned It* [by Billy Preston] – one play was all you needed."

GENE SIMMONS, Kiss

"I knew the man and greatly respected him. My favourite song of his was, ironically enough, made famous by Mott The Hoople. *All The Young Dudes* was one of two songs that David offered to Mott, the other being *Suffragette City*. Those guys couldn't get a foothold and were about to break up, but David really liked them. They didn't like *Suffragette City* but they did like *All The Young Dudes*.

"I've got Bowie's original demo with him singing lead and playing a lot of the instruments. Mott took that demo and put Ian Hunter's vocal on it. The guitar lick is still so iconic. If a new band came out with it now, I'd say, 'Wow, who is that?' That's the mark of a truly great song."

Jay Pepper, Tigertailz

"When I was a kid this song really connected with me. It was an anthem, a call to arms for the young

ICONIC PIX

> "Those lyrics and the song's whole imagery were so seductive. That song was such a big part of what was going on at the time."
>
> **Philip Lewis** on *Moonage Daydream*

people. It felt as though it talked to me directly. It still does."

The Jean Genie
Aladdin Sane, 1973

IAN PAICE, Deep Purple
"I didn't like a lot of Bowie's stuff – it went past me at a time in my life when I was too busy with other things. However, I really love *The Jean Genie*. The sense of groove is superb, and I'm a sucker for a shuffle."

BIG BOY BLOATER
"People might not think of that as being blues, but I can hear so much Howlin' Wolf in there. To me it's an out-and-out blues song. I love that Bowie would add some make-up to it and present it to the public as glam rock. Being able to do that is just pure genius."

RICH ROBINSON, The Black Crowes
"Man, the guitar, when it kicks in, the way he phrases. When I was a kid I was like, 'What's he talking about?' I remember first hearing it. The imagery he painted, he painted as a songwriter. And also delivered in that sort of way – using music as a delivery system.

"I met Bowie. We befriended [Tin Machine guitarist] Reeves Gabrels – his wife was Robert Plant's press agent. We hit it off him with. He was really cool. We were playing in Europe at the end of [The Black Crowes tour] *Shake Your Money Maker*, and Reeves called and said: 'Me and David are going to The Edge from U2's surprise birthday party. Do you and Chris [Robinson, Black Crowes singer] want to go?' Chris and I were, like, 'Yeah, we'll go check it out.' So a sprinter van showed up, and it was me, Chris, David Bowie and Reeves and the Sales Brothers [Tin Machine rhythm section], going to The Edge's house.

"We just talked about music, whatever. It was surreal – I'm sitting in the back of a van with David Bowie and we're going to The Edge's house. I remember talking to Bono and Van Morrison that night, and just how bizarre it all was.

"We used to travel with hotel room stereos, and Chris was trying to get his stereo changed over to British electricity, and Reeves was like: 'David can do this.' And David Bowie came up to his room and said: 'Oh, this is all you have to do,' and he changed the plug so Chris could listen to his music. It was kind of funny."

John, I'm Only Dancing
Single, 1972

The non-album follow-up to *Starman* arrived into full-scale Bowiemania in the UK, but the

Bowie and Ronson, one of rock's truly great partnerships.

US remained so nervous of Bowie's, and indeed the single's, up-front sexual ambiguity that *John, I'm Only Dancing* remained unreleased across the Atlantic until 1976. Apart from the fact that its lyric hinted at the civilisation-undermining possibility that a man might actually be dancing with another man, the track deployed a simplistic Mick Ronson riff so slack-jawed and surly that you could probably bang nails in with it, not to mention a Trevor Bolder bass run that could surely shiver a timber at 50 paces. Simply brilliant.

Drive-In Saturday
Aladdin Sane, 1973

In a mash-up of 50s nostalgia and future-shock science fiction, Bowie's lyric imagines a post-apocalyptic landscape where an artificially reproduced population rediscover sex via vintage pornography. It was written on the road during the US leg of the 1972 tour, like most of *Aladdin Sane*'s tracks – Bowie later referred to the album as "Ziggy goes to America". *Drive-In* was initially offered to Mott The Hoople as their follow-up to *All The Young Dudes*, but they turned it down, causing the man who wrote it to

shave off his eyebrows in frustration (or so he subsequently claimed). Often overlooked, it's a soaring glam classic with a dynamite sax-driven hook.

Rebel Rebel
Diamond Dogs, 1974

JOEL O'KEEFFE, Airbourne
"*Rebel Rebel* is the perfect rock'n'roll song. It's about going out and having a great time no matter how bad you might feel, how you look or the state of the world. That riff and the double-time snare, it changes your mood. There's a pub I know in Melbourne called the Jerry Bar, and it's pretty much on permanent repeat on the jukebox in there because it really gets you going, no matter how much of a shit day you've had."

JOSH FRANCESCHI, You Me At Six
"I'm from the generation that discovered Bowie through their parents, and his music has correlations with being a young kid. Whenever mum and dad had a Christmas party, there would come a certain time of the evening and they'd put on *Rebel Rebel* to get the dancing started. It never failed."

LITTLE STEVEN VAN ZANDT
"I will always love that song, because it's a snapshot of a magical era in music. It's omnisexual. It was quite ahead of its time, though I think it was influenced by Mick Jagger's performance in *Performance* [1970]. Mick didn't get enough credit for that. But it's decadent and disaffecting, and Bowie was carrying that on. I believe that David [not Mick Ronson] played the guitar, actually played the riff, and it really captures the moment." ▷

Diamond Dogs
Diamond Dogs, 1974

Emerging triumphantly from the scene-setting, spoken-word *Future Legend*, *Diamond Dogs'* title track kicks off with a snippet of adulatory cheering that Bowie lifted from the Faces' live album (somewhat bizarrely, Rod Stewart can be heard clearly over the post-*"This ain't rock'n'roll, this is genocide"* opening riff).

It's set in an anarchic future that was gladly embraced as near-utopian by a teenage constituency primed for the advent of punk. Central protagonist Halloween Jack lives atop Hunger City's Manhattan Chase, and it's all street gangs and *'mannequins with kill appeal'* across a swaggering bump-'n'-grind riff.

1984
Diamond Dogs, 1974

DAVE WYNDORF,
Monster Magnet

"It had a huge effect on me, because the first time I heard it I realised that somebody from one genre could reach out and be part of another. David was a rock musician, but here he was stepping right into Isaac Hayes land. That orchestration was straight out of a 'blaxploitation' movie, and David claimed it. I thought that was the coolest thing ever. That song was like something out of a 1984 soundtrack movie. My young brain couldn't conceive that somebody could pick another medium and make it his. It was like somebody took a toothpaste commercial and somehow made it cool. It's a super-cool song.

Fame
Young Americans, 1975

ROGER CHAPMAN

"Bowie's Berlin period fascinated me, especially as I was heavy ensconced in Germany myself at the time. I was never really much of a fan before that era, but I loved the *Young Americans* album. *Fame* is a smashing song and I never tire of hearing it."

Young Americans
Young Americans, 1975

GLENN HUGHES

"David was living at my house in Los Angeles between March and August 1975 when *Young Americans* was number one. There are many different characters of Bowie, and I got the one that was an R&B freak. Which was fine, cos I was an R&B freak as well."

Stay
Station To Station, 1976

Based on a dynamite riff of significant funk conjured up by *David Live* lead guitarist and latterly long-term Bowie associate Earl Slick, *Stay* was recorded, according to second guitarist Carlos Alomar, "very much in our cocaine frenzy". *Station To Station*'s third single, it achieves everything that the 'plastic soul' of *Young Americans* only promised. Here,

a watertight band (Slick, Alomar, bassist George Murray and drummer Dennis Davis) sound so comfortable in each other's company that they take 'off the leash' to beyond the point of 'off the hook'. By 1976's Isolar tour, *Stay* tore the roof off at every venue.

Sound And Vision
Low, 1977

RICHARD JOBSON, The Skids

"*Low* is my favourite David Bowie album, and I've always loved *Sound And Vision*. For me, *Low* was a complete game changer – you could feel it as he progressed with *Station To Station*. *Sound And Vision* was a hit single, yet it doesn't really have any verses, and neither does it have a real chorus. It has a really long fade-in, and ends the same way. It really shouldn't work, but it does.

"I'm also very fond of *Where Are We Now?* [from 2013's *The Next Day*] because it's the first Bowie song that made me weep. It's about ghosts and a man looking back on his life. I knew all of those places in Berlin that he was referring to, so that resonated

immensely with me. It would be very hard for me to separate those two."

Breaking Glass
Low, 1977

In a superb and concise, disturbing but danceable 112 seconds, Bowie casually captures madness. The lyric is little more than a snapshot of the disintegration of lovers: *"Don't look at the carpet, I drew something awful on it,"* and then, schizophrenically insistent, *"See!"* So what's drawn on the carpet? "Kabbalistic drawings of the Tree Of Life," Bowie claimed later.

He had indeed drawn the Tree Of Life on his floor while chemically snow-blind and darkly obsessed with conjuring spirits, prior to reinventing rock in Berlin. So was this short, sharp, synth-slashed descent into insanity and paranoia autobiographical? The clue's in *Low*'s title.

Lust For Life
Released by Iggy Pop, Lust For Life, 1977

When Bowie first hooked up with Iggy Pop, the question had to be asked: who's supposed to be saving whom? Obviously, Iggy had been going through problems,

CAMERA PRESS

Lust for life: on stage with Iggy Pop.

> "The intensity level builds throughout. You can hear him shift through the gears. By the time he gets to *'I remember standing by the wall'*, he's bleeding."
>
> **Dan Baird on *"Heroes"***

but Bowie was only just emerging from a coke maelstrom of his own. Where Iggy's *The Idiot* – written before Bowie properly embarked on what would become his celebrated 'Berlin Trilogy' – been the dark, gothic, industrial flip side of *"Heroes"*, *Lust For Life*'s title track sounded like triumph, an exhilarating celebration.

Hunt Sales's explosive drum tattoo springboards a nagging circular riff Bowie originally wrote on a ukulele, while Iggy's lyric – liquor, drugs, chickens, having it in the ear – is pure Iggy. Who saved whom? Who cares? That they were saved is all that matters.

"Heroes"
Heroes, 1977

DAN BAIRD, Homemade Sin
"I love the way the vocal performance builds from the back. The intensity level builds throughout. If he'd sung it in fourth gear all the way through, it wouldn't mean shit, but he starts in first and ascends all the way to the top. You can hear him shift through the gears. By the time he gets to *'I remember standing by the wall'*, he's bleeding.

Brian Eno's involvement is another huge element of that song's brilliance. Nobody else could have made it sound the way it did. He never gets carried away. It's the vocal that brings the song to a crescendo."

DORO PESCH
"When that record came out, the internet didn't exist, and I had no idea it was made in Berlin. It was such a haunting, beautiful and magical song. I was still at school, and I would listen to it over and over again.

Later on I met David at a rehearsal studio in New York. We had quite a long conversation, and even though we came from different musical worlds we really hit it off. He would always have beautiful women – one on each arm – and they were so tall they towered above us both. His presence and charisma were so inspiring. His eyes were captivating… I had never met anyone with eyes of different colours.

"Bowie released *"Heroes"* in German and French. I always loved *"Helden"*. My version of it was a part of my German-only album *Für Immer* [2017]. I dedicated it to all of my heroes that died, including Bowie, Lemmy and Ronnie James Dio."

V-2 Schneider
Heroes, 1977

While Bowie was a hero to many, he always had heroes of his own, heroes he generally acknowledged in his work – Dylan, Lou Reed, Iggy, Scott Walker. He invariably wore his musical influences on his sleeve, and *V-2 Schneider* is a nod to Kraftwerk

co-founder Florian Schneider. (And to the Third Reich's V-2 rocket, the first ballistic missile, although the best policy when dealing with all things Bowie during this occasionally unfortunate period of unguarded coke megalomania is to adopt Fawlty methodology and not mention the war.) Instrumental, other than a repetition of its much-phased title, Bowie's sax predominates.

Boys Keep Swinging
Lodger, 1979

Bowie and Eno. Who else would have invited their musicians to swap instruments, and therein find pure, chaotic genius? Looking to achieve the garage-band style that the song's mod era-echoing, narcissism-centred lyric suggested, Bowie turned to *Lodger* collaborator Eno, who flipped an Oblique Strategies card that suggested reverse roles. Consequently, guitarist and haphazard percussionist Carlos Alomar took to the drums, while drummer Dennis Davis was let loose on bass. The result was a rolling swagger that suited the song's one-chord-chorus style perfectly. Add an avant-garde Adrian Belew guitar solo and an unforgettable cross-dressing promo clip and you have a stone-cold classic.

D.J.
Lodger, 1979

Another nod from Bowie, this time to David Byrne (a fellow Eno associate) as he clearly mimics the Talking Heads frontman's trademark vocal style across the opening lines of this paean to the increasingly high-profile, powerful and, ultimately, crucial member of the late 70s music business community, the disc jockey. Maybe it was recognition of his subjects' enormous egos that saw Bowie (aka David Jones, aka *D.J.*) release such an uncommercial composition as a single, but a predictable glut of airplay saw Simon House's ▷

Bowie recording with Eno (left) and Robert Fripp.

extraordinary treated violin and Adrian Belew's Fripp-with-added-clang composite guitar break into the charts.

Fashion
Scary Monsters (And Super Creeps), 1980

There's a distinctly robotic feel to *Scary Monsters (And Super Creeps)'* second single, with its in-built stylistic echo of *Golden Years*. Long accorded the status of fashion icon, Bowie addressed the almost fascistic overtones of a blind conformity to fashion's fickle dictates: *"Turn to the left! Turn to the right!" "Bland… tasteless"* are hardly adjectives of approval. Then there are hints at Bowie's love/hate attitude to the clones peculiar to his fan-base: *"Listen to me, Don't listen to me… No!"* Ultimately, Bowie was all about style born of individuality. Fashion? Fashion was, as mod Marc Bolan might have put it, for the 'haddocks'.

Ashes To Ashes
Scary Monsters (And Super Creeps), 1980

ROB CAGGIANO, Volbeat
"Besides the fact that the lyrics and the melody are highly engaging and catchy in a way only Bowie can pull off, the production is so twisted and unique that it draws you in instantly. Combining the funk slap bass with the polar opposite new-wave elements and textures was brilliant and very ahead of its time. I also love how every section of the song is a different musical landscape. It really takes you on a journey. And of course he also brings back Major Tom [from *Space Oddity*] in the lyrics. Bowie and Tony Visconti really outdid themselves with this one!"

Scary Monsters (And Super Creeps)
Scary Monsters (And Super Creeps), 1980

Briefly readopting the caricature cockney of his earliest Anthony Newley-inflected vocal incarnation, Bowie recounts the tale of a woman whose eyes *"were blue but nobody home"*, touched by an insanity that manifests itself in *"a horror of rooms"*. So far, so Dave. But what nudges *Scary Monsters'* title track from greatness to true genius is returning sideman Robert Fripp's truly astounding atonal guitar work, mirroring the lyric's madness, set against a bass riff that pumps along with producer Tony Visconti's era-defining gated bass drum beat.

Under Pressure
Single, 1981

IGGOR CAVALERA, Cavalera Conspiracy
"For my brother Max and I, Queen's *Hot Space* was an absolute game changer. When it came out, people went mad because they'd gone all commercial. At the time, we were listening to much more heavy stuff, but Max and I bought the single. In some ways those metal bands were less explosive. We were like, 'Dude, fuck, this is insane' – the combination of Freddie and Bowie. Those two guys together was like a clash of the titans. I went on to explore a lot of the more experimental stuff that Bowie did, like the things with Brian Eno, but to this day I still think it's one of the coolest things he did."

Modern Love
Let's Dance, 1983

Distinctly touched by the hands of the 80s and a Nile Rodgers co-production which, while surely benefiting its title track, did very little to enhance the music elsewhere, *Let's Dance's* exuberant opener was as straightforward and superficial as anything Bowie ever offered up for public scrutiny. Finally in full commercial control (after years of fulfilling contractual obligations to ex-manager Tony Defries), Bowie was determined to make some real cash, and if anything was going to appeal to mainstream audience it was *Modern Love's* romping Little Richard-inspired repetitions. The climax on 1983's box office-busting Serious Moonlight tour.

Let's Dance
Let's Dance, 1983

JOE BONAMASSA
"As much as I really, really love the stuff that featured Mick Ronson, I'm gonna go with this one. Stevie Ray Vaughan played the lead guitar on it. David at that point was a stadium-level pop artist but decided –as he was often prone to do – to just go and do something different instead. So he allowed Steve to lay down a load of blues guitar over a pop song, and of course it really, really worked."

KIP WINGER, Winger
"It's very un-Bowie, and he came to hate it. I think that's so interesting. Nile Rogers's producing was amazing on that record and it was immensely successful. I think it created havoc in Bowie's psyche, as he had 'sold out'. That's right – sold out every seat in the house. It's the point where his amazing vocal performances became immortalised to the masses, yet he was unhappy with it. I find that so interesting. I love the song and the whole record, as well as all of his more eclectic music. But there's no way around the fact that this record, for better or for worse, blew him up into a massive superstar – and I love irony."

China Girl
Let's Dance 1983 version, with and credited to Iggy Pop, 1977

While it was Bowie's version that engendered the hit, it's Iggy's original interpretation that truly captures its intrinsic magic and, indeed, madness. During *The Idiot's* sessions at the Château d'Hérouville, Iggy fell head over heels in unrequited love with Kuelan Nguyen, but when he attempted to announce his feelings she simply replied: "Shhh." Quite where all the paranoid *"visions of swastikas"* came from is anyone's guess, but, well, we are talking about Iggy Pop here.

While Iggy's take is characterised by claustrophobic post-punk-presaging production and Bowie's toy piano, Dave's has Stevie Ray Vaughan, an inappropriately upbeat Carmine Rojas bass figure and that video.

Loving The Alien
Tonight, 1984

While Bowie always preferred the version captured on his original demo, his passionately delivered (and possibly never more pertinent) Holy Land-based indictment of all forms of organised religion is one of very few highlights to be found on the moribund, time-marking and, depressingly, commercially titanic *Tonight* album.

> "The production is so twisted and unique that it draws you in instantly."
> **Rob Caggiano on *Ashes To Ashes***

One of only two tracks written solely by Bowie for the record (the other being the sparkling single *Blue Jean*), its brilliance lies in an astonishing vocal performance that shines in spite of a laboured, synth-heaped and polite production job so irretrievably 80s that it might as well be wearing deely boppers. But that voice…

Absolute Beginners
Single A-side, 1986

P robably the best thing about Julien Temple's well-intentioned 1986 adaptation of Colin MacInnes's era-defining 1959 book of the same name was its extraordinary title track. Its composition took Bowie – mourning the recent death by suicide of his half-brother Terry Burns, reputed subject of *Hunky Dory* classic The Bewlay Brothers – back to the very peak of his form.

An epic Bowie-Langer-Winstanley production, complete with ABBA-alike Rick Wakeman piano flourishes, it's rendered perfect by a wild-card personnel decision. Bowie wanted someone who sounded 'like a shop girl'. Guitarist Kevin Armstrong said: "My sister works in a shop," and so the entirely untested Janet Armstrong supplied a co-vocal that charms beyond the capabilities of any seasoned pro.

Under The God
Tin Machine, 1989

S ometimes, being a globally acclaimed, fabulously wealthy international superstar simply isn't enough. The urge to be perceived as just another member of a critically derided, suit-wearing metal combo with limited commercial appeal becomes overwhelming. Midlife crisis? Whatever, the media invariably lauded Bowie for his uncompromising penchant for constant change – until he changed into something of which they didn't approve.

Eighties metal was music press poison. Consequently, Tin Machine's first single, an all-guitars-blazing, if relatively conventional, full-frontal assault on the global forces of neo-fascism (take that, Thin White Duke!) fell foul of dismissive reviews and a largely oblivious mainstream. But time has treated it kindly – it stands as a thrilling repudiation of what had come just before.

You Belong In Rock 'N' Roll
Tin Machine II, 1991

RACHEL BOLAN, Skid Row
"Not everybody sees it, but there's a reference to David – '*Some kids think Bowie's just a knife*' – in our song *Monkey Business*, so I'm a massive fan. Besides an obvious choice like *Rock 'N' Roll Suicide*, which is incredible, I'm going to go with something left-field. *You Belong In Rock 'N' Roll* was a single from the second album by Tin Machine. It felt like David was singing directly to me. That happens with some songs. The first time I heard it [in 1991], I had no idea whether we [Skid Row] were going to be doing that any more, so it really connected with me on a one-to-one basis. It reminded me that

Peer Pressure: Bowie and Fredie Mercury.

"The metal bands were less explosive than *Under Pressure*. We were like, 'Dude, f**k, this is insane – the combination of Freddie and Bowie.' It was like a clash of the titans."

Iggor Cavalera

making music was exactly what I should be doing for the rest of my life."

The Buddha Of Suburbia
The Buddha Of Suburbia, 1993

B owie finally emerged from a difficult 80s into his full-scale 90s renaissance by temporarily eschewing forward momentum and seeking inspiration in his own catalogue. Commissioned to provide the theme music for the BBC's adaptation of Hanif Kureishi's 70s-set book *The Buddha Of Suburbia*, he composed a glorious self-parody that sounded like a hugely

welcome return to form for Bowie. Octave-parted double-tracked vocals reminiscent of *The Bewlay Brothers* and especially *All The Madmen* ("Zane zane zane, Ouvrez le chien"), an acoustic bridge straight out of *Space Oddity* and a soaring sax break are deployed in a nostalgic and emotive fan-directed masterpiece that effortlessly transcends mere pastiche.

The Hearts Filthy Lesson
Outside, 1995

T hat this intentionally apostrophe-free descent into disconcerting industrial darkness was adopted as the closing theme to David Fincher's self-consciously disturbing serial-killer movie *Se7en* really tells you everything you need to know about it. As a nagging, distorted, dirty, Eno-treated guitar figure repeats insistently, Mike Garson hurls eccentric, avant-garde piano ejaculations into the mix, while Bowie's stressed vocal unravels subterranean yarns of extraordinary madness. Sterling Campbell's robotic drums drop away briefly as Bowie drawls an enigmatic '*Paddy, who's been wearing Miranda's clothes?*' and it's pure *Psycho*. Trent Reznor's alternative mix cranks the psychosis yet further.

No Control
Outside, 1995

ARJEN LUCASSEN, Ayreon
"I love the intro, the melody and the way Bowie arranged it. It's a totally modern song from his *Outside* album. For me it's all about the melody. *No Control* is so hummable and memorable. I tried to cover it on my solo album *Lost In The Real New* [2012], but of course I couldn't better or add anything new to the original so I gave up on it." ▷

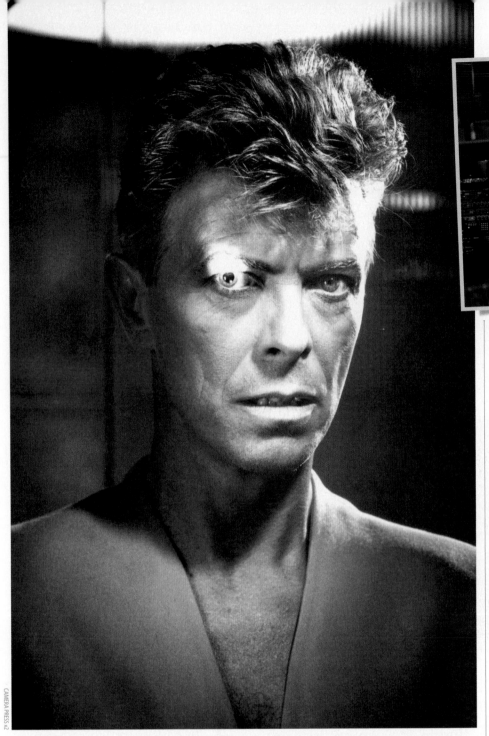

> "It has the aggressive sound that I like, and for this day and age and the climate that we live in, its lyrical message seems appropriate."
>
> **Dweezil Zappa on *I'm Afraid Of Americans***

drum'n'bass-themed tracks sound a little dated now, but this still sounds great, I reckon."

JONNY LANG

"I first saw him sing that one during a televised concert and I loved it. His delivery was masterful. I won't presume to say I know what David was talking about in the lyrics, but the song's honesty and sincerity really connected with me. I love its sense of art."

CHRIS ROBERTSON, Black Stone Cherry

"The [remixed] version that he did with Trent Reznor [for the expanded edition of *Earthling*] is incredible. The video of David walking about in the street and being followed around and then chased by Trent in New York is just fascinating. For the life of me I don't know what the song is really about [laughs], but it always stuck out to me as something really special and unique."

DWEEZIL ZAPPA

"I love all of the elements to that song. It has the aggressive sound that I like, and for this day and age and the climate that we live in, its lyrical message seems appropriate [laughs]. In fact in a couple of days I'm actually going to cut my own version of it. I thought that might be fun, though at the moment I'm not sure how I will release it."

The Pretty Things Are Going To Hell
Hours, 1999

This track is thematically pessimistic and, tragically, probably more pertinent to our unfolding future than it was at the dawn of the millennium. The Pretty Things of the song's title are the spiritual progeny of Evelyn Waugh's 'bright young things': carefree youth, the likes of which Bowie celebrated on *Hunky Dory*, yet that he now imagined were facing extinction in the *"tough times"* of the contemporary zeitgeist. Allied to an engaging Reeves Gabrels guitar hook and a propulsive, driving chug, *Pretty Things* sounds less like a requiem for doomed young dudes (*'They wore it out, but they wore it well'*), more a brooding rock monster.

Thursday's Child
Hours, 1999

This lush, reflective ballad was inspired by Eartha Kitt's autobiography of the same name. Along with DH Lawrence,

Hallo Spaceboy
Outside, 1995

With the spirit of Tin Machine proving hard to exorcise entirely, Bowie rekindled his relationship with old compatriot Brian Eno set to work with Tin Machine/*Outside* guitarist Reeves Gabrels on the latter's *Moondust*, a hitherto instrumental composition that rapidly mutated into a pounding *"this chaos is killing me"* sound collage of punishing drums, wildly panning guitars and claustrophobic industrial-rock devices. On the US leg of 1995's *Outside* tour, Bowie and band would share the stage with Nine Inch Nails for *Hallo Spaceboy*. As if his of-the-moment approximation of 'the metal Doors' didn't sound cutting-edge enough, he then gave it to Neil Tennant for a Pet Shop Boys remix.

I'm Afraid Of Americans
Earthling, 1997

BRUCE SOORD, The Pineapple Thief

"When I heard the *Earthling* album it blew me away. The production is high-quality but aggressive, and it still sounds great today. Maybe some of the

"Thank you, and goodnight..."

PRESS

it provided the 14-year-old Bowie with some of his "favourite bedtime reading", according to his VH1 *Storytellers* appearance. There's no deeper significance here. Despite the nursery rhyme's insistence that "Thursday's child had far to go", Bowie was born on a Wednesday. There's something of *The Buddha Of Suburbia* in this Reeves Gabrels co-production's mood, and its intrinsic melancholia is accentuated by a dreamlike Holly Palmer backing vocal. Having passed through the cleansing fire of *Outside*, Bowie's narrator finally appears to be finding inner peace.

Slip Away
Heathen, 2002

The first Bowie classic of the new millennium, *Slip Away* addresses the ephemeral nature of fame from the perspective of abandoned puppets. While appearing in the 1980 Broadway production of *The Elephant Man*, Bowie took to watching *The Uncle Floyd Show*, which disappeared from schedules in 1999. Meditating on life after celebrity, *Slip Away* imagines the puppets Oogie and Bones Boy's post-*Floyd* limbo: "*Once a time they nearly might have nearly been, Bones and Oogie on a silver screen,*" and the poignancy of Bowie's impassioned delivery universalises the silent pain of the abandoned glazed-eyed puppets' sense of loss. Which is no mean feat.

New Killer Star
Reality, 2003

With an abstract lyric that's haunted by 9/11, oblique religious/pop culture references ("*Like seeing Jesus on Dateline*") and a conciliatory central core ("*I'll never said* [sic] *I'm better… than you*"), *New Killer* (nuclear) *Star* benefits from the vintage sparkle of Tony Visconti's hands on the desk. Just as you're settled into the solid, dependable groove of what first appears to be a perfectly acceptable chorus, it suddenly reveals itself to be a diversion, a mere bridging section that soars into a chorus as magical as anything you'd expect from Bowie and Visconti in harness. Bowie was back! And then gone…

Where Are We Now?
The Next Day, 2013

Ten years on from the release of *Reality*, following a decade of significant speculation as to Bowie's state of health, the surprise-released *Where Are We Now?* arrived into an unsuspecting world on his

66th birthday, to universal acclaim. Supported by an extraordinary promotional video featuring the wife of its director Tony Oursler – artist Jacqueline Humphries – and Bowie as conjoined puppets, it's a composition loaded with backward-glancing melancholia. Heavy with nostalgia, specifically for 70s Berlin, Oursler's promo is cut with vintage clips of the divided city Bowie briefly called home from 1976. *Where Are We Now?* confirms Bowie's lifelong ability to deliver the heartbreakingly brilliant.

Blackstar
Blackstar, 2016

DAVE MATTHEWS
"The song and the album are both unbelievable. I find it almost infuriating that somebody could be such an unrelenting artist. Staring at one's own mortality and calmly producing something of that magnitude – also doing it in secret! – is barely conceivable. I mean, put yourself in the place of his band. When they find out that he was there singing and making that music, knowing his time was dwindling… good grief, what kind of a human being could do that?"

CARL PALMER
"The whole *Blackstar* album is tremendous, and I love the title track. Try to forget about the fact that he knew he was dying when he made it. It's an unbelievable piece of art. The sparseness of the production and the voice… the videos were chilling. You can talk about *Space Oddity* and *Let's Dance* all you like, but this one was just… deep."

The Resurrection Of David Bowie

Rumours of Bowie's demise proved to be premature when he released new album *The Next Day* in March 2013. This is how he made his surprise comeback.

Words: **Johnny Black**

Even the most optimistic David Bowie fan had given up on their hero releasing any music ever again. The singer had largely vanished from public life following serious heart problems in 2004, prompting rumours that he had retired or was seriously ill. Consequently, the announcement on Radio 4's *Today* programme on the morning of January 8, 2013 was a bombshell: Bowie would be releasing a brand new single, *Where Are We Now?*, that day, and it would be followed by his first album in a decade, *The Next Day*. What made the news even more surprising was that both had been recorded in total secrecy, in the heart of Manhattan, with everyone from his record label to the general public kept in the dark.

Tony Visconti (producer): We all know he had a health scare. I hate to hear it described as a major heart attack – it was not a major heart attack – but he had surgery in 2004 and he's been healthy ever since. Because he hasn't come out and said anything, people suspect the worst. And it was frustrating. I would have lunch with him and I'd tell people that he looks fantastic and he sounds great and all that, and people would not believe me.

Gail Ann Dorsey (longtime Bowie bassist): I'd had some correspondence with him where he'd said that he just wasn't interested in writing music anymore, because he didn't have anything to say.

Tony Visconti: Music didn't interest him until two years ago; that's when he made the call. He said: "How would you like to make some demos?" He just said: "I feel like writing again." I don't know how long prior to that he began writing. He came up with [demos of] about eight songs. He wrote them at home.

Gerry Leonard (Bowie's guitarist and musical director): David sent me an email asking if I was free for a week during November 2010 to get in a tiny basement rehearsal room in the East Village with him, [drummer] Sterling Campbell and Tony Visconti to play through some ideas he had. The title of the email was "Schtum", and that, apart from "bring your guitar", was the main instruction.

Tony Visconti: David prefaced every session [saying] that it was experimental and that it might not be an album, so let's just get together and make some music. Even when we made the first demos we were sworn to secrecy.

Gerry Leonard: We would arrive at 10, play through one or two song ideas until lunch, then after lunch play through another couple. For some, David had rough-sketch recordings on his little four-track recorder. Or he would play us chord changes for sections on piano or guitar, or sing melody ideas. But he always had a definite idea and direction for the song. Most of them had simple one-word working titles, or sometimes even a number. We would knock off around five or six pm. We did that for four days. And then, on the last day, we made a super-fast recording where we replayed everything we did all week, just as a memo.

Tony Visconti: Then he disappeared for four months and said: "I'm gonna start writing now." So he wrote more songs and then fleshed those out even more.

Mario J McNulty (engineer/producer): I had lunch with Tony, right at the start of January 2011. We went to Tony's studio, and while I was there David called him. That's when they broke the news to me and asked if I'd be interested in getting involved. Like everybody else, I had to sign a non-disclosure agreement.

Tony Visconti: The members of the band, the engineers, the people who bring us coffee in the studio, everybody who was involved had to sign, to keep this a secret.

Kabir Hermon (project manager, The Magic Shop studio): Tony Visconti came down to get a feel for the studio in February or March of 2011, but we didn't know who the artist was until the day he came in.

Zack Alford (drummer): David sent me an email asking if I was available in the first two weeks of May. It was out of the blue. He wouldn't even say where it was or what it was. I remember Gail Ann Dorsey and I talking about it, like, "Oh, did he contact you too?" "Yeah, he contacted me." "What's it for?" "I don't know."

Kabir Hermon: David and the musicians came in on May 2, which I remember because it was the day Bin Laden died.

Steve Rosenthal (owner, The Magic Shop): I've owned this studio for 26 years, but I've never experienced the level of secrecy we had to achieve for David's album. Each time David came to the studio we allowed about 60 per cent of our staff to take time off, because the more people who knew, the more danger there was of the story getting out. We're in SoHo, in Manhattan, right across the street from Bloomingdale's, but I keep the studio entrance low-key. David was usually able to ➧

> ## "Music didn't interest him until two years ago; that's when he made the call."
> ### Tony Visconti

Tony Visconti (left), Bowie and staff enginneer Brian Thorn at The Magic Shop.

"During the recording he was smiling, he was so happy to be back in the studio," says Visconti,

come and go, but there was one occasion when someone nearby thought they saw him, and we just denied it, like, "Naw, c'mon, man. No way."

Mario McNulty: During the first phase at The Magic Shop, which was about three weeks, I believe he had about 16 or 18 demos to work on.

Tony Visconti: During the recording he was smiling, he was so happy to be back in the studio.

Gerry Leonard: I really enjoyed the spontaneity of those sessions. One day, for example, I was doing overdubs and Tony says: "Do you want to try it on Marc's guitar?" It turned out to be Marc Bolan's Stratocaster. Another time David had me come in and said: "Trust me, just bring a favourite guitar." He and Tony had recreated Mick Ronson's set-up from an old photograph from a rehearsal back in the day. They had me plug into it and do some overdubs.

Gail Ann Dorsey: The sheet music that was handed out as each new song was introduced was always meticulously and purposefully collected from our music stands at the end of the day so that there wasn't even a chance of a piece of paper with some chords scribbled on it being leaked or entering into the world. It was something from a spy movie.

Kabir Hermon: One day Emily Haines and James Shaw of the band Metric dropped by to see Brian Thorn, the engineer, to see when they could next come in for a session. We had to keep them at the door, and Brian told them they couldn't come in. I think they were super-confused by that.

Tony Visconti: Robert Fripp was asked to play on it. He didn't want to do it. And then he wrote on his blog that he was asked. And nobody believed him. It was a little flurry for a few days, but everyone said, how could that be true, we haven't heard it from anyone else.

Kabir Harmon: They returned to The Magic Shop in the second week of January 2012, for another two weeks.

Tony Visconti: His [Bowie's] stamina was fantastic. It was as if he never stopped doing this for a 10 year period. He was singing with every live take; quite often he'd play piano or guitar at the same time. And when it came time to do the final vocals, he was as loud as he ever was.

Brian Thorn (assistant engineer): The distinctive drum sound on *Where Are We Now?* was partially obtained from the use of a random microphone that was set up for another instrument that wasn't being played. It was just in a spot in the room that everyone thought just sounded great.

Tony Visconti: I didn't hear the lyrics until about five months after it was recorded. It was called something else. He came in one day and said: "I've written words for that. I wrote a song about Berlin." And I thought: "That's really cool." And he gave me a copy [of the lyrics], and got on mic and started warming up. I read the lyrics and it gave me goose-bumps, because I spent quite a while in Berlin, too, making the three [of Bowie's] albums that are called the Berlin Trilogy.

Mario McNulty: Earl Slick came in to do guitar overdubs for about a week in July 2012.

Earl Slick: It's just a really relaxed, casual, hanging out. The only thing was that it had a lot more secrecy going on. I mean, one day I went out to have a cigarette in front of the studio. And something felt weird. I peered across the street, and there was a guy there with a camera on a tripod. So I put my cigarette out and went back inside. 'Cos if they see me, they can put two and two together.

Tony Visconti: Earl Slick was the tearing-it-up lead guitarist, and then both Gerry and David have different versions of ambient guitar, very dreamy, washy kind of guitar sounds. So the three guitarists were very complementary.

Mario McNulty: *Valentine's Day*, the fourth single, was mostly Slick, maybe all Slick.

Kabir Hermon: Their last lot of sessions at The Magic Shop were in early September of 2012.

Tony Visconti: We over-recorded – I think 29 songs in all – and some of them were abandoned within weeks. They just didn't work out.

Mario McNulty: One thing I'm really pleased about was that I was able to take all of the different parts, different instruments, recorded in separate

> **"On one occasion someone saw David near the studio. We just denied it: 'C'mon, man. No way'."** Steve Rosenthal

The news of Bowie's new album was as much a surprise as seeing him playing banjo.

studios with different players, and make them all sound like one seamless, cohesive body of work.

Tony Visconti: Rob Stringer [President of Sony Music Group, Bowie's label] came to the studio in December 2012. He was thrilled. He said: "What about the PR campaign?" And David said: "There is no PR campaign. We're just going to drop it on eighth of January. That's it."

Julian Stockton (publicist, the Outside Organisation): We first heard about it on Friday [January 4]. Alan [Edwards, Outside's MD] was called to New York for a meeting and told about the album and the single, and instructed to get the message out on the *Today* programme. I was in the office at 4am on Tuesday, waiting to hear a single that I had to write a press release for by 5am.

Tony Visconti: When it was released, I stared at my computer for 15 minutes until the first person realised it was simply dropped in iTunes.

Mario J. McNulty: This record is one for the history books. I can't ever see an artist like David, with his status, pulling off a secret album like this again. ●

WHAT HAPPENED NEXT?
The Next Day was released on March 11, 2013 and debuted at No.1 in the UK chart. Bowie refused to break his silence to promote the album. His only statement was a 'work flow diagram' made up of 42 words, among them 'Cthonic', 'Miasma' and 'Comeuppance'.

TOGETHER WE'RE
LOUDER
LOUDERSOUND.COM

ROCK   HAMMER   PROG   BLUES

On January 8, 2016, David Bowie released his 26th album, *Blackstar*. Two days later, news of his death was announced. This is how he turned his final exit into one of his greatest works of art.

Words: **John Aizlewood**

"LOOK UP HERE...

What next? 2013's *The Next Day* did its job like no David Bowie album since *Let's Dance*, back in the last century. His first British No.1 since 1993's *Black Tie White Noise*, it was also his highest charting album in the US where it soared to No.2. Moreover, for all that *The Next Day* took fewer chances than much of his 21st Century output, it was objectively a superior effort: the songs were better.

Having retreated – though not retired – from public life since his heart attack of 2004, the release of *The Next Day* came as a surprise. Bowie had regained his aura of mystery. The question remained, though. What next?

With no touring duties to fulfil and no interviews to give, Bowie submerged with as little fuss as he'd surfaced. To the outside eye, he disappeared, but walked his daughter Alexandria, aka Lexi, to school every day; he frequented Puckfair, a bar opposite his apartment on Lafayette Street, SoHo; he'd wander around Manhattan with a Greek newspaper prominently visible, so passers-by would assume he was a Greek guy who looked a little bit like some famous rock star.

Of course he didn't disappear, he took stock and went back to work. The stocktaking was very Bowie. He retained the secrecy of recording, he retained Manhattan's Magic Shop and Human Worldwide studios and he retained the signing of NDAs for collaborators. *The Next Day*'s co-producer Tony Visconti was back too, but Bowie instinctively grasped that the album had opened a new world of opportunities. Just as the success of his 70s and 80s albums enabled him to

take unexpected new directions, to kill Ziggy Stardust, to embrace soul, electronica, rock'n'roll, cover versions and, lest we forget, unashamed commercialism, *The Next Day* gave him artistic freedom and people were listening again.

He dumped both *The Next Day*'s band of star-sessioneers and long-term bassist Gail Ann Dorsey. In June 2014 he had his people contact Maria Schneider's people via Facebook. Bowie had seen the jazz composer and bandleader in concert some years before. Bowie was such a fan that a friend had asked for a signed set of Schneider's albums made out "To David" as a birthday present.

"He had a song he'd started that he wanted to collaborate on," she remembered in 2017. She brought in her saxophonist Donny McCaslin and guitarist Ben Monder. The result was *Sue (Or In A Season Of Crime)*, which would become the single from November's *Nothing Has Changed* compilation. Something had changed though: around the time of the *Sue* sessions, Bowie was diagnosed with liver cancer. He started chemotherapy. None of the musicians had an inkling. It was a battle he was convinced he would win, but beyond wife Iman, Lexi Corinne 'Coco' Schwab (his assistant of 43 years), Visconti and archivist Jimmy King, he would fight it in private.

For the rest of 2014, Bowie busied himself writing and demoing songs. He'd enjoyed working with McCaslin and Monder and decided their jazz style would be the launchpad for the sound of the next album, already destined to be more experimental and avant than *The Next Day*. McCaslin became the band leader and he recruited drummer Mark Guiliana, keyboardist Jason Lindner and bassist

Tim Lefebvre. All were technically brilliant but musically flexible, just as Bowie required. By the end of the year, the musicians had Bowie's first demos. Such was Bowie's enthusiasm at what his new band brought, he took another crack at *Sue (Or In A Season Of Crime)* and its b-side, *'Tis A Pity She Was A Whore*, on which he had played everything. LCD Soundsystem leader James Murphy added percussion in February and Monder returned in March.

His condition notwithstanding, Bowie was in a hurry. The band recorded tracks at Magic Shop for both *Blackstar* and what would become the musical *Lazarus* (only the musical's title track would make both). Other than the studio creation *Dollar Days*, the method was the same: Bowie sent demos, the musicians brought their magic to short studio sessions (11am to 4pm) and voila.

Francis Whately, director of *The Last Five Years* documentary, which detailed the making of *Blackstar* without interviewing Bowie, said of the sessions: "Everyone would like me to say he was turning up to the studio to record *Blackstar* and he was terribly ill, but I don't think he was. There were musicians in the *Blackstar* band who didn't even know".

By April, the musicians' work was complete. Bowie had sung guide vocals at Magic Shop and only his work on *Lazarus*'s *No Plan* would make the final cut. He and Visconti moved to Human Worldwide, where they could properly record the vocals. By the end of May, everyone was happy.

Damien Hirst collaborator Jonathan Barnbrook, responsible for Bowie's album artwork since 2002's *Heathen*, designed the stark sleeve. It was full of hidden treasures, not least the squiggles under the black star itself, forming the word B-O-W-I-E. ▷

..I'M IN HEAVEN"

David shot by Jimmy King in New York during his last ever photoshoot.

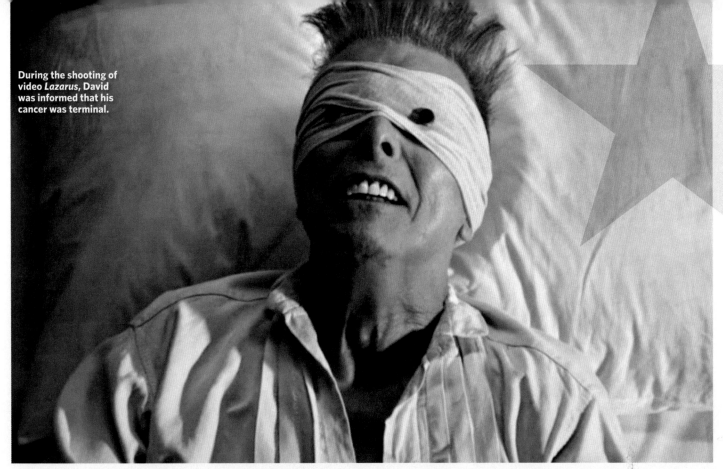

During the shooting of video *Lazarus*, David was informed that his cancer was terminal.

"From the beginning, we discussed not revealing everything," explained Barnbrook of the artwork. "There are certain things about the cover which haven't been discovered. Bowie didn't know about some of them."

All that remained was for two videos to be filmed, both directed by Johan Renck, the Swede formerly known as dance act Stakka Bo. The surreal mini-epic *Blackstar* itself was filmed in September; *Lazarus* a month later. Both featured Bowie with a bandage around his head.

Lazarus finds Bowie partly filmed in what hindsight may suggest was a deathbed. During the week of shooting, Bowie was informed that his cancer was terminal and his treatments would be stopped. Renck, however, says the ideas for the video were already in place.

Bowie had attended *Lazarus* rehearsals and when that became too difficult, he had a camera installed at home so he could observe and pass on notes. On December 7, the *Lazarus* musical, which updated the saga of *The Man Who Fell To Earth*'s Thomas Newton, opened at the New York Theatre Workshop. Still, somehow, in a whirlwind of creativity, Bowie had already demoed songs for *Blackstar*'s sequel, including a potential duet with Lorde. The opening would be Bowie's last public

appearance. If *Lazarus* director Ivo van Hove's recollections are accurate, Bowie was still denying what so few very knew to be inevitable.

"He got through the night," van Hove said. "I'm convinced that he was fighting death and he wanted to continue and continue. Afterwards we were sitting behind the stage and he said 'let's start the sequel to *Lazarus* now'. It reminded me of Dennis Potter, who wrote right up to his deathbed. Bowie put up an incredible fight. He really didn't want to die."

Titled after an Elvis Presley song, a cancerous lesion which appears in the shape of a black star, or something else entirely, *Blackstar* was released on January 8, 2016, Bowie 69th birthday. Bowie's death in the SoHo apartment – and, finally, the cancer which caused it – was announced two days later. There was no funeral. He was cremated in New Jersey on January 12. His ashes were scattered in Bali in accordance with his interest in Buddhism.

Blackstar was a British No.1 and his first American chart-topper. Much of his back catalogue charted in the UK. The city of Berlin, his muse in the late 70s, commemorated him with a plaque (it may not seem much, but it's officially a five-year wait for the newly deceased). Belgian astronomers registered a constellation (near Mars of course) in his name.

There were tributes from sources likely (his musical contemporaries) and unlikely ("musically, creatively and artistically, David Bowie was a genius," said then-British Prime Minister David Cameron, although he couldn't name a favourite track), vigils and in June, a lock of his hair sold for $18,750. In November his art collection was sold for £32.5 million in London.

Half of Bowie's £70 million will and the SoHo apartment went to Iman. Son Duncan received 25% of the estate, as did Lexi, who also received the family's mountain retreat in Ulster County, New York. Schwab received $2million and the

still-mysterious company, Opossum Inc, while Duncan's Scottish nanny Marion Skene – who looked after the then-Zowie while Bowie and first wife Angie were keener on narcotics than nappy changing – was gifted $1 million.

Inevitably there was a rush to find clues to his demise that Bowie may or may not have left, both in his actual death, which Visconti suggested was "a work of art", and his final work.

Even without Bowie's passing distorting the issue and for all the tendency to read final farewells in *Lazarus*'s opening line *"Look up here, I'm in heaven"* and *I Can't Give Everything Away*'s *"seeing more and feeling less/Saying no but meaning yes/This is all I ever meant/That's the message that I sent"* (wait until people read the lyrics to *Ashes To Ashes*), the seven tracks have retained their charms.

It's a great Bowie album; it's a great album full stop. It's brave, full of both reflection and promise and while it was an extraordinary way to finish an extraordinary career, it wasn't meant to be a full stop. There was clearly so much more to come. What next? Simple: he wanted to carry on living and carry on creating. ❼

Just where is the best place to start with the bewildering extensive back catalogue of one of the greatest popular music artists of all time? From the landmark albums to the forgotten gems, here's our guide...

While most of his peers softened into water-treading middle-age, David Bowie's view on art was that it was almost worth drowning for. "If you feel safe in the area that you're working in, you're not working in the right area," he once advised. "Always go a little further into the water than you feel you're capable of being in. Go a little bit out of your depth. And when you don't feel that your feet are quite touching the bottom, you're just about at the right place to do something exciting."

It was a soundbite that Bowie lived by. Flying in the face of that tiresome 'chameleon' tag, the songwriter preferred to innovate and let the rock landscape blend in with him. Then, once that musical skin became too snug, he would cast it off and forge ahead. We watched Bowie repeat this thrilling trick countless times, right the way to the release of 2016's swansong, *Blackstar*, recorded with a troupe of previously esoteric New York jazzers. The catalogue he leaves behind is, quite simply, one of the bravest in rock'n'roll.

A Bowie reinvention was nothing less than a bonfire of the old ways. When he was reborn, everything that went before was scattered to the winds. The musical direction might flip from crunching glam-rock to breezy plastic soul. The production might trade sumptuous strings for buzzsaw distortion. The persona could switch from rock'n'roll spaceman (Ziggy Stardust) to emaciated sieg-heiling provocateur (the Thin White Duke). Even Bowie's musicians – always a vital strand of each new era – had precious little job security, as the artist amicably hired and fired according to his muse.

Bowie's flair for tearing it all down made him both irresistible and inconsistent. He junked genres and collaborators when it seemed there was more gas in the tank. He hung around longer than we'd have liked in such divisive waters as electronica and dance. Occasionally, his taste for the new seemed contrived – and during his torrid late 80s, there's a case that he missed the target as often as he hit it.

And yet, as he proved with his restorative millennial output, you discounted David Bowie at your peril. While most rock legends settled into their groove, this questing songwriter refused to be tied down: surprising, wrong-footing and kicking out against familiarity, right until the end.

Henry Yates

BUYER'S GUIDE
David Bowie

GETTY

The Man Who Sold The World

(RCA, 1971)

The recruitment of Hull-born guitarist Mick Ronson was a transformative move and the sea change was evident immediately on *The Man Who Sold The World*, a third album that shredded Bowie's early acoustic folk-pop sensibilities and set him up as a bona fide rock star.

While not quite as front-to-back brilliant as the 70s work to come, thrilling moments abound, from the primitive punch of *Black Country Rock* to the descending intro of *The Width Of A Circle* (a riff that feels like the template for stoner rock). Towering above it all is the title track, its haunted guitar hook still one of the loneliest sounds in rock'n'roll.

Hunky Dory

(RCA, 1971)

The album that floating fans take off the shelf – for good reason. Stick a pin in even Bowie's best records and you'll find missteps, but the songs he tracked at Trident Studios over the summer of 1971 are solid gold.

From the opening swell of *Changes* to the shivering epic *Life On Mars?*, the sunshine of *Fill Your Heart* to the punky smash-and-grab of *Queen Bitch* (a backhanded tribute to former Velvet Underground frontman Lou Reed), this is Bowie at his most unashamedly melodious, serving up hooks that remain deathless more than half a century later.

A stone cold classic, and the only release that gives *Ziggy* a serious run for its money.

The Rise And Fall Of Ziggy Stardust And The Spiders From Mars

(RCA, 1972)

The back sleeve advised that Bowie's fifth was 'To Be Played At Maximum Volume', and these songs deserved nothing less. At the sweet spot between experimentation and route-one rock, equally good on headphones or heard in snatches on the radio, this loose concept album saw the Ziggy character lead us from the impending doom of *Five Years* to the agonised *Rock 'N' Roll Suicide*, via glorious pop hooks like *Starman* and the title track.

Bowie would never be better, but there's a case that Ziggy belongs equally to Mick Ronson.

Aladdin Sane

(RCA, 1973)

After the springboard of the previous year's *Ziggy*, Bowie was a megastar in motion, and much of this sequel was penned as he watched America whip past the windows of the tour bus.

In lesser hands, the circumstances might have resulted in a transitional work, but *Aladdin Sane* felt like anything but a dashed-off postcard, offering a run of gems from *Ziggy*-esque rockers (*The Jean Genie*) to flesh-creeping anti-ballads (*Lady Grinning Soul*), and from blues-rooted shuffles (*Panic In Detroit*) to blue-eyed pop (*Drive-In Saturday*).

Most exciting of all is *Watch That Man*, whose build-back-up outro stands amongst the most exciting sounds Bowie ever made.

Diamond Dogs

(RCA, 1974)

When Bowie was denied permission to stage a theatre production based on George Orwell's *Nineteen Eighty-Four*, the redundant songs wound up on *Diamond Dogs*.

Those cut-and-paste roots led to a semi-concept album that loosely riffs on a vision of a decaying future, but it works, thanks to some of Bowie's toughest songs, taking in the full-throttle title track, the trashy riff cycle of *Rebel Rebel* and a dystopian lyric sheet he deemed a "precursor to the punk thing".

Coolly received but growing in stature since, the only frustration of *Dogs* is that these songs would surely have punched even harder with the Spiders lineup.

Young Americans

(RCA, 1975)

Bowie had broken into a strut by the mid 70s, confident enough to toss out tired influences and indulge his fresh fixation with Philly soul at the city's Sigma Sound studio.

All clipped beats, exuberant brass and airtight guitars from incoming sideman Carlos Alomar, *Young Americans* was an adroit engagement with black genres and demanded the listener's movement from the spring-heeled title track to the glittering funky finale, *Fame*. Always ambivalent about the record, Bowie deemed *Young Americans* "the squashed remains of ethnic music… written and sung by a white limey".

A pastiche, perhaps, but one of the best you'll ever hear.

Station To Station

(RCA, 1976)

Bowie's herculean mid 70s drug intake meant he claimed not to remember making *Station To Station*. For anyone less addled, this tenth record ranks amongst his most memorable.

Comprising six extended tracks whose brittle emotions hold up a mirror to Bowie's mindset (at this point, he was trading as the Thin White Duke), *Station* bore the aftertaste of *Young Americans'* funk-soul stylings on moments like *Stay*, while hinting at the chillier electronic leanings the Berlin Trilogy would soon explore.

For instant gratification, it has to be *Golden Years*, while slow-burn *Wild Is The Wind* demands headphones and full focus.

Low

(RCA, 1977)

Heralding critics favourite Berlin trilogy, *Low* was as fractured and inconstant as Bowie's headspace as he clawed back from the cocaine blizzard of the *Station To Station* era at the city's Hansa TonStudios.

Alongside co-producer Tony Visconti – with a defining contribution from ex-Roxy Music man Brian Eno on synth and general vibes – Bowie crafted an often-unsettling soundscape that roamed from caustic post punk like *What In The World* to nuclear-winter instrumentals (*Warszawa*).

Aside from the welcoming side one crowd-pleasers like *Sound And Vision* and *Speed Of Life*, *Low* is hardly Bowie's most accessible work, but there's an argument that it stands amongst his bravest.

"Heroes"

(RCA, 1977)

On the mother of all hot streaks, Bowie followed up *Low* the same year with his second Berlin-inspired record.

Once again recorded with Visconti at Hansa, *"Heroes"* shares a noticeably similar atmosphere with its predecessor, particularly on austere moments like *Sense Of Doubt* and *Neuköln*, but there's more light creeping beneath the curtain here, from the spiky riffing of *Joe The Lion* to the barrelhouse stomp of *Beauty And The Beast* – and of course the peerless reunification anthem, *'Heroes'*.

This time, too, Bowie's secret weapon was the envelope-pushing fretwork of Robert Fripp, the King Crimson guitarist roaming the studio floor to find the perfect flavour of feedback.

Scary Monsters (And Super Creeps)

(RCA, 1980)

Emerging from the Berlin period with critical acclaim but falling sales, Bowie began the 80s with a record that made it to the UK No.1 spot without compromising an inch on his artistry.

Scary Monsters was once again bolstered by the spidery guitar lines of the returning Fripp (not to mention Pete Townshend on *Because You're Young*) and added at least two anthems to the canon in the form of *Ashes To Ashes* and *Fashion*'s robotic crunk (a song that still sounds like the future four decades later).

His commercial clout would peak with 1983's *Let's Dance*, but *Scary Monsters* was Bowie's one inarguable classic of the decade. ◆▸

Lodger

(RCA, 1979)

Recorded at Montreux's Mountain studio in a break between Isolar II tour dates, Lodger has often laboured under its reputation as the runt of the Berlin litter.

In fact, with a little distance, it's highly underrated: standouts like the disco-tooled *D.J.*, the propulsive *Look Back In Anger*, the epic sweep of *Fantastic Voyage* and the strutting, stomping *Boys Keep Swinging* pushed artistic boundaries while supplying impressive hooks that could be whistled on a building site. *Yassassin* even fused funk, reggae and middle eastern motifs without sounding contrived.

Commercially, *Lodger* would stutter, lapped by one of Bowie's own acolytes, Gary Numan. It deserved better.

Let's Dance

(EMI, 1983)

Let's Dance represented a new dawn for Bowie, who quit RCA Records in frustration and entrusted Chic's Nile Rodgers as the architect of his new sound.

Working at New York's Power Station, Bowie caught two of the finest singles of his career in *Modern Love* and *China Girl*, while the title track was not so much a song as a phenomenon: a frosty, dancefloor-ready, sax-blown anthem with stunt guitar from a rising Stevie Ray Vaughan, that topped the transatlantic charts and still sounds like nothing else.

Those three cuts aside, however, the album was a little patchier than its career-best sales might at first suggest and Bowie's decade would go sharply downhill from here.

Earthling

(VIRGIN, 1997)

A Union flag-coated Bowie's keywords for *Earthling* were "jungle, aggressive rock and industrial", and the songwriter and guitarist/right-hand-man Reeves Gabrels would place as much emphasis on sampling and looping as instrumentation as the band set to work at Mountain Studios in Montreux.

Some critics of the period argued that the album represented a brazen attempt to hop aboard the prevailing drum 'n' bass bandwagon – and that beneath the tooth-rattling production lie some fairly pedestrian songs. But that is to overlook highlights like the visceral charge of *Dead Man Walking*, the block-rocking *Little Wonder* and Eno collab, *I'm Afraid Of Americans*.

Heathen

(ISO, 2002)

Following a patchy 90s, Bowie hit the new millennium like a train, pulling together offcuts from his then-unreleased *Toy* album, rocket-fuelling covers like the Pixies' *Cactus* and Neil Young's *I've Been Waiting For You*, and underlining his sustained relevance with cameos from young guns like Dave Grohl and Dream Theater's Jordan Rudess.

Bowie wouldn't necessarily take the term as a compliment, but *Heathen* felt familiar, lightly tipping a hat to his 70s output (you could imagine the stunning *Slip Away* sat neatly beside *Life On Mars?*). And though he insisted it predated the September 11th attacks, wistful opener *Sunday* (opening line: *"Nothing remains…"*) bottled the atmosphere.

Reality

(ISO, 2003)

Bowie's post-millennial purple patch continued apace along with restored longtime producer Tony Visconti on a record which attempted to make sense of a post-9/11 world in which *"truths seem to have melted away, there's nothing to rely on any more"*.

He didn't have all the answers, but this close cousin to *Scary Monsters* made his bewilderment listenable and danceable, especially on the wonky call-and-response rock of *New Killer Star* and *Never Get Old*'s clipped funk.

Reality made a credible No.3 in the UK, but underperformed in Europe and sunk in the US. Its tour was curtailed when Bowie suffered a heart attack, but it was a record to cling to during the long wait for Bowie's return.

The Thin White Duke: Bowie's post-glam mode.

The Next Day

(ISO, 2013)

After a decade of studio silence following 2003's *Reality*, sparked by his heart attack the following year's A Reality Tour, *The Next Day* arrived like a thunderbolt on Bowie's 66th birthday.

Once the shock subsided, the songs revealed themselves, from the wistful beauty of lead-off single *Where Are We Now?* (its heartbreaking video a clear nod to the Berlin that had inspired Bowie so much as a younger man) to the thrashy stomp of *The Stars (Are Out Tonight)*.

Sounding like the work of a musician with gas still in the tank, *The Next Day* felt like the start of an imperious, if unexpected late-career run – though of course fate had other plans.

Blackstar

(ISO/COLUMBIA, 2016)

Just as he had lived as an artist, so Bowie died as one, releasing *Blackstar* two days before his shock death from liver cancer and sprinkling valedictory messages across this seven-track release.

Marking his most adventurous and uncompromising collection in years, the cut-up vocals of the title track and *Girl Loves Me*'s jittery beats confirm he was curious to the end, but the most powerful moment is the pure-hearted, piano-driven *Dollar Days:* a song that completely and utterly defies you to remain unmoved.

Tony Visconti subsequently described it as a "parting gift", and as *Blackstar* swept the board at that year's Grammys, Bowie's death lost just a little of its sting.

GETTY

Good Worth hearing

David Bowie

(PHILIPS, 1969)

Securing a new record contract and entering into the orbit of sometime bandmate/producer Tony Visconti for the first time, the album universally known as *Space Oddity* was a few notches above Bowie's debut, even if there was far better to come, and soon.

The centrepiece, of course, was his extraordinary tale of an astronaut's blast-off and eventual burnout: an entire sci-fi movie told in five minutes flat, still icily brilliant after all these years. Elsewhere, Bowie settles a little too often on a slight brand of psych-folk, but there are further highlights, including the gloriously chaotic seven-minute gang-chant finale, *Memory Of A Free Festival*, inspired by a real-life gathering in Croydon Recreation Ground.

Black Tie White Noise

(SAVAGE, 1993)

By the early 90s, any uptick was seized upon by Bowie fans as a renaissance, and *Black Tie White Noise* was the first of several bestowed with the sobriquet: "His best since *Scary Monsters*".

While this reunion with Nile Rodgers isn't as good as the claims of a grand comeback, it has spark and purpose. The songwriter's ears are pricked up on a record that juggles genres with the confidence of old – a trumpet solo, a techno exploration – and returning wingman Mick Ronson anchored an enjoyable cover of Cream's *I Feel Free*. Single *Jump They Say* defied grunge to put Bowie back in the UK Top 10, while the title track was the funkiest he'd sounded in years.

Go carefully Mixed bags

Pin Ups

(RCA, 1973)

Having blazed across the rock'n'roll landscape with *Ziggy Stardust* and *Aladdin Sane*, Bowie and his Spiders returned with a whimper on *Pin Ups*, strolling through a rum batch of covers he described as "my favourites from the '64-'67 period of London" as a sop to the record label.

The album is not without merits: his take on the Merseybeats' *Sorrow* still holds a elegant thrill (and gave him a Top 5 UK hit to boot), the military chop of *Shapes Of Things* matches up to the Yardbirds original and a punchy reading of Syd Barrett's *See Emily Play* was a natural fit. But misty-eyed nostalgia didn't suit Bowie, and a proposed second volume was quietly dropped.

Tin Machine/Tin Machine II

(1989/1991, EMI/VICTORY)

Fretting that he had "lost his vision" after 1987's *Never Let Me Down*, Bowie fell in with maverick American guitarist Reeves Gabrels and Iggy Pop's old rhythm section, Hunt and Tony Fox Sales.

Tin Machine is often lazily used as shorthand for Bowie's turn-of-the-decade travails, but the band's first volume, at least, is better than its reputation, with a combative and chaotic sound that makes standouts like *Bus Stop* and *Under The God* hard to square with an artist supposedly in stasis.

Aside from the breakneck *Baby Universal* and glistening *You Belong In Rock 'N' Roll*, the sequel offered diminishing returns and the band would be gone within a year.

Hours

(VIRGIN, 1999)

Released in the run-up to the new millennium in September 1999 *Hours* (styled *"hours…"*) might have been culturally significant as the first album by a marquee artist available to download from the web, but Bowie's loose approach to quality control actually suits the streaming era better.

Tracks to cherrypick include the serene, string-draped opening ballad *Thursday's Child*, the folky chime of *Survive* and *Seven's* muscular jangle-pop, but the focus soon fades and the album's back end is scarcely notable for anything bar a general wash of sleepy atmosphere. It's the most transitional of his works, not bold enough to be either good or bad, just there.

Outside

(BMG, 1995)

As Britrock's faux-working class heroes monkey-walked around him, Bowie marched to the beat of his own idiosyncratic drum, enlisting Berlin-era collaborator Brian Eno for a concept piece that played out like a cyber-age film noir (a chief inspiration was *Twin Peaks*) and plumbed new depths of dystopia.

Mostly improvised in the studio – "We decided to go in with not even a gnat of an idea," Bowie explained – these tales of art and murder are patchy, and at times the sonic murk feels like a Nordic winter. Yet the scattershot approach also birthed some compelling moments on *Outside*, particularly the itchy industrial groove of *Hallo Spaceboy*.

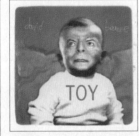

Toy

(2021, ISO/PARLOPHONE)

No cynical posthumous cash-in, Bowie intended to release the *Toy* material – mostly fresh takes of his 60s-into-70s output – straight after tracking it in New York at the turn of the millennium. Instead, the label buried it, Bowie rolled on to *Heathen*, and *Toy* waited two decades to be officially exhumed.

Largely, it was worth the wait. The stunning, aching, *Ziggy*-era piano ballad *Shadow Man* or *Space Oddity's* b-side *Conversation Piece*, here reborn as a bruised, country-inflected 12-string strum, belie the idea that Bowie was artistically lost. But perhaps inevitably, *Toy* feels more like a ragbag than an album in the true sense: more like the garnish on your collection than any kind of centrepiece.

Avoid For completists only

David Bowie

(DERAM, 1967)

The falsest of starts. The sleeve billed this 1967 release as the debut of David Bowie, but here he still sounded like plain old David Jones, an earthling fumbling for the zeitgeist with a ragbag of sub-Small Faces fare so mannered and twee that even producer Mike Vernon subsequently disowned the results ("I do wish it would go away," he told this writer. "It didn't do anything for me").

The nudge-nudge-wink-wink *Love Til You Tuesday* was the musical equivalent of eating too much cake icing, *We Are Hungry Men* little more than a skit, *Rubber Band,* a cringey vocal. But soon, DB would be unrecognisable and no-one would miss this debut.

Tonight

(EMI, 1984)

Running on fumes from the previous year's *Let's Dance*, even Bowie admitted he was merely "keeping his hand in" with this tepid follow-up.

Commercially, *Tonight* was another UK No.1, but the numbers couldn't disguise an artist spinning his wheels on a run of limp originals and covers that needed no improvement, from The Beach Boys' *God Only Knows* to Leiber and Stoller's *I Keep Forgettin'*. The still-wonderful *Blue Jean* only serves to amplify the stench of the clunkers. "There's stuff on *Tonight*," said Bowie in 1989, "that I could really kick myself about. When I listen to the demos, it's, 'How did it turn out like that?'"

Never Let Me Down

(EMI, 1987)

It might be tight at the top of the Bowie discography, but it's also a squeeze at the bottom, where several mid-period duds could conceivably be tarred, feathered and paraded as his lowest ebb.

Never Let Me Down makes a strong case for the wooden spoon, thanks to noisy, goonish misfires like *Day-In Day-Out* that sound like the great visionary clutching at straws. Marking the rock bottom of Bowie's weakest half-decade, to paraphrase the footnote on the *Ziggy* sleeve, this was a record to be played at minimum volume. Even Bowie recognised it: his next move would be to go back to basics with Tin Machine.

*"Time may change me,
but I can't trace time..."*

David Bowie 1947-2016